War Without Mercy

FOR

Penny and Karen
With our admiration and love

James Kirby Martin (1943–2024)
A brilliant historian and the best of friends

War Without Mercy

Liberty or Death in the American Revolution

Mark Edward Lender &
James Kirby Martin

OSPREY PUBLISHING
Bloomsbury Publishing Plc
Kemp House, Chawley Park, Cumnor Hill, Oxford OX2 9PH, UK
Bloomsbury Publishing Ireland Limited,
29 Earlsfort Terrace, Dublin 2, D02 AY28, Ireland
1385 Broadway, 5th Floor, New York, NY 10018, USA
E-mail: info@ospreypublishing.com
www.ospreypublishing.com

OSPREY is a trademark of Osprey Publishing Ltd

First published in Great Britain in 2025

© Mark Edward Lender and James Kirby Martin, 2025

Mark Edward Lender and James Kirby Martin have asserted their right under the Copyright, Designs and Patents Act, 1988, to be identified as Authors of this work.

For legal purposes the Acknowledgments on pp. 12–13 constitute an extension of this copyright page.

All rights reserved. No part of this publication may be: i) reproduced or transmitted in any form, electronic or mechanical, including photocopying, recording or by means of any information storage or retrieval system without prior permission in writing from the publishers; or ii) used or reproduced in any way for the training, development or operation of artificial intelligence (AI) technologies, including generative AI technologies. The rights holders expressly reserve this publication from the text and data mining exception as per Article 4(3) of the Digital Single Market Directive (EU) 2019/790

A catalog record for this book is available from the British Library

ISBN: HB 9781472872678; eBook 9781472872661; ePDF 9781472872685;
XML 9781472872708; Audio 9781472872692

25 26 27 28 29 10 9 8 7 6 5 4 3 2 1

Artwork in the plate section previously published in the following
Osprey title: MAA 450: *American Loyalist Troops* 1775–84 (p. 8 bottom)
Maps by www.bounford.com
Index by Alan Rutter

Typeset by Deanta Global Publishing Services, Chennai, India
Printed and bound in Great Britain by CPI (Group) UK Ltd, Croydon CR0 4YY

Osprey Publishing supports the Woodland Trust, the UK's leading woodland conservation charity.

To find out more about our authors and books visit www.ospreypublishing.com. Here you will find extracts, author interviews, details of forthcoming events and the option to sign up for our newsletter.

For product safety related questions contact productsafety@bloomsbury.com

Patrick Henry wasn't fooling. Too often, the choices really were "Liberty or Death!"

Contents

	Preface	8
	Acknowledgments	12
	List of Illustrations	14
	List of Maps	16
	Prologue	17
	Introduction: Toward War Without Mercy	22
1	"Fighting Justly"? *Jus in Bello* and its Problems	41
2	"Exposed to Both Internal and External Enemies": War to the Knife in New Jersey	65
3	Theater of Fear: Existential War in the West	103
4	"A Contagion of Violence": The New York Frontier	135
5	Target New London: Benedict Arnold from *Jus in Bello* to "Hard Line"	159
6	The South: Terror from the Start	185
	Epilogue: A Word from Thucydides	211
	Notes	218
	Bibliography	259
	Index	280

Preface

This is a book about a cruel and ruthless war – a war without mercy – in which those caught up in it believed they had nothing to lose by fighting without regard for the rules of so-called "civilized warfare." It was the War for American Independence. At its grimmest level, this was a confrontation in which military restraint was more the exception than the rule, a struggle in which combatants believed their very existence was in question. This reality led to an acceptance of violence against persons and property as preferable to a defeat equated with political, cultural, and even physical extinction. It was war with an expectation and acceptance of ferocity and brutality – *anything* to avoid defeat.

Any number of insightful historians have concluded that America's founding struggle reached a level of ferocity that few modern Americans have associated with the movement for independence. With few exceptions, however, these studies have described *what* happened over the course of the war, generally scanting *why* the conflict took so violent a turn. Surely brutality of such scope and pervasiveness calls for a fuller explanation. Using the lens of "existential warfare" – a term encompassing the unforgiving and merciless nature of revolutionary violence – this book is our attempt to supply that understanding. Our purpose is twofold: to further clarify *why* the conflict became so violent; and, stemming from this better understanding of *why*, to define the very nature of the war. These matters cry out for attention, for we believe Patrick Henry's clarion call to arms was more than just rhetoric.

For many combatants the choice *really was* one of "Liberty or Death!" – and they fought accordingly.

Our book has a long and wide-ranging genesis. In various individual or co-authored essays published over the past decade or so, we explored the roots of political and military violence during the War for Independence. Much of what we learned about that violence, and existential warfare in particular, we pulled together in a paper – "Liberty or Death!" – presented at a conference on "just war" convened at the Union League of Philadelphia in late 2015. It was our first comprehensive attempt to explain how the colonial rebellion transformed into a genuinely vicious conflict. The reaction from conference participants was gratifying, with one prominent scholar of the Revolution commenting that our title might better have been "Liberty *and* Death!" A revised version of that paper appeared in a 2018 volume, *Justifying Revolution*, edited by Glenn Moots and Phillip Hamilton. Again, we were pleased with the response. And just as conversations with colleagues and lecturing inform further research, we decided to delve deeper into the admittedly grim subject of revolutionary violence – especially its manifestation in unrestrained military actions. That effort, tied with some of our previous work, has produced this book.

After a Prologue and Introduction which delve into the matter of existential warfare and outline the structure of the book, we proceed to a chapter on the tenets of *"jus in bello"* (just war theory). These were the Enlightenment-inspired rules as 18th-century Europeans and Americans understood them of how "civilized" nations ideally were to conduct themselves in war. *Jus in bello* is the baseline against which we assess how far from the ideals of justice and compassion in war the revolutionary struggle diverged. We then move to a theater perspective, looking at how combatants actually fought in five regions we believe are reflective of the War for Independence as a whole. In each theater we explore why various factors – cultural, ideological, political-military, and even psychological – led virtually all combatants outside of the regular armies to ignore the ideal norms of just war and to adopt the unrestrained realities of existential war. We will draw heavily on the voluminous military literature of the Revolution and also on the literature of terror as a political tool. It is all something of a lesson in the consequences of irretrievably fractured political outlooks, harrowing ethnic and racial hatreds, the breakdown of capable political and military authorities, and inflammatory rhetoric that fueled virtually unstoppable cycles of violence, revenge, and retribution.

Throughout, we have found that individuals *mattered*. Yes, there were broad trends and social, cultural, and political forces at work. But individuals – patriots, tories, American Indians, the enslaved, whoever – made conscious decisions to pursue an existential war. While we did not set out to write a history "from the bottom up," in a sense that is what we have produced because that was how most of the war developed. It was an overwhelmingly local war in which the regular armies often played little or only peripheral roles. And in the belief that they had nothing to lose, untold numbers of individuals of all political allegiances, acting locally and fighting for their own reasons, and employing all means at their disposal, ultimately did as much – perhaps more – than General George Washington, Sir William Howe, or any other senior military leader did to shape the nature and character of the revolutionary conflict.

A word is in order on the use of certain terms. While many loyalists considered themselves "patriots" in their loyalty to George III, we will use "patriots" – with a lowercase "p" – to denote Americans in rebellion against the Crown (which gets a capital "C"). From time to time we also call them "rebels" or "whigs" (a term many patriots preferred). "Loyalists" and "tories," used interchangeably, of course denote those remaining loyal to the King (who gets a capital "K"). In general, although it sometimes can be tedious, we will use the actual ranks of military personnel. For example, when he served as British commander-in-chief after 1778, Sir Henry Clinton was Lieutenant General Clinton; prior to that, as Sir William Howe's subordinate, he was Major General Clinton. Actual lieutenant colonels will be Lieutenant Colonel So-and-So, not Colonel So-and-So (there are purists to whom this kind of specificity *matters*). Interchangeably, Indians will be American Indians or (less frequently) Native Americans, if we do not use a specific tribal name (e.g., Oneida, Mohawk, Shawnee, Cherokee, etc.).

Here, then, is our history of the War for Independence as an often merciless contest – an existential war in every sense of the term.

Mark Edward Lender
Richmond, VA
James Kirby Martin
Houston, TX
2024

Acknowledgments

As *War Without Mercy* came together over the past decade, we were fortunate enough to enjoy assistance and encouragement from many quarters. Tracking down obscure volumes and reading manuscripts took us variously to (among other repositories and collections) the libraries of Virginia Commonwealth University, the University of Richmond, Special Collections at Rutgers University, the collections of the David Library of the American Revolution (now at the American Philosophical Society in Philadelphia), the Pennsylvania Historical Society, the Library of Virginia, the Virginia Museum of History and Culture, the New York Public Library, the New-York Historical Society, and the Fort Ticonderoga Museum. The staff at all of these institutions have our profoundest thanks. We thank as well those institutions and publications for permission to use portions of our previously published work: the University of Oklahoma Press, Westholme Press, the *Journal of Military History*, and the *Journal of Military Ethics*.

We are in the special debt of colleagues who took the time to review our book's chapters and to share their comments. Garry Wheeler Stone, John (Jack) Buchanan, T. Cole Jones, Brian Mack, John Maass, Ricardo (Rick) Herrera, Maxine Lurie, and Jonathan Lurie all lent their expertise, and their criticisms not only saved us from many a slip, but also strengthened our narrative. As always, Penny Booth Page read everything with her sharp editorial eye. Nothing (at least from Mark Lender) goes to other readers without her blessing. She really is the best.

ACKNOWLEDGMENTS

Our agent, Roger Williams, truly believed in our manuscript, and he connected us with Bloomsbury/Osprey, for which we are deeply grateful. Kate Moore, our editor, offered helpful advice and encouragement every step of the way, copy editor Julie Frederick caught any number of slips and added polish to the book, and working with desk editor Alex Boulton has been a pleasure. All of the above have our profoundest thanks.

All errors, of course, are ours.

List of Illustrations

The Bloody Massacre by Paul Revere, showing the March 5, 1770 confrontation in Boston. (Metropolitan Museum of Art, Gift of Mrs. Russell Sage, 1910)

The author of *The Law of Nations*, Emer de Vattel (1714–67). (Photo by Fine Art Images/Heritage Images via Getty Images)

William Franklin (1730–1813), the royal governor of New Jersey before the Revolution. (From the New York Public Library, EM9850)

William Livingston (1723–90), the governor of revolutionary New Jersey. (Photo by Hulton Archive/Getty Image)

George Rogers Clark and the surrender of Fort Sackville, Vincennes, on February 25, 1779. (Signal Photos/Alamy Stock Photo)

The Gnadenhütten Massacre, March 8, 1782. (Henry Howe, *Historical Collections of the Great West*, 1852)

Joseph Brant (Thayendanegea) by George Romney (1776). (GL Archive/Alamy Stock Photo)

Incident in Cherry Valley – Fate of Jane Wells by Alonzo Chappel. (Library of Congress)

Oneidas at the Battle of Oriskany by Don Troiani (2005). (Private Collection © Don Troiani. All Rights Reserved 2025/Bridgeman Images)

Major General John Sullivan, leader of the 1779 Sullivan Expedition. (Library of Congress)

LIST OF ILLUSTRATIONS

Schooner Ajax leaving Delaware from the William H. Meyers diary. (From the New York Public Library, b16044202)

Gathering of Overmountain Men at Sycamore Shoals by Lloyd Branson (1915). (Tennessee State Museum)

Nancy Hart (*c.*1735–1830). (Photo by Fotosearch/Getty Images)

A soldier serving in the Ethiopian Regiment recruited under Virginia royal governor John Murray, Lord Dunmore. (Artwork by Gerry Embleton © Osprey Publishing Ltd)

List of Maps

1	The New Jersey Theater	66
2	The Trans-Appalachian West	104
3	The New York Frontier	136
4	The Battle of Groton Heights, September 6, 1781	169
5	The Southern Theater	186

Prologue

On March 5, 1770, patches of snow were still on the ground in Boston. Early that evening Private Hugh White, a redcoat sentry, stood his chilly vigil near a sentry hut in front of the Customs House. He was part of a British garrison, the 29th Regiment, dispatched to the Massachusetts capital in 1768. The troops had arrived in the wake of colonial truculence born of resentments against British policies intended to tighten imperial controls over the colonies long accustomed to a large measure of self-government. The garrison's presence had exacerbated already fraught tensions, and on this night White drew the attention of a rowdy group of Bostonians. Earlier in the evening he had had an altercation with a local youth, and now he became the focus of serious intimidation. The veteran private – a redcoat for 11 years – called for help, which arrived in the form of seven soldiers under the command of Captain Thomas Preston. Incensed by Preston's arrival, the growing crowd turned belligerent.

The mob became riotous, pelting Preston's redcoats first with snowballs, then with a hail of stones and muck containing feces. Some rioters even dared the soldiers to fire. The outnumbered troops faced injury or worse; and although the captain tried to maintain discipline, one of the beleaguered soldiers fired. Whether a deliberate act or the twitch of an anxious finger, the shot sent events spiraling out of control. Without orders, the rest of the frightened redcoats unloaded a volley. At point-blank range they could hardly miss, and musket balls tore into the shouting Bostonians, killing three, mortally wounding two others, injuring six more, and scattering the rest. Patriots quickly decried the "Horrid Massacre" or the "Bloody Massacre," which became the "Boston Massacre" in American lore.[1]

But a massacre? Really? Look up "massacre" in almost any dictionary, and in no case will the definition fit the events of that dramatic Boston night. With differences in phrasing, as either a noun or a verb the word implies a merciless intent to kill the defenseless under circumstances of wanton cruelty. A massacre is a calculated atrocity, the word deriving from the French for "carnage" and "butchery."[2] Nothing of the kind occurred on March 5, 1770. The musketry that cut through the aggressive mob came from soldiers fearing for their lives, and the harassed men fired without orders. This reality was obvious to John Adams, as staunch an advocate of colonial rights as any in America. When he defended the redcoats at trial against charges of murder, the public took notice. The facts were plain: The troops had fired in self-defense, and the Boston jury acquitted all but two of the accused. The "guilty" soldiers, convicted of manslaughter, received a brand on their thumbs and were sent on their way. There had been no "massacre," and Boston knew it.

But patriot fire-eaters ignored the verdicts. To paraphrase the old aphorism: They were not about to let mere facts stand in the way of a good story. Radicals now thundered against the dangers redcoats posed to colonial liberties. They made much of the perils supposedly inherent in maintaining regular armies in times of peace – they were the tools of tyrants! – the proof of which was now visible on the bloodied cobblestones of the Massachusetts capital. Paul Revere – Boston silversmith, illustrator, patriot provocateur, and five years later he of the famous "Midnight Ride" – drove the point home brilliantly. In a damning print of the troops confronting unoffending Bostonians, Revere had Preston, sword upraised, ordering his sneering men to fire into the bleeding "unhappy Sufferers." Poor Boston! "Thy hallowed Walks besmear'd with guiltless Gore."[3] Nonsense. But it was masterful hyperbole; no one was allowed to forget the heinous massacre.

And they didn't forget. Bostonians organized an annual "Massacre Day" to keep the memory alive. Beginning in 1771 a speaker expounded on the evils of standing armies and, more generally, on British threats to traditional English – and thus colonial – liberties. The first orator to commemorate "the bloody 5th of March" was Boston schoolmaster James Lovell, a republican radical and future long-serving Massachusetts delegate to the Continental Congress. His oration was noteworthy. Balancing a professed loyalty to King George III with scathing denunciations of Parliament, Lovell warned listeners that "we are [either] slaves or freemen." He spoke stridently of the consequences of accumulating political frustrations, cautioning that "Anger produces anger; and differences, that might be accommodated by kind and respectful behaviour may by imprudence be enlarged to an incurable rage." Partisans could actually forget the roots of their differences, their minds instead focusing on their present ill will. "When feuds have reached that fatal point, considerations of reason and equity vanish; and a blind fury governs, or rather confounds all things. A people no longer regard their interest, but a gratification of their wrath."[4]

This was tough talk, and it pointed toward a scale of violence far greater than the events of that unfortunate March 5. Lovell's was hard-headed realism about the dangers of political acrimony becoming "blind fury": It *could* become "incurable rage," and the "gratification of wrath" *could* evolve into genuinely horrific ferocity. There was also the implication – even a belief – that the controversies leading up to the "massacre" left little room for any middle ground. The choices facing American whigs (a term patriots frequently adopted) were simple and blunt: "we are slaves or freemen." This was not the stuff of moderation. Lovell was prescient, for as the imperial crisis deepened, others echoed his uncompromising stance. In his view, American patriots had to choose...

Many did. Abigail Adams was one of them, and by 1774 she saw the American mood as dangerously volatile. While her husband, John, represented Massachusetts in the First

Continental Congress, she opened a correspondence with the English historian Catharine Sawbridge Macaulay, an author of considerable reputation and openly sympathetic to the American cause. Adams' missive was full of foreboding. Most Americans were no longer "unfealing or insensible" to the growing "calamity," she reported, and she predicted a resort to "the Sword" if colonials were unable to peacefully "obtain a release from our present bondage." "The only alternative which every american thinks of," she warned, "is Liberty or Death."[5] These were the choices; she saw no middle ground.

Several months later, of course, Patrick Henry supposedly exclaimed "Liberty or Death!" as a literal call to arms. Whether Henry actually uttered precisely the rousing words attributed to him, he certainly captured the spirit of the moment, and he confirmed the rebellious enthusiasm that Abigail Adams had sensed – and that Lovell had proclaimed four years earlier. And Henry was not the only one breathing fire. Addressing the Georgia Provincial Congress, rebel governor Archibald Bulloch stated the case with equal fervor: "This is no time to talk of moderation," he proclaimed, "in the present instance it ceases to be a virtue."[6] From Massachusetts to Georgia – from North to South – for many the message was the same: No compromise, Liberty or Death!

Our contention is that for American whigs these fiery outbursts – the warnings of James Lovell and Abigail Adams, the rallying cries of Henry and Bulloch – were more than rhetoric. They were reality, or at least perceptions of reality. Whigs were convinced they were victims of a vast conspiracy against the traditional rights of Englishmen, and they saw "Liberty or Death" as actual alternatives. We further believe that very real consequences flowed from these stark convictions. You were with the Revolution or you were its enemy; and if "moderation" had "ceased to be a virtue," then what sense did it make to pursue any other than a radical course, especially when protest exploded into rebellion and war? We think the "rage" and "wrath" James Lovell had so feared quickly spiraled out of control, leading to a conflict of startling and often unrestrained violence. Even individuals who came late to the patriot cause would catch fire in the blast of war. "They are actuated by resentment now," John Adams would observe, "and resentment coinciding with principle is a very powerful motive."[7]

Indeed it was. And the motives for the "resentments" ran deep and, as we will see, so did the violence derived from them. As the Revolution devolved into civil war, frontier conflicts, and ideological divides, the line between soldiers and civilians frequently dissolved. There would be genuine atrocities – actual massacres that dwarfed the casualties inflicted by the frightened redcoats defending themselves that Boston evening. One wonders if James Lovell grasped the point that he, along with so many others of his generation, tacitly came to accept virtually any form of violence that served the cause of victory – as opposed to a defeat they equated with the extinction of everything they held dear?

Introduction: Toward War Without Mercy

For over two centuries the American military narrative of the Revolution has favored a relatively temperate view of the contest for independence – at least on the part of the winning patriot side. The nation's founding myth dwelled largely on the nobility of the struggle and the heroic sacrifices of the revolutionary generation as it confronted and overcame British, tory, and American Indian depredations. A triumphal narrative emphasized what we might call a "revolutionary immaculate conception" – a victory wrought without patriots resorting to the hideous violence and horror associated with many subsequent revolutions. The French, Latin American, Russian, and Chinese revolutions represent cases in point. This perspective – a blind spot, actually – began with early historians sympathetic to the Revolution, including such accomplished writers as Carlo Botta, Mercy Otis Warren, and David Ramsay. Although perfectly willing to see patriots as victims of British malevolence, they scanted mention of any similar conduct among the revolutionaries.[1]

For generations this generally benign perspective on the patriot war effort has prevailed in the popular narrative of the Revolution, and even among many academic historians.[2] More recently, however, this view has been changing. With many whigs having seen Liberty or Death as literal alternatives – with no room for middle ground – much evidence of serious violence became all but inevitable once warfare erupted.[3] Opinions have differed on the extent of the consequent ferocity of the fighting and who was most to blame.[4] Among the closest students of the conflict there is now general agreement that combatants (especially those engaged in combat beyond the regular armies) showed little remorse or sympathy toward their opponents.[5]

Any number of accounts on the war in particular regions or in specific incidents also have found violence to be pervasive, with combatants often making few distinctions between soldiers and civilians. Places like Cherry Valley, New York; Augusta, Georgia; Monmouth County, New Jersey; Wyoming, Pennsylvania; Gowen's Fort, South Carolina; New London, Connecticut; Gnadenhütten, Ohio; and so many others would see the blood of innocents and combatants alike shed with deliberate cruelty – along with racial strife, psychological shock, and incalculable property destruction. Tens of thousands would be driven from their homes as exiles and refugees. Such were the realities of the war, as many well-researched histories have concluded.[6]

The incidents related in these studies comprise a catalog of horrors. As James Lovell had predicted, the rival combatants came to loath one another and "blind fury govern[ed]" their conduct.[7] Patriots in particular had few scruples when it came to stifling royalist voices. Well before independence, whigs orchestrated local efforts to impugn the dignity and social standing of prominent loyalists. These were campaigns of character assassination, and in the honor-driven world of 18th-century elites, they frequently shattered the morale and political influence of their targets.[8] From this it was an easy step toward harsher measures. In various protests against British policies, whigs openly threatened royal officials or anyone suspected of royalist sympathies with social ostracism and physical violence. Intimidation of suspected tories was commonplace, and tarring and feathering – a brutal torture – was the fate of more than a few individuals with courage enough to openly disagree with rabid patriots.[9] And as T. H. Breen has thoroughly shown, much of this activity was the work of local *ad hoc* whig committees acting independently of and without the sanction of patriot elites – a precursor of how many local patriots later (and not too much later) would fight their war.[10] Friends of the King lived at the sufferance of local activists, answerable only to themselves for their conduct.

Rebels did not shy away from employing outright terror. In late 1775, to cite a hideous example, a mob of Georgia patriots confronted loyalist Thomas Brown and insisted he pledge support for the rebel cause. When Brown refused, whigs fractured his skull with a rifle butt, tarred his legs, and held them over a fire. Then they cut off his hair, scalped him, and left him for dead. The patriot Georgia Council of Safety considered the matter something of a lark: "The said Thomas Brown is now a little remarkable, wears his hair very short, and a handkerchief around his head in order that his intellect ... may not be affected." The council would regret its levity. Brown – "Burntfoot" Brown ever after – lost two toes but recovered to become a talented guerilla commander and scourge of southern patriots for the rest of the war.[11]

Northern patriots were no more tolerant. In early 1777 at Morristown, New Jersey, patriots hanged two tories and the same day would have executed dozens of others had they not "volunteered" for service in the Continental Army.[12] Fighting for "liberty" did not imply compassion for contrary opinions; revolutionaries were not (and usually *are not*) champions of free speech.

We could pile example upon example, but the pattern is clear: No one involved – patriot, loyalist, American Indian, or redcoat – had a monopoly on military excesses, which often rose to the level of atrocities and tore at the very social fabric. The lament of New Jersey pastor Nicholas Collin, who saw his congregation ripped apart by civil discord, captured the calamitous state of affairs: "Everywhere distrust, fear, hatred, and abominable selfishness were met with. Parents and children, brothers and sisters, wife and husband were enemies to one another."[13] The distraught pastor's cry from the heart was the stuff of high tragedy.

There is a name for this kind of war. Historians have rarely applied it to the American War for Independence, but we will insist that it captures the essence of the revolutionary struggle. This is "existential warfare."[14] One of the best definitions comes via Canada's Mackenzie Institute, a highly regarded think tank focused on security, military, terrorism, and related concerns. The Institute describes human conflict at its grimmest level:

> Existential war is a war for existence, not for status, power, territory or resources, but for existence itself – as a nation, as a people, and ultimately as an individual. When human beings fight for those stakes, there are no limits. The choice of survival or extermination doesn't leave many options open for negotiation; and if given a choice like that, all that a real human being can do is fight with all the ferocity, cunning and strength he or she can muster.

Mackenzie's conclusion is glib, but spot on: "To do anything else is to flunk out of life and get expelled."[15]

Bear with us briefly, as the modern term "existential" requires a bit of explanation. It is usually associated with the philosophical school of that name, "existentialism." With origins traced to the 19th century, interest in existentialism peaked in the mid-20th century primarily in the works of such European writers as Albert Camus, Jean-Paul Sartre, and Simone de Beauvoir, among many others. But exactly what is existentialism? There has *never* been any agreement. Princeton University philosopher Walter Kaufmann has written that it is not really a formal philosophy; rather – in a definition that Mackenzie likes – Kaufmann explains existentialism is a "refusal to belong to any school of thought, the repudiation of the adequacy of any body of beliefs" as "the heart of existentialism."[16] For our purposes, we can also note that existentialism generally posits that individuals must justify their existence through their own choices. They must do so without reference to "any body of beliefs," including traditional moral codes. Existentialists consider life meaningless unless people act through their individual choices; and the corollary to this is that we are responsible for our choices. We must decide individually what is good or evil, what is right or wrong. If individuals choose to be just or compassionate, they do not necessarily do so from any conventional mores, sacred or otherwise. They do so for personal reasons and make choices accordingly.[17]

The Mackenzie Institute has focused on this matter of personal choice in existential thinking. "We decide to be merciful, to be compassionate, to restrain ourselves; not out of any higher moral code, but because we choose to do so for our own reasons." From this follows an alarming conclusion: "In existential war, therefore, there is no absolute requirement for mercy, compassion or restraint, unless you choose to behave this way." And then comes an even more alarming question: "But if your enemy has none of these limitations, then why should you?"[18] Under these circumstances, fighting without restraint is a choice to exist. And it is certainly a choice made without reference to (or despite) the codified tenets of "civilized warfare" – *jus in bello* (which we discuss at length in the following chapter).

Australian military writer Strobe Driver takes this point even further. Existentialism, he claims, holds individuals free "to make decisions" unencumbered by "historical and social constraints." He specifically cites Enlightenment ideals as among such "constraints," which, as we will see, would include *jus in bello*. This conclusion echoes Mackenzie's observation (via Kaufmann) that existentialists act "not out of any higher moral code," but from individual motives. Such freedom from established mores even allows terrorists to act out of personal convictions regarding what is right. At the same time, Driver points out that "what is an existential threat is dependent on perspectives." That is, action depends on who feels threatened and the seriousness of the perceived threat. Anti-Western terrorists (as labeled by Western nations), for example, see the West as an existential threat, while many in the West see non-Western terrorists in a similar light.[19] Either way, passionate emotions are in play, with stakes James Lovell, Abigail Adams, Patrick Henry, and Archibald Bulloch would have understood.

None of this framework is to argue that 18th-century combatants were existentialists – *certainly not!* But we are saying that the resort to existential war – war without mercy – during the Revolution stemmed from reasons any modern existentialist would have comprehended. It came from the fear, often grounded in harsh reality, that your enemy intended to wage war without restraint, and that for you to do anything less in response would risk your personal destruction. The resort to existential warfare was a choice based on reasons that various combatants and populations not only considered proper, but inescapable given any lesser alternatives. Why should you hold back if you were convinced the other side meant your utter subjugation – or even obliteration?

The rise of existential warfare didn't happen all at once, and it didn't happen everywhere or all of the time. But during the War for Independence a substantial number of combatants across political and ethnic divides, caught up in the cycles of attack and retribution, came to believe their very existence was in question. Consequently, they *chose* to fight without limitations on their behavior – behavior prevalent enough to characterize the war as a whole.

The "*Whys*" of War

But why was the Revolution so violent? Why existential warfare? The question is, of course, complicated. People take up arms for any number of reasons and often reluctantly, and the American revolutionary generation was no exception. Motives did vary by region. Land hunger – "greed," if you will – among white colonists certainly exacerbated tensions with the Indians along all of the frontiers. In New Jersey a religious schism within the Dutch Reformed Church played a role in civil strife. In many cases family and social allegiances – or resentments – weighed in decisions on whether to fight or on what side to fight. Ethnic animosities were sources of conflict as well. Looking at the war as a whole, however, we have identified six central factors — the "whys" — as chiefly responsible for the war's brutality and which accounted for the marked disparity between the ideals of *jus in bello* and the lived experience of conflict. Violence deriving from particular local sources can be subsumed within these broader categories.

The chapters that follow will investigate these "whys" in considerable depth, but allow us to introduce them briefly here.

First, we will maintain that much of the war's ruthlessness and ferocity (although hardly all of it) lay in its local context. This factor emerges from the arithmetic of the war — the statistics of who fought, where, and under what circumstances. These numbers, rough as they are, are important here. In 1974, in anticipation of the upcoming American Revolutionary Bicentennial, historian Howard H. Peckham published a compilation of revolutionary war engagements and casualties. It was the first serious attempt to quantify the scale and human costs of military activity during the conflict. However, Peckham decided not to count many Indian raids, incidents involving a few individuals, or operations such as foraging that "met cries of protest from civilians" without actual combat. Thus, his count was conservative, and he made no claim of complete accuracy.

Peckham conceded that defining a military action was often a judgment call.[20] Yet in mining archival collections, local histories, and other sources, Peckham (and his various research assistants) counted 1,546 land and naval actions between 1775 and 1783. Significantly, of the 1,331 land actions, fewer than 100 involved the regular armies as the primary opponents (albeit often with militia or other forces involved). The rest were engagements, not necessarily small, in which regular soldiers played only peripheral roles, if any at all. That is, roughly 93 percent of revolutionary engagements were primarily the business of local militias, irregular forces, tribal groups, or even families defending individual homesteads.

Moreover, we stated that Peckham's count was conservative — and it certainly was. New Jersey's revolutionary experience illustrates the problem. Peckham counted 238 engagements within the borders of the future Garden State; and there is general agreement that New Jersey, situated as it was between the chief British garrison in New York City and the *de facto* rebel capital in Philadelphia, saw more fighting than any other state. But we also know that Peckham's findings for New Jersey – and elsewhere – represent a significant undercount. A detailed tally by New Jersey archivist David Munn, based on much deeper archival research – and including all incidents involving any level of violence – has documented almost 600 engagements fought in all sections of the state, on its rivers and bays, and off of its immediate coasts.[21] Of these, perhaps 20 (some 4 percent) were engagements that saw the bulk of the fighting conducted by the main British and American regular armies.[22]

So we have to ask: Why would the undercount in New Jersey be unique? How many other engagements, how many killed, wounded, and missing have escaped notice? We don't know, but it's a safe bet that the answer is "plenty." While Peckham noted more engagements in New Jersey than elsewhere, he also cited New York as not far behind with 228, with South Carolina in third place with 155.[23] However, even a cursory reading of the modern literature of the Revolution in the South renders these numbers questionable. In a 1776 South Carolina campaign against the Cherokees, for example, Peckham could only cite "an ambush and other attacks" for the month of September – hardly an observation approaching precision.[24] We now know that in South Carolina, where small-scale actions were endemic, the figures are dramatically wrong. In an important corrective, researcher John Parker tracked through archives and local sources to provide a considerably more precise understanding of the conflict in the Palmetto State. Parker has documented over 400 engagements of various intensity, from pitched battles to brief skirmishes – that is, well over double Peckham's count of 155.[25]

The total for New York is certainly an undercount as well. Absent a New York David Munn or John Parker, we probably never will know the extent of the shortfall. But even using Peckham's count of 228, and subtracting the major engagements and raids between 1776 and 1781 – more or less some 26 actions – it is clear that local combatants were responsible for the overwhelming proportion of New York's fighting.[26] There is no reason to suspect that circumstances were appreciably different in other states or on the western frontiers.

Why are these numbers important? Or, put another way, what were the implications of this enormous number of small battles and incidents? An obvious and key observation is, simply stated, *the war was a very local conflict*. In this truism lies much of the disparity between the canons of *jus in bello* and the brutal realities of the war – and thus any argument that the Revolution followed a relatively moderate course. The vast majority of revolutionary engagements pitted local forces against one another in regions often far removed from effective governmental or military authorities who might have attempted to rein in the worst of military excesses. There were times when there were no functional political authorities, at least none capable of influencing – let alone actually controlling – military activities. Without the restraining hand of senior Continental or British officers or of established political structures, local forces were left to fight according to their own rules, which quite often meant no rules.

To be clear: Effective political and senior military oversight was *frequently* lacking. In South Carolina, for example, at one point the harried state government actually decamped to North Carolina, leaving the fight to militia officers, some of whom were very turbulent characters. In North Carolina, at another juncture, loyalist raiders captured the governor, again leaving the fighting to local commanders. In southern New Jersey, patriots, exasperated by the state's inability to control loyalist raids, formed the extra-legal Association for Retaliation, which waged a private war. In the state's northeast, the Hackensack Valley became known as the "Neutral Ground" because no political faction could establish effective control as patriots and loyalists raided one another in a vicious cycle of revenge and retribution. There was nothing to stop it.

These hundreds of small battles won and lost, actions often without names fought by individuals equally nameless, provided the overall context for more specific sources of revolutionary violence. Of these, the military legacies of the colonial wars were especially significant. Such as local combatants observed any rules of war, they followed military practices in place since white settlers arrived in North America. Violence was nothing new to Americans; to be honest, fighting was endemic in colonial America. As colonists fought various Indian wars, they freely employed scorched-earth tactics, striking at tribal villages and frequently targeting women, children, and the elderly as well as warriors, thereby erasing the line between combatants and noncombatants. These were wars of annihilation aimed at removing threats once and for all.

Historian John Grenier has called this acceptance of and resort to unrestrained military violence America's "first way of war."[27] There was nongovernmental brutality as well. In December 1763 the massacre of some 20 defenseless Conestoga Indians by the so-called Paxton Boys near Lancaster, Pennsylvania, was a prominent case in point.[28] But all of the colonial frontiers witnessed attacks by various tribes on isolated farms and settlements, and the possibility of frontier violence was simply an almost endless fact of life.

Moreover, colonial authorities did not limit violence to dealings with American Indians; they were apt to employ it relatively freely against truculent white populations. New England authorities showed little reluctance in using the bludgeon to keep white laborers in line. In New York and New Jersey, violence occasionally flared as tenants clashed with landlords over rents and real estate titles. In 1771 North Carolina fought a civil war pitting the colonial government against backcountry Regulators who resented the corruption of local officials and the domination of the eastern planter elite.[29] And across the colonies only brute force kept enslaved black people in submission. In short, violence lurked just below the surface in the colonies, and in times of crisis (or apparent crisis) Americans willingly enough resorted to terrible brutality.[30]

The Regulator crisis in North Carolina underscored the relevance of another military legacy: Established governments did not like rebels and did not hesitate to use force against them. Rebels occupied an ambiguous status under the rules of "civilized war," and the monarchies of Europe traditionally accorded them little respect, let alone mercy. Much of the brutality inherent in the Revolution stemmed from this reality, as many British officers brought their disdain for rebels with them to America in 1775 and beyond. They had shown little compassion to the Highland Scots after the Jacobite rising of 1745–46, and they saw no reason to treat American rebels more kindly.

Ironically, after declaring independence patriots used the same reasoning to crack down on loyalists. No longer considering themselves rebels (if they ever did), revolutionary authorities cast that opprobrium on loyalists – now seen as rebels against newly legitimate American governments. And if patriots had moved quickly to eradicate symbols of imperial connection, they also adopted the traditional international posture against rebels and linked the Declaration of Independence *directly* to efforts to stamp out loyalism. Less than two weeks before passage of this key document, John Adams, never especially bloodthirsty, argued that a declaration of independence was just what patriots needed to deal effectively with loyalists. "The Advantages, which will result from Such a Declaration," he told Harvard professor John Winthrop, were "very great. After that Event, the Colonies will ... establish Tests and ascertain the Criminality of Toryism. The Presses will produce no more Seditious, or traiterous Speculations. Slanders upon public Men and Measures will be lessened."[31]

Adams' Massachusetts colleague Elbridge Gerry was of like mind. Congress, he wrote to Major General Horatio Gates, anticipated "a speedy Declaration of Independence & Confederation," and already had urged the states "to make provision for punishing all Inhabitants, & other persons ... who shall be found affording aid or Comfort to the King of G[reat] Britain or other Enemies of the united States of America." Delaware's delegate Caesar Rodney was even more emphatic. With independence declared, he informed his younger brother Thomas, time was up for the loyalists. "Their wings must and will be Clipped. The Declaration has laid the foundation – and will be followed by Laws fixing the degree of Offence, and punishment Suitable. Some people have done things, which if done in future nothing less than life will be Sufficient to Attone for."[32]

This was tough talk, and Adams, Gerry, and Rodney were quite accurate in describing the fate awaiting loyalists. The Declaration helped clear the way for the new states to initiate some of the most repressive measures in the Revolution's history. One example from the tory pen of Anglican reverend Samuel Peters offers a glimpse of how quickly the Declaration gave patriots cover for "clipping" loyalist "wings." No sooner was the Declaration announced than local patriots "pulled him [Peters] out of his desk, put a rope around his neck," and dragged him through a local river "to cool his loyal zeal." Perhaps whigs saw the action as one of their "inalienable rights."[33] But willingness to use repression and violence was (and is) central to most revolutions.

Political ideology was an important factor as well. Whigs shared the general republican outlook that historians have long identified with the popular colonial intellect. Liberty, republicans held, was under constant threat from would-be tyrants, and it behooved "virtuous" individuals to defend their rights upon which liberty depended. This was the thinking that James Lovell and Patrick Henry lived and breathed. But republicanism was also, in many respects, an ideology of suspicion and even fear; patriots in particular believed traditional English rights were under assault and that British conspiracies were afoot to "enslave" Americans.[34] Indeed, it was easy for whigs to believe in all sorts of conspiracies involving loyalists, Indians, and slaves all in league with the British. Confronted with such odds and such malevolence, what was a virtuous people to do but fight with all available means?

Terrorism became a prominent part of the equation. If people honestly believed a malignant conspiracy threatened their rights and future, then why wait for your enemy or oppressor to complete your subjugation? Would it not make sense to strike preemptively? Commonly in the rebellious colonies, patriots struck first, which brings us to the matter of terrorism. Studies of terrorism approach the subject from any number of directions, but there is general agreement that terrorists employ violence against defenseless populations or specific groups on behalf of a political, religious, social, or other possible specific agendas. The goal is to compel and enforce obedience and to repress or eliminate opposition.

Historian John A. Lynn II goes further, noting that terrorists aim at initiating rapid revolutionary action while eroding the will and ability of established authorities to counter them. If successful, terrorism would then evolve into more formal military operations as the terrorists gained traction with a broader range of supporters.[35] The process Lynn has identified was, we shall see, very much what American whigs employed against the enemies of the Revolution – and not just in certain regions, but *everywhere*. Repressed loyalists learned that they had little chance to oppose the revolutionary onslaught, and early in the war most resistance was ineffectual. But when they had the chance – as they did later, in conjunction with British or Indian forces – they also knew they had little to lose in returning terror for terror. That is, if patriots were not disposed to show mercy, why should they?

There was also the factor of race. Tensions between white settlers and Indians were high before independence, but once committed to the war – with but a few exceptions on the side of the Crown – Native Americans saw no reason to hold back. Why should they? They knew full well what a patriot victory would bring to them in its aftermath: land-hungry settlers marching west, more Indian homelands lost, more forced removals, more of their culture destroyed, more death. Then there were the slaves. Black people, free and enslaved, fought on both sides, but more gravitated to the British, who offered freedom for those who fled patriot masters. And this, of course, fed whig fears of slave revolts and conspiracies encouraged by the British. As the reader will learn, this was true not only in the South. Any region with a substantial black or Indian population found white patriots living in fear of black–Indian–British (including loyalist) conspiracies and of a two-front war: the British as an external threat and Indian and black people as potential (and often very real) internal enemies.

Then there was the factor of psychological disconnect to consider. Many (and probably most) loyalists simply could not understand the motives of their rebellious fellow Americans. They were utterly unprepared to deal with what, after 1774, seemed an inexplicable surge in anti-British sentiments. The advent of actual revolution the following year absolutely confounded them. Thousands of tories could not grasp why so many Americans were unhappy with the empire, at least to the extent that they would take up arms. Besides, little more than a decade before, Americans and the British had stood together against the French and allied Indians. Ties of tradition and sentiment mattered deeply to many colonists. Repeatedly in tory comments on the rebellion, the word "unnatural" appeared; the Revolution was incomprehensible.[36] Psychologically, loyalists were unable to fathom the patriot rationale for a revolution that, to the King's friends, made so little sense. Nor could they account for the violence directed at them from erstwhile neighbors. They reacted initially with bewilderment and resentment, then with fear – and later with fury.

Fury took a number of forms, but feelings among many tories were such that they considered actions barely imaginable before the war. Without suffering a profound psychological shock, why, for example, given the long-standing racial and historical animosities between white and Indian populations, did white loyalists fight willingly alongside Indians? Why, in some cases, did they fight voluntarily under Indian command? And given white prejudices and even fears of slave rebellions, why did white tories willingly serve alongside black raiders in New Jersey and elsewhere? We can only surmise that it was a deep well of hatred for the revolutionaries that motivated cross-racial alliances.

Finally, there was the issue of momentum. For whatever motives revolutionaries and their opponents took up arms, the War for Independence developed in cycles of retribution and revenge. Violent incidents led to reprisals, then to counter-reprisals, and so on, as in killer disease epidemics, literally becoming uncontrolled contagions of violence when notions of restraint all but ceased to exist. It was just as James Lovell had predicted: *Hatreds, fears, and the thirst for revenge escalated and became driving forces in and of themselves.* This was less true in battles between the regular armies, but we will insist it was certainly true at the local level as rival militias, tribal, and irregular forces confronted one another.

Gruesome as all of this was, it was fully understandable. Was anyone willing to endure terror and attack without striking back? Most whigs and loyalists – it didn't matter – were not. For most of the war the only promise of ending regional mayhem was a truly knock-out blow by one side or another, and as we will find, such decisive victories were few and far between. Even such successes, as bloody as they may have been and as important as they briefly appeared, were only temporary. Sooner or later, and usually sooner, the defeated rival regrouped and came back to reclaim lost ground – and for revenge. Like a perverse variant of a law of physics, once in motion armed violence tended to stay in motion.

What Follows

This volume is not a chronological narrative. We proceed from a discussion of the tenets of just war, as 18th-century European and American elites understood that concept. Then, *War Without*

INTRODUCTION

Mercy is a collection of five case studies indicative of the course and nature of the War for Independence in specific theaters and specific circumstances. They will support our argument that the violent and unrestrained character of the war – the horrors of an existential struggle – stemmed directly from the overwhelmingly local nature of the conflict.

Chapter 1 looks at how "civilized" nations ideally were to wage war in a context of humanity and restraint. The Enlightenment ideals of *jus in bello* embodied these rules, which defined the boundaries of what was acceptable conduct in war. They defined the nature of legal combatants, and proposed limits on military violence – especially in relation to prisoners of war, civilians, private property, and, significantly, what was permitted when an opponent transgressed the bounds of *jus in bello*. These canons are the touchstone of our narrative, the baseline against which we assess the level and nature of military excesses during the Revolution. In effect, we will be measuring ideals against realities.

The next chapter focuses on the long-settled province of New Jersey, which was anything but a hotbed of revolutionary fervor. However, when the shooting started, the colony descended into a bitter fratricidal struggle that, in one of the smallest provinces of the British Empire, reflected virtually all of the elements we have cited as contributing to existential warfare. Located between the *de facto* rebel capital of Philadelphia and the chief British garrison in New York City, the state saw more fighting than any other of the rebellious colonies and was also a battleground that often saw few distinctions between soldiers and civilians. That New Jersey could descend into the maelstrom of an existential war was a prime indicator of how quickly more militant regions could do the same – or worse. There would be some notable exceptions, as there were some voices calling for moderation, but if such trauma could strike in New Jersey, it should surprise no one to find it prevalent virtually everywhere.

Chapter 3 investigates a much larger geographical region. The Trans-Appalachian West witnessed embittered racial fighting as western tribes, allied for their own reasons with the British, contested fiercely for their homelands and ways of life. White populations responded with the scorched-earth tactics settlers had employed against Indians for over a century. No one was safe, and distinctions between civilians and combatants largely evaporated. For every good reason we have called the West the "Theater of Fear."

The northern New York frontier (Chapter 4), especially in the Mohawk Valley, saw a desperate struggle between settlers defending homesteads and lives against an equally determined Iroquois effort to do the same for their homelands. Here we find furious loyalists fighting alongside the Iroquois in a widespread biracial alliance – white tories and Indians against white patriots, who also attracted significant levels of support from the Oneidas and Tuscaroras. As deadly civil discord wracked white and Indian communities alike, no one living in this northern frontier was truly safe.

In Chapter 5 we turn our attention to a local case study, the controversial September 1781 British raid on the Connecticut privateer port of New London, led by turncoat brigadier general Benedict Arnold. Arnold, who always claimed to be fighting within the parameters of just war, nevertheless brought the "hard line" of war to the patriot town. In so doing he raised questions of who was a legitimate target of military violence. There was no question about privateers and other active combatants – they were fair game. But what about the civilians and privately owned facilities and port infrastructure that supplied, maintained, and *invested in* the privateers? What did *jus in bello* allow when the lines between combatants and civilians blurred?

Over the vast landscapes of the South (Chapter 6) the war developed in two distinct phases. From 1775 through most of 1778, patriots held sway, resorting to terror tactics to intimidate and silence opponents of the Revolution. In doing so they were utterly unapologetic – we have mentioned the ordeal of Burntfoot Brown and the perverse levity patriots enjoyed at his expense. But with the return of the Crown in late 1778, loyalists would rise and return measure for measure. While the regular armies campaigned, the war at the local level rapidly spun out of control. At critical times civil authorities virtually dissolved or became impotent in the face of unrestrained violence. In the absence of political control or the effective occupation of regular armies, rival militias and irregular bands clashed in a civil war that rivaled the worst of the Revolution's existential havoc. Race, ideology, historical precedent, bewilderment, terror, and certainly the momentum of war – all of the "whys" underlying revolutionary violence – played a role in unleashing existential havoc.

Our Epilogue draws the geographical threads together, looking for common strands in the evolution of the existential struggle across the revolutionary landscape. How did the war so quickly depart from the ideals of *jus in bello*? Indeed, in the face of genuinely fundamental differences along ideological, racial, and even psychological lines, did these just war notions matter at all? The war confronted Americans – whig, loyalist, free, enslaved, indigenous – with an array of challenges, the "whys" of our narrative. Any one of them was serious enough, but in combination the threats in each was magnified, and we will advance some observations on how the momentum of war overwhelmed any regard for human restraint or compassion. Was James Lovell right in 1771? Did "Anger," as he predicted, produce a "blind fury" – a war without mercy, an existential war – that "confound[ed] all things"? Was Liberty or Death, as Abigail Adams and Patrick Henry declared, the actual reality that legions of Americans faced? Our research concludes that the answer is an unambiguous *yes*.

I

"Fighting Justly"? Jus in Bello *and its Problems*

War is a grim business. As American rebels took up arms, and as Britain mobilized against them, all concerned recognized that any war would produce its share of death and destruction. John Adams knew that independence was impossible without a serious fight, which he predicted would be long and brutal: "A bloody Conflict We are destined to endure."[1] At the same time there were reasons to hope that the conflict – however long it lasted – would not be unnecessarily ruthless or cruel. Colonial and European elites shared a generally recognized doctrine defining what was and was not permissible in warfare; and these rules, if observed by "civilized" combatants, ideally would constrain the worst excesses of military violence. Or such optimistic thinking reflected their hope. These rules, and how they fared when tested in the severe realities of war, will be our immediate focus here.

Jus in Bello

Jus in bello is translated from the Latin as "justice in war," or "fighting justly." It is distinct from the related doctrine of *jus ad bellum*, which deals with justifications for going to war. *Jus in bello* pertains to the conduct of combatants, no matter what the reasons for going to war or the justice of those reasons. The idea has an ancient lineage. The Greeks and Romans paid some attention to ethical concerns about what was proper in conducting war; and early Christian writers, who considered making war a sin, sought to define the circumstances under which war was ethically appropriate and to place limits on military excesses when war occurred.[2]

Christian thinkers generally recognized two categories of conflict. There was "holy war," waged over matters of faith and, supposedly, under "divine authority" – and which could morph into an actual crusade under the leadership or blessing of senior ecclesiasts. Such conflicts could become unrestrained affairs with little mercy accorded opponents. "Just war," by comparison, concerned with justifications for taking up arms – questions of whose cause was in the right – was usually more secular in character. Combatants "fought on public authority for more mundane goals," including territorial defense, treaty violations, various rights, or other political considerations. "Codes of right conduct" sought to limit military excesses and curb efforts to utterly destroy an opponent.[3] Of course actual combat, even in just war, could lead to genuine mayhem – the Middle Ages would see plenty of examples – but the ideal of restraint in war at least had a theoretical foundation.

Early modern Europe inherited this interest in the nature of just war, but secularizing Enlightenment thinkers gradually altered the direction of the inquiry. By the 17th century Enlightenment scholars largely had divorced conceptions of just war from religious roots, and writers focused less on the right to wage war than on allowable conduct during war. The goal was to mitigate brutality inherent in armed conflict, no matter who initiated hostilities.

Of all the early Enlightenment thinkers writing on *jus in bello* – and there were several of note – one stood out. This was the Dutch diplomat and humanist Hugo Grotius (1583–1645). In 1625, while the Thirty Years War still raged, Grotius published On the Law of War and Peace: Three Books (*De Jure Belli ac Pacis Libri Tres*). The Dutchman asserted in Book Three that no matter what the cause of the war or who started it, "natural law" bound all combatants to certain standards of humane conduct. In particular, Grotius sought to protect the persons and property of noncombatants.[4]

For the next century, Grotius influenced a host of other Enlightenment writers, including Thomas Hobbes and John Locke; their ideas probed the possibilities and moral duty of limiting warfare through formal rules. Increasingly they saw war as the business of the sovereign states then taking shape in Europe whose monarchs – at least ideally – would fight within the constraints of natural law. Grotius' *Law of War and Peace* stood as the premier statement of *jus in bello*. Today his ideas on natural law as a restraining hand on military violence continue to resonate.[5] Modern authorities have cited the *Law of War and Peace* as roughly "synonymous" with today's International Humanitarian Law. *Jus in bello*, the International Red Cross explains, "seeks to minimize suffering in armed conflicts, notably by protecting and assisting all victims of armed conflict to the greatest extent possible." It "is intended to protect victims of armed conflicts regardless of party affiliation."[6]

Much of this Enlightenment interest in *jus in bello* had tragic roots – a reaction to events we can only describe as horrific. Between 1618 and 1648, the Thirty Years War tore apart central Europe. It began as a religious conflict, triggered when the arch-Catholic king of Bohemia (and soon-to-be Holy Roman emperor), Ferdinand II, attempted to force Catholicism on his Protestant subjects. The Protestant aristocracies of Bohemia rebelled, and the resulting strife engulfed much of Austria, many of the German principalities, and parts of northern Italy. The ferocity grew in intensity as the initial religious fervor meshed with emerging dynastic, territorial, and economic goals. Eventually, the Swedes, French, Poles, Spanish, Danes, British, and even the Ottomans were drawn in as alliances shifted and various monarchs and factions jockeyed for advantage. Mercenaries filled many of the armies, and when they went unpaid (which was often) they lived off the land, preying on virtually defenseless peasantry. Thousands of these soldiers deserted from formal armies and roamed as gangs of pillaging and murdering banditti, sometimes joined by individuals cast adrift as regional societies collapsed. These non-state actors were marginally more terrifying than the monarchial troops, but the formally constituted armies also plundered with a free hand. Unrestrained murder, destruction, and rapine were commonplace; vast regions were virtually depopulated.[7] Much of Europe was shaken to its very foundations.

The toll was staggering. The Bohemian phase of the war effectively ended in 1620 following Ferdinand's victory at the Battle of White Mountain, after which he dealt decisively with the defeated rebels. He had prominent Bohemian (Czech) leaders executed, and he confiscated the estates of Protestant nobles. Tens of thousands of Czech Protestants fled, and of some 151,000 farmsteads on Bohemian Crown Lands in the early 1620s only some 50,000 were left by 1648. Only 800,000 inhabitants remained out of an original 3,000,000.

Bohemia was not alone in its tribulations. Germany (then an agglomeration of dozens of principalities) lost an estimated 20 percent of its population, with some regions suffering a 50 percent loss. The Thirty Years War was one of the most destructive ever waged, and one estimate of military and civilian casualties from all causes has placed the toll at some 8,000,000 fatalities. These losses equaled or surpassed the military and civilian fatalities endured during the devastating Napoleonic Wars (1803–15).[8] Europe would not see violence on this scale again until the First World War.

The horror ended with the Treaty of Westphalia in 1648, but the memories of an enervated Europe lingered. Grotius wrote while the Thirty Years War raged, and it was his fervent hope that if there must be war – and he and subsequent Enlightenment writers had no illusions on that score – perhaps a recognized ethical code might limit or avoid the savagery that convulsed Europe for three long decades.

The most polished work on the subject, however, appeared just over a century after the treaty. In 1758 the Swiss-born lawyer and

"FIGHTING JUSTLY"?

German diplomat Emer de Vattel (1714–67) published *The Law of Nations* (*Le Droit des Gens ou Principes de la Loi Naturelle Appliqués à la Conduite et Aux Affaires des Nations et des Souverains*).[9] Vattel, deeply schooled in the Enlightenment philosophers, was heavily influenced by Grotius and the works of Gottfried Wilhelm von Leibniz (1646–1716) and Christian Wolff (1679–1754). These latter scholars wrote on any number of subjects during the later 17th and early 18th centuries, contributing to discussions on the nature of rational thought, good government, and general ethics. Vattel not only read them, but he began his own work as a translation (from the Latin) of Wolff's *The Law of Nations According to the Scientific Method* (*Jus Gentium Methodo Scientifica Pertractum*). As Vattel worked through the translation, he incorporated his own ideas, interpretations of previous authors, and what he saw as lessons from history. The result was an opus that delved expansively into the philosophical and political relationships between states and between governors and the governed – and of *jus in bello*.

Vattel wrote with the hope of marking the "just bounds" of war, and "by the rules of justice, equity, and humanity" to moderate deadly military conduct.[10] There is general consensus on the main elements of *jus in bello*, although here we offer only a brief summary of Vattel's work. The first element is "distinction," an agreement that war is confined to active combatants, meaning that civilians, wounded soldiers, prisoners of war, and any others posing no military threat should suffer no violence. Only legitimate military targets are subject to attack, thus sparing most private property and non-military facilities. "Proportionality" ideally limits military action only to measures necessary to gaining military advantage or accomplishing a specific objective. Under *jus in bello*, measures beyond the strictly necessary are considered excessive and reprobated; the goal is to limit needless violence and destruction. The related tenet of "necessity" again emphasizes the obligation to focus military actions on legitimate military targets, and when such operations unavoidably harm noncombatants or civilian property – what today we call "collateral damage" – such harm should be held to a minimum. *Jus in bello* also specifically prohibits the mistreatment of prisoners and the use of inappropriate weapons or methods (*malum in se*).[11]

The American Context

The doctrine of *jus in bello* did limit military savagery in 18th-century Europe, where states fought primarily over limited territorial or dynastic objectives. And it is true the Enlightenment ideal, along with a related sense of military honor, played a role in curbing excesses during the War for Independence. Most senior British officers and many in the colonial elite were familiar with the *jus in bello* ideal. Translations of Grotius had been available in America for some time. The first English translation of Vattel's *The Law of Nations* appeared in 1760 and apparently crossed the Atlantic soon thereafter.[12] In 1773 George Washington ordered copies of both authors for a relative (although he may not have read Vattel himself until the 1790s); and at least one colonial governor cited Grotius in questioning the legality of capturing Indians taken during a formal truce.[13]

Vattel also was in evidence as the imperial crisis came to a head. John Adams noted citations to *The Law of Nations* in debates with Massachusetts royal governor Thomas Hutchinson; and Adams and Thomas Jefferson consulted Vattel in deciding points of law (especially on naval or military prize seizures) during the Revolution. Benjamin Franklin owned a copy of *The Law of Nations*, and he indicated delegates to the Continental Congress knew of it.[14] Indeed, historians generally consider Vattel "the most influential" proponent of the rules of just war; and as one authority has observed, among the elites of the revolutionary generation Vattel's writings were virtually "canonical."[15]

There was something of great significance to this reality. For with or without direct familiarity with *The Law of Nations*, the ethos of *jus in bello* did permeate the thinking of numerous patriots. As one observer has correctly stated, "no nation in the history of the world has made the law governing the conduct of armies in war more crucial to its founding self-image than the United States."[16] For whatever purposes Congress intended the Declaration of Independence – a statement of principles, an appeal for international recognition, a justification for the resort to arms – the delegates also used America's inaugural document to broadcast their commitment to the tenets of "civilized warfare," their belief that military violence should be limited and bound by universally recognized constraints. Pointedly, they used the Declaration to seize the high moral ground, stridently denouncing multiple British violations of the canons of *jus in bello*. Among other alleged outrages, the Crown had "plundered our seas," "ravaged our Coasts," and destroyed American towns and livelihoods; had also unleashed merciless Indian assaults that fell on all ages and sexes; encouraged slave rebellions; and employed German mercenaries who had committed unspeakable crimes "scarcely paralleled in the most barbarous Ages." These were appalling acts, shameful behavior on the part of supposedly civilized Great Britain.[17] Hardly disguised was the Declaration's implication that in their struggle against tyranny American patriots would never stoop so low.

At least some senior officers in the revolutionary military shared these sentiments – again, whether or not such opinions reflected any actual reading of Vattel. Moreover, ranking officers of the Continental and British armies belonged to their respective national social and political elites, and as "gentlemen" they were certainly familiar with the mores and codes of honor of the day. On the American side, we may note two examples. The first is obvious: General George Washington, commander-in-chief of the Continental Army. Washington had been a soldier since his youth, and in 1754, as a 22-year-old lieutenant colonel of Virginia militia, he had been involved in a questionable affair in western Pennsylvania (modern Fayette County). Sent to deter French claims in the Ohio River Valley, he launched a surprise late-night attack on an encamped French party that had sortied from Fort Duquesne (today's Pittsburgh). In confusing circumstances, his men killed, wounded, or captured over 30 French soldiers (some of whom were Canadian), including their commanding officer, Ensign Joseph Coulon de Jumonville.

Washington later insisted it was a fair fight; the French protested that Jumonville's mission had been diplomatic, not military, and that the wounded Jumonville and other French had been murdered – a gross violation of the rules of war. That incident, never conclusively resolved, left Washington touchy about his reputation. Thereafter, he was scrupulous in observing the canons of *jus in bello*.[18] During the Revolution he cautioned his army about respecting private property, enforced prohibitions against pillaging, insisted on the humane treatment of prisoners – even as the British held patriot prisoners of war in abominable conditions – and did his best to maintain cordial relations with civilian authorities. Instances of not "fighting fair" met his principled objections. Washington and British commander-in-chief William Howe, for instance, both denounced the practice of soldiers cutting incisions in lead musket balls in order to inflict greater damage to opponents (although soldiers continued to do so).[19] Given his preferences, the Virginian would have waged as restrained a war as possible.

We may take the Continental Army's chief of artillery, Brigadier General Henry Knox, as our second example. Knox was a self-taught soldier. A Boston bookseller before the war, much of what he learned had come from the books in his shop. He was no revolutionary zealot; having climbed from very modest origins, he took seriously his social position as a successful merchant. Knox had "arrived" socially – including a marriage "above himself" to Lucy Flucker, daughter of Thomas Flucker, the staunchly loyalist colonial secretary of Massachusetts – just as revolutionary sentiments were reaching critical mass. When he joined the Continental officer corps, Knox brought with him the social perspectives of the colonial elite, even if he was *nouveau*. In his view, honor and justice required that he wage "civilized" warfare, eschewing the military excesses of which he would accuse the British. To do otherwise would disgrace him as an individual and the country for which he fought. As far as we know, Knox came to this belief without any specific reference to *The Law of Nations*, Grotius, or any other Enlightenment text.[20] He simply modeled his conduct and outlook on what he considered most proper for an officer *and* a gentleman.

Washington and Knox were hardly alone. Other officers, not always of senior rank, also tried to avoid needless carnage and to restrain the conduct of their troops out of regard for what was proper in war. Lieutenant Colonel John Graves Simcoe of the Queen's American Rangers – a crack regiment of loyalist regulars – deplored the practice of firing on sentries if no greater action was intended. Others shared Simcoe's sentiments. During operations near Charleston, South Carolina, in 1776 British captain William Dansey was enraged when a rebel picked off one of his sentries. The rebels were "cowardly Scoundrels, who came upon their Hands and Knees to get a shot at him as one wou'd at a Duck."[21]

Such conduct violated elite conceptions of fair play, and gentlemen supposedly did not condone such behavior. In 1779, after the dramatic storming of Stony Point, Anthony Wayne, whose command Major General Charles "No Flint" Grey had devastated at Paoli in 1777, permitted no abuse of British wounded and prisoners. As his troops marched across New Jersey in 1778, Sir Henry Clinton, impressed with the courage of a dying militia officer who refused to disclose the location of his comrades, had the man's remains buried with the full honors of war (a separate grave, a religious observance or formal recognition of the deceased's courage, and a musket salute). After the Battle of Monmouth, rebels returned the compliment. They buried Grenadier lieutenant colonel Henry Monckton, the senior British officer killed during the battle, with military honors. Also at Monmouth, Continental doctor William Read walked the field caring alike for patriot and British wounded. After the patriot fiasco at Penobscot (in modern Maine), British brigadier Francis McLean treated rebel prisoners with humanity; he even provided shipping to repatriate some of them.[22] Citing similar examples, historian Wayne E. Lee found restraint and the influence of *jus in bello* characteristic of key facets of the American war effort – specifically among Washington's regular troops.[23] As grim as military realities were, things could have been worse.

In these views of what was and was not fair, regular officers were abiding by European standards of military etiquette, including the tenets of *jus in bello*, as matters of professionalism, principle, and military culture. A final example will help establish the point. Again, we look at the highest reaches of command. In May 1781 Charles, Second Earl Cornwallis (1738–1805), invaded Virginia. The earl had matters pretty much his own way on campaign, laying waste to economic targets, scattering Virginia's political leadership, and hoping to destroy any rebel forces willing to stand and fight. Yet Cornwallis had every intention of observing the "rules of civilized war." He insisted that his officers and soldiers protect loyalist civilians and do their utmost to win the populace to the royal cause. That meant scrupulous efforts to avoid plundering and all gratuitous violence. His was hardly a successful appeal; British commissary operations were stretched thin, and soldiers on short rations foraged persistently just to feed themselves. But Cornwallis was determined to restrain excesses, a policy he continued in Virginia, and his headquarters repeatedly issued orders against illegal foraging and violence against civilians. He applied the death penalty for rape and desertion, and – in an extraordinary proclamation – he even called on paroled rebels "to seize, & Bring to head Quarters all stragglers from the British Army, particularly those whom they may detect in committing depredations & Robberies in the Country, that they may be punished."[24]

Although hardly any insurance against all depredations toward civilians, Cornwallis made a good-faith effort, obviously combining practical and gentlemanly motives. And whatever their motives, they kept violence within sufficient bounds to avoid provoking a popular rising akin to the outraged reaction against British behavior in New Jersey in late 1776. Thus *jus in bello*, while not observed or interpreted universally, was not entirely a dead letter – at least among some regular forces.

Shared martial values frequently allowed the mutual understanding of correct conduct in specific situations, conduct that fully reflected the tenets of *jus in bello*. Opposing officers frequently exchanged messages under flags of truce, for example, and the violation of a flag (such as firing on a flag party) was held to be grossly dishonorable.[25] There was a preference for offering opponents honorable terms of surrender rather than forcing bloody battles to the last man. The classic examples here were Saratoga, Charleston, and Yorktown. True, at Charleston and Yorktown the victors denied the surrendering American and British armies the "honors of war" – marching to the formal ground of capitulation under arms and with colors flying – but at least the negotiations provided for the fair treatment of prisoners and the parole of senior officers.

On the other hand, there was an understanding that a besieged opponent, or an opponent otherwise *hors du combat*, refusing terms of honorable surrender, could expect little mercy. In this instance Vattel was very much in evidence. *The Law of Nations* specified that a military formation in utterly hopeless circumstances, in which fighting on would serve no purpose, *ought* to surrender. Vattel appreciated valor. "Resistance carried to extremity" was laudable; but when resistance became "fruitless," then fighting on was only "obstinacy, and not firmness or valour." When "no succour is to be expected," he explained, an opposing commander may be "summoned to surrender; and he may be threatened with death in case of his persisting in a defence which is absolutely fruitless, and which can only tend to the effusion of human blood. Should this make no impression on him, he deserves to suffer the punishment with which he has been justly threatened."[26] This section of *The Laws* had a merciless sound to it, but the intent was to avoid useless bloodshed.

Of course, beyond any philosophical obeisance to *jus in bello*, efforts to encourage martial restraint often had very practical motives. Senior commanders on both sides knew wanton violence, the plundering of unoffending civilians, and the mistreatment of prisoners and wounded would likely lead only to retaliation from opponents (which even Vattel conceded was justified). Rather, the goal was to win popular support for the respective British or American causes.

For whatever other reasons Washington wanted to fight "justly," he also wanted no part of a conflict that would shatter society to its foundations. Accordingly, he stressed the fair treatment of the civilian population, and he strictly forbade his troops from plundering or otherwise abusing civilians. Washington rightly feared that ill-disciplined American troops would drive the populace to the British; indeed, he was so averse to incurring popular wrath that during the Valley Forge winter Congress had to prod him to impress foodstuffs even from loyalists.[27]

Sir Henry Clinton, who replaced William Howe as British commander-in-chief in 1778, shared a similar fear. He was convinced that a key to victory lay in the ability "to gain the hearts and subdue the minds of America" (we may credit Sir Henry as one of the first to use the language of "hearts and minds" in a military context). A campaign of wanton destruction, he was sure, would only further alienate the rebellious colonials and further complicate the royal war effort. There would be times when he would try to hold in check fire-breathing subordinate officers who would have preferred a campaign of fire and sword (and more on them shortly).[28] During his raid in Virginia in 1781, even turncoat Benedict Arnold studiously avoided needless damage to private property and harm to noncombatants in an effort to woo Virginians back to the King's standard. His orders for restraint were entirely practical, but he tried to enforce them.[29] Martial restraint did have many useful purposes.

The Limits of Restraint ... and Other Problems

Convincing as they initially appear, however, examples of humanity and mitigated violence are too few to sustain an argument for any controlling influence of *jus in bello*. However canonical in theory, the "lived experience" of the Revolution revealed the ideal of martial restraint carried less weight than some historians have suggested, even among rebels aware of Grotius, Vattel, and other such commentators.

Part of the problem was that the rules of just warfare were seldom clear; there was never full agreement on what *jus in bello* precisely condoned or forbade. James Lovell, our "Massacre Day" orator, was clear on this point. Lovell, now a Massachusetts Continental congressional delegate, wanted John Adams to consult Grotius and Vattel and others on the technicalities of dealing with John Burgoyne's army, captured at Saratoga in October 1777. Lovell favored breaking the proposed surrender agreement (called a "Convention" to assuage British feelings) and holding Burgoyne's soldiers in strict custody as prisoners of war. The congressman noted interpretations of the *jus in bello* authors offered little guidance; they could "support reason and commonsense or destroy both." *Jus in bello* was open to all sorts of interpretation, Lovell noted, and looking for unambiguous answers would likely "cause a vast expenditure of ink" and nothing more. In addition, interest in *jus in bello* was often quite utilitarian, focused on rather mundane points of law rather than the mitigation of military violence.

When Virginia governor Thomas Jefferson sought a legal opinion on the ownership of captured enemy horses, attorney general Edmund Randolph cited *The Laws* on the spoils of war (the state owned the horses). But Randolph also noted that even among Virginia's elites there was limited "access to Vattel," and one assumes a similar unfamiliarity with other writers on *jus in bello*.[30]

Depending on who was reading and interpreting Vattel, there were caveats in *The Laws* that seemingly left many civilians and irregular combatants outside of the theoretical protections of just war. *Jus in bello* stressed lawful combat between formal military organizations — that is, fighting between the regularly enlisted, uniformed, organized, and officered forces of sovereign states. Vattel grouped those serving on privateers with regular forces as long as they could produce valid letters of marque (an official permission from a legal government to cruise against enemy shipping and split the prize money with the issuing government).[31] Yet *jus in bello* was unambiguous on a key point: soldiers were distinct from civilians, and civilians were *not* under *any* circumstances to meddle in military activities. Vattel insisted war was the exclusive business of regular troops. "The peasants, the citizens," he warned, "take no part in it." "[T]he [regular] troops alone carry on the war, while the rest of the nation remain in peace."[32]

All such matters were often problematic even in Europe, but they failed to reflect North American realities. Elite familiarity with *jus in bello* was not an indication of its influence beyond patriot military and social leaders. For example, frontier warfare recognized few distinctions between soldiers and civilians. It was much the same with militia warfare elsewhere, which could blur the line between combatants and noncombatants. The farmer tilling his field one day could be the citizen-in-arms the next. It was just such an "embattled farmer" that had mercilessly tomahawked a helplessly wounded redcoat near Concord Bridge.[33]

Civilians, including women and children, were prime sources of intelligence, served as messengers, and marshaled supplies for rebel forces. Dealing with hostile civilians was a constant source of apprehension and irritation for the British. How was a redcoat to know who the enemy really was? Civilians or anyone out of uniform mixing in military affairs crossed a dangerous line. If civilians remained peaceful, Vattel wrote, they should have "nothing to fear from the sword of the enemy ... [and] they live in as perfect safety." But "if the peasants of themselves commit any hostilities, the enemy shows them no mercy, but hangs them up as he would so many robbers or banditti."[34] Few British soldiers did any such thing, but no amount of restraint on the part of their senior officers could prevent frustrated troops from lashing out at local populations they perceived as hostile.

"FIGHTING JUSTLY"?

When British soldiers did vent their anger at civilians, they generally chose their targets deliberately along political lines. The example of a single campaign makes the point: in June 1778, as Sir Henry Clinton's army retreated from Philadelphia across New Jersey, his troops selectively burned the homes and farmsteads of active patriots. Tories abandoning the state with the British willingly pointed out appropriate targets. In Burlington County, the homes of William Shreve and Peter Tallman went up in smoke – Shreve being a senior militia officer and Tallman a prominent politico. Such were the risks of leading rebel military and political figures. But less prominent patriots suffered similar losses. In Monmouth Courthouse (Freehold, New Jersey), out-of-control soldiery sacked the town, looting and torching the shops, homes, and barns of local whigs. Loyalist properties were unmolested. Here was an example of the divide between the ideal and the reality of war – and of the limits of *jus in bello*. Clinton had done his best to leave civilians alone during his retreat; he issued strict orders against pillage and offered generous rewards for anyone turning in looters. But no one talked; and if most senior officers were willing to abide by the rules of war, or at least to follow Clinton's orders, the reality on the ground indicated that many (if not most) junior officers and NCOs honored them only in the breach.[35] After all, soldiers bearing the brunt of the campaign considered that hostile civilians deserved everything they got.

Yet even when commanders maintained strict control, *jus in bello* left plenty of room for violence. Under certain conditions armies could wreak considerable havoc while remaining within the rules of "civilized warfare." "Since the object of a just war is to repress injustice and violence," Vattel explained that states had the right to use all means necessary against an unjust enemy "in order to weaken him, and disable him from resisting us and supporting his injustice: and we may choose such methods as are the most efficacious and best calculated to attain the end in view, provided they be not of an odious kind, nor unjustifiable in themselves."[36] "Efficacious" methods included the pillage "of a town taken by assault." "It is lawful to take away the property of an unjust enemy in order to weaken or punish him, the same motives justify us in destroying what we cannot conveniently carry away."[37]

This was a grave enough business, but Vattel counseled that "on certain occasions ... matters are carried still farther: A country is totally ravaged, towns and villages are sacked, and delivered up as prey to fire and sword. Dreadful extremities, even when we are forced into them! Savage and monstrous excesses, when committed without necessity!" But they were necessary when "checking" the brutality of "an unjust and barbarous nation" and "preserving ourselves from her depredations." Vattel then offered a striking example of when such dire measures were appropriate — one that would resonate later in the War for Independence. "Who can doubt," he asked rhetorically, "that the king of Spain and the powers of Italy have a very good right utterly to destroy those maritime towns of Africa, those nests of [Barbary] pirates, that are continually molesting their commerce and ruining their subjects?" As we will see, this reasoning would spell trouble for any number of American coastal towns serving as privateer bases.

Thus, even within *jus in bello* there was a slippery slope. War itself develops a momentum of its own (which we have cited as a central element of existential warfare), and short of a premeditated massacre of prisoners or of unoffending civilians, or the needless destruction of non-military property, where did one actually draw the line in justifying martial behavior? Who defined "unoffending," "needless," or "non-military"? To what extent did one retaliate against an attack, event, or behavior perceived as a violation of the "rules"? Stated bluntly, there was never full agreement on what *jus in bello* precisely condoned or forbade. The humane spirit was clear enough, but how to put that spirit into practice was anything but easy to accomplish.

Then there were instances of senior commanders professing complete ignorance of *jus in bello* or reasoning that the canon did not apply to particular circumstances. Admiral George Rodney's conquest of Dutch St. Eustatius (1781) was a case in point. While the Dutch were not in formal alliance with the Americans, their Caribbean island was a bustling entrepot transshipping arms, munitions, and the sinews of war of all kinds to the rebels. When the Anglo-Dutch War broke out in December 1780, St. Eustatius was a logical target, and Rodney took it with a minimum of fighting. But the admiral then proceeded to the systematic pillaging of private and public property. He might have claimed that as a key source of supplies for the Americans, St. Eustatius had crossed a line – that it had fatally blurred any distinction between military and civilian affairs and had thus made itself a legitimate target for retaliation. But Rodney acted with a hand heavy enough to incite parliamentary calls for his prosecution. The admiral, however, made no such defense. He claimed instead that he was a military man with no knowledge of *The Law of Nations*.[38] This was ridiculous, but Rodney's disingenuous excuse for his conduct was reflective of sentiments found in other British officers who took exception to at least some of the rules of war.

The "Hard Line": Woe to Rebels

Many ranking British officers believed that rebels fell outside of the protections of *jus in bello*, and they saw little point in waging war with a velvet fist. And there was recent precedent for their point of view. In 1746 the immediate aftermath of the Battle of Culloden – the last serious engagement during the Jacobite rebellion of 1745–46 – saw brutal retaliation against wounded Scots, followed by a determined British effort to root out Jacobite sympathizers in the Scottish Highlands. Eventually, hundreds of Scots were exiled, many Jacobite leaders were executed, and property confiscations were extensive.[39] Culloden and the Jacobite rebellion were recent memories in 1775, and any number of British officers saw no reason to see the American rebellion differently.

Redcoats of this mind firmly believed the only way to bring the Americans to heel was to liberally apply the blade and the torch — and worse. These "hard-line" men (historian Stephen Conway's helpful term) had come to America angry; they saw the American rebellion as thoroughly unjustified and American rebels as deserving of no sympathy or recognition under the canons of "civilized war." Captain William Glanville Evelyn, 4th Foot, put the hard-line perspective into a nutshell: British authorities, he wrote, "must permit us to restore to them the dominion of the country by laying it waste, and almost extirpating the present rebellious race." He was happily willing to torch as many American towns as it took to bring the rebels to their senses.[40]

Officers of Evelyn's mind refused to recognize the legitimacy of the patriot Congress or state governments, and the soldiery generally took their cues on allowable conduct from their officers. If officers hinted (or openly avowed) that rebels, military or civilian, should pay a price for disloyalty to their sovereign — and how else can we interpret Evelyn's attitude? — troops acted accordingly. And for every officer who sought to "fight justly," there were probably just as many Captain Evelyns. Woe to rebels!

Vattel saw things differently. In *The Laws* he specifically frowned on rebellions against duly constituted authority. He stated that rebels ordinarily deserved little mercy. But when a rebellion assumed sufficient popular scope and political organization, with formally organized and officered armed forces, Vattel conceded that rebels had as much right to protections under *jus in bello* as the combatants of sovereign states.[41] But who defined things like "sufficient scope and organization"? It was another arguable point, and the hard-line camp held that nothing was too harsh for those in rebellion against the Crown. If a campaign of fire and sword was the only way to break them (considering that they had it coming), then so be it.

The results could be horrific. During the Battle of Bunker Hill on June 17, 1775, for example, the outspoken Massachusetts patriot leader Dr. Joseph Warren fought on the front lines. When His Majesty's forces finally overran the rebels, a British officer who recognized Warren, a man who had regularly disparaged British redcoats, took aim and shot away part of the agitator's face, killing him instantly. Other soldiers poured in and repeatedly bayoneted the lifeless body to the point of mutilation. This was in the heat of battle when passions ran high. But two days later, another British officer allegedly – the account is disputed – sought out Warren's remains, "spit in his face," then "jump'd on his Stomach and at last cut off his Head and committed every act of violence upon his Body."[42]

There were similar incidents. On January 2, 1777, in Trenton, New Jersey, 63-year-old Presbyterian minister John Rosbrugh failed to escape as Lord Cornwallis' troops moved into the town. He surrendered to a Hessian detail under command of a British junior officer. Rosbrugh, a College of New Jersey (Princeton) graduate, was serving as a Pennsylvania militia chaplain, and under the canons of *jus in bello* he was entitled to humane treatment as a prisoner of war. He didn't receive it. The soldiers supposedly were under orders to take no prisoners; and with the reverend pleading for mercy "for his family's sake," the Hessians plundered him, sabered him in the head, and repeatedly bayonetted him before leaving his body where he fell. "The British officer at whose command he had been put to death," a patriot account later claimed, then "exhibited the dead Chaplain's watch, and boasted that he had killed a rebel parson."[43] So much for humanity and honor.

The Americans had their "Captain Evelyns" as well – and in high places. If they usually eschewed the blood-curdling rhetoric of Evelyn, they could be strident enough. Remember the war cry of Georgia governor Archibald Bulloch: "This is no time to talk of moderation; in the present instance it ceases to be a virtue."[44] And moderation quickly disappeared. Recall the fate of Georgia loyalist Thomas "Burntfoot" Brown in 1775. The treatment of Brown was an egregious example of what loyalists faced across the rebellious colonies.

As noted, the Declaration cleared the way for the new American states to initiate some of the most repressive measures in American history. We should recall that the catalog of what loyalists endured is shocking: forced exile, property confiscations, trials and executions for treason, murder without trial, imprisonment in fetid conditions (including in old mines), and all manner of small and large daily harassments. Matters only got worse as the war deepened.

By the end of the war, British raids on American coastal towns had so exasperated patriots that Congress seriously contemplated ordering summary executions of captured British officers. Such would be fit retaliation, the delegates averred, for depredations "contrary to the laws of war among civilized nations."[45] One can wonder how "civilized" summary executions may have been. But major hostilities in the East ceased only weeks later after Yorktown, and luckily we will never know if patriots would have followed through on their threats.

Combatants

Yet the outlook and conduct of hard-line officers like Captain William Evelyn, or of a vengeance-minded Congress, provide only a partial insight into the war's excesses. The chief reason for the disparity between the ideal and the actual — that is, between the desire for military restraint and the realities of widespread and uninhibited violence — is not hard to find. It lies in who the combatants actually were, and most were not the Captain Evelyns of the war. If senior commanders of the regular armies were the most likely to urge moderation in war — and they were, even given what we have seen about the excesses of many British troops — this reality is fatal to any argument for a pervasive *popular* acceptance of *jus in bello*. For most of the combat between 1775 and 1783 was neither the business of the regular British or Continental armies nor of their ranking officers.

Most combatants, including American Indians, were not regulars. The largest share of the fighting over the eight years of conflict fell to local militia and other irregular forces, and if much of this small-scale combat involved the regulars, it did so only marginally. We actually have numbers to support this contention, and here we return to compilations of revolutionary engagements by Howard Peckham, David Munn, and John Parker. Recall that Peckham counted 1,546 land and naval actions between 1775 and 1783; and of the 1,331 land actions, only 60 were primarily engagements between regular armies. Parker's count in South Carolina showed a myriad of local engagements, the vast majority not involving regular forces.[46] Although not precise, these numbers do provide a sense of the scale and nature of the combat. It was a grinding sort of war, and revolutionary America bled steadily from many pores.

Then there was the matter of where the fighting occurred. The majority of engagements took place in widely dispersed "military frontiers."[47] These were the regions in which neither side had established firm military, political, or social control. Vast tracts of the North American interior were, in effect, "borderlands" or "no-man's-lands." Different groups variously traversed them, contested others for control, and fought over them. Virtually all of Trans-Appalachia and much of the southern, Pennsylvania, and New York State backcountries were such frontiers, as were the eastern shores of Virginia and Maryland. So were the New Jersey counties fronting British-occupied New York City and the British garrison in Philadelphia.[48] These military frontiers encompassed spans of territory too immense for either of the regular armies to pretend to control.

Peckham and Munn made clear how much of the war took place in these military frontiers. Peckham places well over half of the fighting on the western frontiers of the South, in northern and western New York, in western Pennsylvania, and in Trans-Appalachia. Munn found most of the New Jersey engagements – easily some 75 percent – occurred in areas closest to British-held New York City and Sandy Hook. This largely included the "Neutral Ground" of Bergen County and large sections of Monmouth County and the Pine Barrens of southern New Jersey. We can add to these the New Jersey actions during the British occupation of Philadelphia. Again, bear in mind that these numbers are suggestive rather than precise, but there is little reason to doubt the general validity of the picture they present. That is, most revolutionary combat occurred in areas beyond anyone's effective military control or political authority. That meant when combat spilled over into unrestrained mayhem, no one was in a position to stop it. It was a local war fought with local rules – meaning there generally were no rules.

Toward Existential War

How do we sum up our narrative to this point? What is clear is that while *jus in bello* was a widely shared ideal that did carry some weight, its tenets were porous. Emer de Vattel understood that it was impossible to take all of the violence out of war and that in certain circumstances such violence was justified. What those circumstances were, however, remained contentious. It was also beyond question that not everyone agreed on who fell under the protections of *jus in bello*. Vattel was guarded in recognizing rebels as legitimate combatants, and there were those – British and American – who frankly considered that rebels deserved everything they got, no matter how grim and brutal. Thus, even among elites, including senior officers and political leaders, *jus in bello* was hardly a firm barrier against military excesses, especially when perceived military and political necessity seemed to require draconian measures.

The War for Independence was not largely a war of elites, at least not at the level where the "better sort" actually did most of the fighting. There were some obvious (and ominous) implications in the numbers we have presented. The war more often than not was a conflict fought by ordinary local troops. Be they whig, tory, or American Indian, combatants generally served and fought in local contexts, often in defense of homes and communities. Without regular officers and functional political authorities to urge restraint, the military frontiers were rife with the sort of combat that most lent itself to unrestrained mayhem – violence very much akin to the events that convulsed Europe during the Thirty Years War. Entire regions lived in a perpetual state of anxiety and often naked fear; raids, pillaging, murder, and all manner of viciousness were constant possibilities. We can only guess at the psychological impact on all concerned.

We can end with an observation: It appears generally to be the case that the farther one got from the main armies – those of George Washington, Nathanael Greene, William Howe, Henry Clinton, or Charles, Lord Cornwallis – the more merciless the violence became. We will explore the specifics of this observation in the following chapters as we investigate the Revolution's descent into the maelstrom of existential war.

2

"Exposed to Both Internal and External Enemies": War to the Knife in New Jersey

New Jersey was one of the smallest of the rebellious colonies. With 120,000 or so residents, it was physically larger only than four others.[1] The province was overwhelmingly agricultural, and most white Jerseymen (enslaved and free black people comprised something over 6 percent of the population, perhaps a bit more) were yeomen of middling circumstances. Their produce, livestock, timber, and related products sold well in New York and Philadelphia and hence to markets overseas. It was not yet the Garden State, but New Jersey was one of the empire's breadbaskets. After 1763 Jerseymen shared most colonial discontents with various imperial policies; but with the exception of the Stamp Act, which did arouse considerable indignation in 1765–66,[2] the province did not share the depth of wider colonial alarm at British regulatory initiatives. The colony was not necessarily tranquil. Local politics could be heated, and residents occasionally rioted over disputed land titles. But those were largely internal squabbles, and for the most part New Jersey residents were happy enough as British subjects. With a large pacifist Quaker population, little in the way of an Indian frontier, scant commerce subject to imperial regulations, and a generally popular royal governor in William Franklin (son of Benjamin Franklin), the province seemed anchored to the empire.

Yet the façade of imperial loyalty fell away with the coming of the Revolution. New Jersey not only became a battleground –

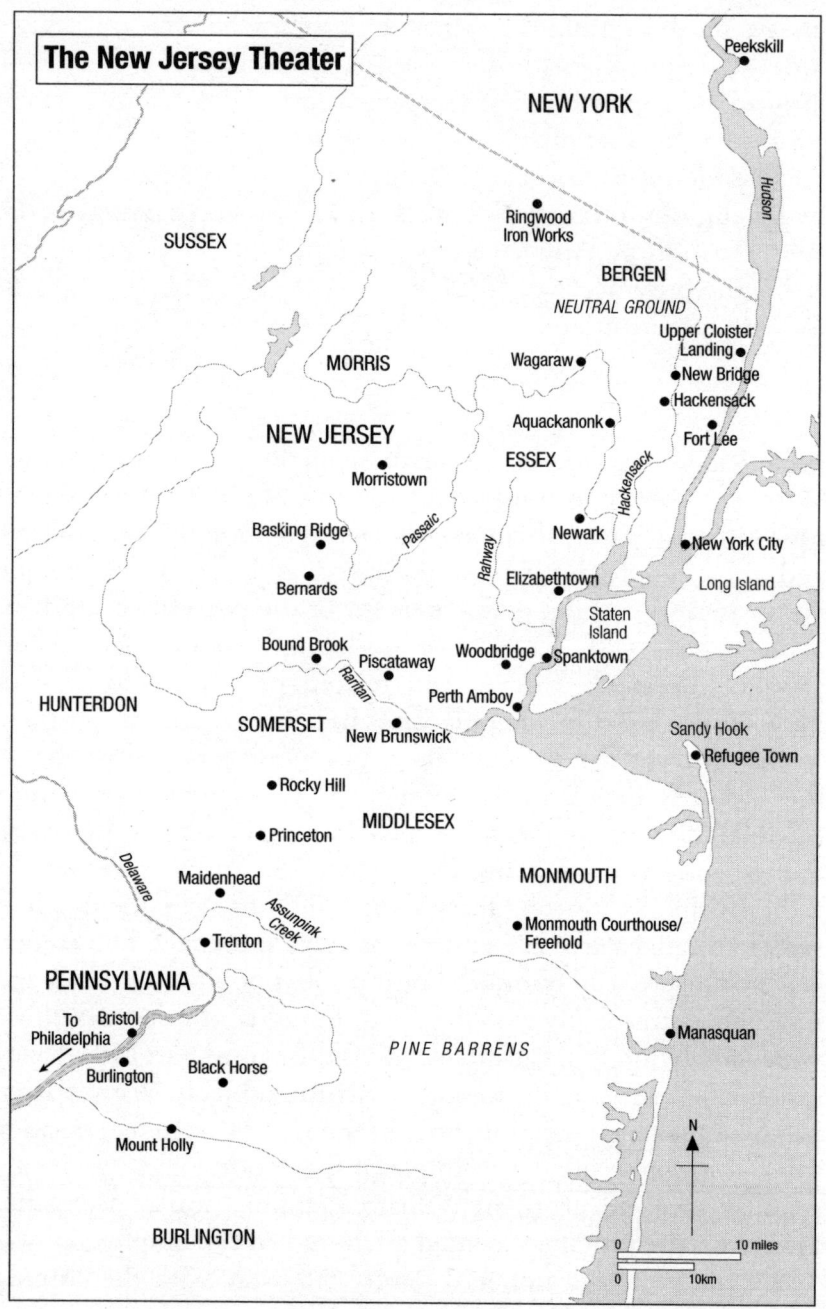

MAP I

it saw more fighting than any other state[3] — it also witnessed a tidal wave of pitiless violence. Once unleashed, the viciousness proved unstoppable, as it overwhelmed voices of moderation and martial restraint. New Jersey would suffer under the vicissitudes of invasion and enemy occupation, a fratricidal civil war, religious and racial strife, and harrowing cycles of revenge and retribution. Anything but a hotbed of revolution before 1775, the province would fall prey to all of the dire tribulations of existential warfare.

A State Fissures: 1775–76

New Jersey came to the Revolution slowly. Opinion was divided on how far to go in opposing imperial policies (if at all), and there was little enthusiasm for a showdown with the parent nation. There probably was none. Still, as the post–Tea Party crisis at Boston dragged on, sympathy for supporting the patriot cause gradually waxed. New Jersey whigs, in agreement with the First Continental Congress, organized an "Association" to boycott British trade and were increasingly threatening against neighbors who lacked appropriate sympathy for put-upon Massachusetts. Jerseymen who evinced support for the British ministry, objected to the Association mandates, or were even suspected of loyalist sympathies, were to be shunned, taunted, and even intimidated as emotions flared up. There were few acts of actual violence, but people were taking sides, and there were strong hints that matters would turn ugly.

That turn came with news of the fighting at Lexington and Concord in April 1775, which galvanized New Jersey patriots. Extra-legal committees moved quickly to purge militia units, courts, and governmental institutions of assumed tories — effectively seizing political and military control of the colony. A provincial congress for all practical purposes replaced the colonial assembly, and the rebel government mobilized its militia and sent three regiments into Continental Army service before the end of 1775.

Open intimidation of loyalists began in earnest. In Piscataway Township, local patriots considered loyalist Thomas Randolph too unimportant to rate serious punishment (whatever that may have been) – so Randolph was "stripped naked, well coated with tar and feathers and carried in a wagon publicly around the town."[4] Patriots hauled one Nathaniel Haten before the Bernards Township committee, which found Haten "an enemy to the liberties of *America*." The committee proclaimed that all residents should shun this man – or else. "Otherwise they will expose themselves to the resentment of the friends of *American* liberty, and will be dealt with accordingly."[5] Patriots similarly harassed and threatened any number of other New Jersey residents, rounding them up and forcing them to pledge allegiance to the whig cause, disarming them, and intercepting shipments of all manner of goods destined for anyone judged inimical to whig sentiments.[6] Even political neutrals were right to be alarmed.

Still, the Crown enjoyed considerable support. Why? Loyalist motives have defied any easy explanations, and generalizations are risky as questions of political loyalties cut across socio-economic and geographical lines.[7] New Jersey inhabitants with long attachments to the royal government, including officeholders, generally remained loyal to King and Parliament. So did Anglican clergy and some major landowners, whose titles derived from early grants from the Crown. Many Quakers, while avoiding overt political commitments, remained at least passively loyal. Personal and family connections, and certain religious affiliations, played roles as well. And recall that many in New Jersey had few serious grievances against the empire; they simply wanted to maintain a traditional socio-political order they found congenial. Why on earth were radicals rocking a generally satisfactory boat? For whatever reasons they chose to stand by the Crown, however, the rebellion simply made no sense. There was a profound psychological disconnect between bewildered loyalists and those actually in rebellion, an inability to grasp the reasoning and conduct of erstwhile neighbors now in arms against the King. Over and over tory voices bewailed the "unnatural" rebellion. Indeed, the conviction that the war was somehow "unnatural" was something of a unifying factor, a common thread of understanding (or misunderstanding) in the loyalist experience.[8]

This pattern was nowhere more evident than in the experience of Sussex County farmer James Moody. Events left him utterly bemused. "When the present ill-fated Rebellion first broke out," Moody wrote, he was a prosperous and "happy farmer" with good neighbors, "a beloved wife, [and] three promising children." Moody was largely apolitical, but considered "he had every possible reason to be grateful for, and attached to, that glorious [British] Constitution to which he owed his security." Thinking of the Association, he found the proceedings of the First Continental Congress a threat to the constitution, "but he was completely miserable when, not long after, he saw it totally over-turned." No one ever put the loyalist case better. Moody's world was shattered, a world he saw as benign and just; and he felt it only right to act in its defense.[9] When the time came, Moody was willing to take up arms, while other tories were happy to cheer on the redcoats as they fought to put down a "destructive and unnatural rebellion ... inexcusable in the sight of God and Man."[10]

New Jersey whigs were fully aware of loyalist sentiments – and of the numbers of Jerseymen who held them. So hesitant were New Jersey patriots of their ground that they did not feel strong enough to move decisively against Governor William Franklin, Benjamin's illegitimate son, until January 1776. They placed him under house arrest, but took him into actual custody only after the Continental Congress issued the Declaration of Independence. Franklin endured a harsh captivity in Connecticut before being exchanged in 1778.[11] He never conceded the legitimacy of the new patriot government, and he always considered himself the rightful governor of New Jersey. Deeply embittered, Franklin became one of the most implacable hard-line men of the war, and New Jersey would hear from its former governor again.

The announcement of the Declaration was a defining moment. The news was traumatic. Moderate Jerseymen – probably the majority of the populace – were now caught between impassioned radicals and desperate tories. Ardent patriots, of course, rejoiced at the turn of events, and for them the new political calculus was simple: America was now independent, and those who opposed independence were no longer just contrarian neighbors – they were *traitors*.

In New Brunswick, "K. L. a Mechanic" warned Frances Lagrange, wife of loyalist attorney Bernardus Lagrange, that it was now "high treason to revile against the states of America, or at the ruling Body of them." Bernardus could either mend his ways, flee, or face the consequences. The same scribbler followed with a direct threat to Bernardus. "Have we not the sufficient reason," he rhetorically asked, "to pronounce you are an enemy of your country, and to brand you with the **odious** [emphasis in original] name of traitor?" Then an ominous conclusion: "if neither reason, justice or humanity are able to change your sentiments ... [be] assured there is a fatal day approaching which will bring ruin to your devoted head."[12] Lagrange, no fool, decamped to British lines.

So did many others. They faced essentially three choices: fight, flee (like Lagrange), or keep quiet and out of the way. Plenty of Jerseymen did try to affect neutrality, some successfully doing so for years. Others resorted to "situational loyalty," ingratiating themselves with whichever side seemed to be winning at the time. But in mid-1776 many New Jersey tories, their spirits buoyed by the expected British assault on New York City (the first redcoats landed on Sandy Hook and Staten Island in June), now boldly took up arms and determined to defend themselves, their property, and the empire.[13]

Fighting spread across the state. There were clashes between loyalists and patriot militia in Hunterdon, Essex, Gloucester, and Bergen Counties. In Bergen affairs were particularly heated.

"EXPOSED TO BOTH INTERNAL AND EXTERNAL ENEMIES"

The county was heavily Dutch, and loyalties split very roughly along the lines of a schism in the Dutch Reformed Church – a conflict between those who favored ordaining ministers in America, who generally were rebels, and those who insisted clergy be ordained in Holland, who were mostly tories. Security evaporated as rival militias, raiders, and patriot groups little better than gangsters clashed in small-scale actions so frequent that state authorities never could establish firm political control. The county's Hackensack Valley became known as the "Neutral Ground," and violence, semi-deserted villages, and fear became the regional norm.[14] "The good people of Bergen County," a militia commander noted, "Lay Greatly Exposed to Both Internal and External Enemies."[15] And they would be so exposed – in a state of civil war – until 1782.

Violence flared south of the "Neutral Ground" as well. The independence announcement in July sparked a full-blown loyalist counter-insurgency movement in Monmouth County. Hundreds of Monmouth residents, including many alarmed patriots, switched sides or declared themselves neutral; others actively took up arms. Rebels quelled the uprising with the help of militia from neighboring Burlington County and a contingent of Pennsylvania Continentals. But tory outbreaks continued, and only the arrival of additional Continentals, many of them from Monmouth County, shifted the balance of power – at least for the moment.

The Continental commander was Colonel David Forman, a Monmouth man. Loyalists called him "Devil David," and he was as zealous and uncompromising a radical as New Jersey produced during the war.[16] Sweeping through the county, Forman's troops arrested at least a hundred Monmouth residents and sent them to out-of-state prisons; they intimidated countless others. But when the Continentals disbanded in December, loyalists returned the favor. Leading patriots were rounded up, rebel properties pillaged, recruiting began for loyalist regiments, and tories attempted to take over the reins of civil administration. The year ended with loyalists very much in control and with the British commander-in-chief, Lieutenant General William Howe, exceedingly pleased with Monmouth's so-called "Tory Ascendancy."[17] But "Devil David" Forman had escaped the tory net, and like William Franklin, New Jersey would hear from him again.

The new state fissured along racial lines as well. Black people, free and enslaved, comprised about 6 to 7 percent of the population — around 9,000 individuals — the second-largest black population north of the Mason–Dixon Line. The largest concentrations of slavery were, respectively, in Bergen, Somerset, and Monmouth Counties.[18] How would black people, especially slaves, react to a civil war among the white populace? Would the enslaved flee, or even join the British and fight? There were plenty of rumors about black plots and restiveness, and rebel fears that New Jersey slaves might use the revolutionary turmoil to strike for freedom added a new dimension to the war.

In Somerset County patriots thought they had discovered a slave conspiracy, probably encouraged by British prisoners and local tories. Details of the affair are murky, but rebels became convinced the threat of a black insurrection was real.[19] This was not an isolated fear. In Monmouth, where enslaved and free black people constituted some 10 percent of the county's population, patriots knew that local slaves were restless. During the summer of 1776 any number of slaves (we don't know how many) escaped to British lines, and militia did not hesitate to arrest black individuals "on Suspicion of intending to join the Enemy."[20] The war was still in its infancy, and it was too early to predict if hatred of the rebel cause might forge an interracial alliance, however informal, between white and black loyalists. New Jersey whigs, like most republican-minded patriots elsewhere, were disposed to fear conspiracies anyway; the situation bore watching.

As the prospect of large-scale hostilities grew, so did a feeling among the state's white patriots that black people represented part of a triad of threats. The looming British threat — the enemy without — was clear enough, as was the tory enemy within. The idea occurred to some patriots to view the state's slaves as the

"EXPOSED TO BOTH INTERNAL AND EXTERNAL ENEMIES"

natural allies of the Crown and the loyalists. In July 1776 the patriot committee of Essex County, meeting just across from British-garrisoned Staten Island, informed Washington of fears the British would raid into the county "and ravage our country" and render the county "destitute of inhabitants, our wives and children unprotected either from the enemy without or the Tories and negroes in the midst of us."[21]

New Jersey whigs were hardly alone in their trepidation, as similar worries were as acute in neighboring regions. In Philadelphia, one congressional delegate warned that "I have great reason to think we shall have a severe trial this summer with *Britons, Hessians, Hanoverians, Indians, Negroes,* and every other butcher the gracious King of *Britain* can hire against us."[22] In the South, as we will see, the much larger enslaved population accented the alarm. In particular, news that Virginia's royal governor, John Murray, Lord Dunmore, had offered freedom to slaves willing to fight for the King was met with genuine consternation among the northern white population. Thus, almost from the beginning of the rebellion, there was no mistaking the profound uneasiness New Jersey rebels shared as they considered the possibilities of a black alliance with the Crown.

Thus, even before the first British redcoat set foot in the state, for all practical purposes New Jersey already was at war. Residents had experienced the dissolution of royal government, political and social turmoil, the first stages of civil war, and lived with fears born of racial tensions. Neighbors eyed one another warily. And things would only get worse.

Invasion and the Hard Line

In late 1776 New Jersey felt the shock of full-scale invasion. In November the British moved into the state against largely ineffectual resistance, and hundreds (if not thousands) of Jersey residents took advantage of Howe's proclamation asking that they renew their allegiance to George III and return peaceably to their homes. Many who did so were not necessarily tory in sympathy, but they considered it senseless to maintain a losing fight against an apparently invincible professional army, especially when all Howe required of them was to return peaceably to their homes. Many tories openly welcomed the redcoats, hundreds even organizing in tory militia units or joining provincial battalions in the British service. Memories of whig persecution were raw, and regional loyalists moved to settle scores. In so doing, however, legions of tories publicly identified themselves, which would come back to haunt them – but not quite yet.

Despite the welcome from loyalists, the British invasion was anything but gentle. In addition to his appointment as commander-in-chief, William Howe held (with his brother Admiral Lord Richard Howe) a brief as a peace commissioner; and General Howe wanted nothing more than to cap his victories with a successful effort to reestablish a willing American allegiance to King and Parliament. The British army, however, received mixed messages on the best way to conduct military operations. During the Trenton–Princeton campaign, a number of British orderly books fell into American hands, and whigs were mortified at Howe's orders. "His Excellency the Commander-in-Chief," one book read, "orders that all inhabitants that shall be found with arms, not having an officer with them shall be immediately taken and hung up." Another volume said the same in slightly different language. "Small straggling parties not dressed like soldiers and without officers, not being admissible in war who presumes to molest or fire upon soldiers or peaceable inhabitants of the country, will be immediately hanged without trial as assassins."[23]

All of this is instantly recognizable as Vattel's injunction against civilians mixing in hostilities. Recall the warning in *The Law of Nations*: "The peasants, the citizens take no part in it [the fighting]." Regulars were to do the fighting "while the rest of the nation remain in peace." But "if the peasants of themselves commit any hostilities, the enemy shows them no mercy, but hangs them up as he would so many robbers or banditti."[24] Of course rebel militia, generally without uniforms and often without a recognizable (to the British) command structure, easily fit Vattel's characterization of "banditti" or of Howe's "assassins." If rebels chose to fight outside the bounds of "civilized warfare," then in British eyes they also did so outside the protections of *jus in bello*. Howe condoned no mass hangings, but there were reliable reports of redcoats killing wounded militiamen.[25] Further, there would be plenty of instances when, especially in close-quarter combat with the bayonet, British and Hessian regulars showed little mercy.

Many of Howe's junior officers (and for at least a time probably most of them) absorbed the spirit of Howe's general orders. If rebel irregulars ignored the conventions of civilized war, then it was easy enough for the British to direct their ire at civilians who sympathized in some way with the rebels. Redcoat officers and their soldiers viewed New Jersey as a province in rebellion – much as Scotland in "the '45" – and they readily adopted the hard line with the locals. The results, if often tragic, were predictable. Howe's army plundered its way across the state. Troops, often with loyalist support, pillaged with abandon, burned homes and mills, appropriated food and forage, drove off or killed livestock, tore up fences, and threatened and beat civilians. It was a performance anything but calculated to endear Americans to the Crown or to bolster Howe's mission as a peacemaker. Most junior officers simply didn't care or, more charitably, had lost control of their men. When officers did try to intervene, there were instances of rank and file ignoring them with impunity.[26] Overall, Howe's army alienated thousands who might otherwise have returned to the royal standard.

Worse, there were frequent documented instances of rape. Indeed, any number of New Jersey women and girls (we don't know how many, but more than a few) suffered brutal assaults. According to Thomas Olden, a Princeton resident who lived through the invasion, at least some victims, perhaps most, kept silent to avoid "miserable and lasting Reproach." "I am, of the Opinion That many honest virtuous women have suffered in this Manner and kept it Secret for fear of making their lives miserable and so many of these Capital Crimes escape Punishment."[27]

There is little reason to believe Olden was exaggerating. The horrific ordeal of Abigail Palmer of Pennington, a village just north of Trenton, graphically illustrated the invasion's excesses. She was 13 years old when the British arrived, and for days a number of soldiers repeatedly raped her and a number of her friends. The young Palmer detailed her story of what amounted to sexual abuse and torture in a formal deposition — she was one of six New Jersey women to do so — that became grist for the revolutionary atrocity mill.[28] In January 1777, Thomas Nelson, Virginia congressman and Signer of the Declaration of Independence, wrote Thomas Jefferson that Howe's troops had "play[ed] the very Devil with the Girls and even old Women to satisfy their libidinous appetites. There is Scarcely a Virgin to be found in the part of the Country they have pass'd thro'."[29]

Conceding that whigs may have exaggerated accounts of rape for propaganda purposes, there is no question that much of the narrative of sexual predation was all too true. Benjamin Franklin found accounts of the rapes so shocking that, in the interest of the reputations of the victims, he wanted Congress to suppress the worst details in a public report of the incidents.[30] But Congress published everything, detailing what today we would call war crimes. These included "the wanton and oppressive devastation of the country, and destruction of property"; the "inhumane treatment of" prisoners; the "savage butchery of many who had submitted or were incapable of resistance"; and "the lust and brutality of the soldiers in abusing of women." The report alleged "many instances of the most indecent treatment" and rape.[31] Reprinted in northern newspapers and in pamphlet form, Congress did its best to assure that the report had a wide circulation.[32] The impact was what all whigs could have hoped: Thousands of Americans were unsurprisingly enraged and more motivated in various ways to support the rebel cause.

"EXPOSED TO BOTH INTERNAL AND EXTERNAL ENEMIES"

Not all British officers turned a blind eye to such abominable behavior. But in 1776 the worst punishment one of the rapists at Pennington endured was to be locked up for a few hours.[33] Overall, violence against civilians was common enough to sustain a view that, at least early in the war, British troops saw sexual assault and brutality against noncombatants as integral to their campaign against the Revolution. Everything alleged in the congressional report was a violation of the tenets of *jus in bello*, and it described British conduct that mirrored treatment meted out to the Scottish Highlanders after Culloden. And the comparison, at least from the whig perspective, was apt. Rather than recognize the Americans as freemen "defending their rights on principle," "those who are officers, and call themselves gentlemen" had disposed their troops to view patriots as "desperadoes and profligates, who have risen up against law and order in general, and wish the subversion of society itself."[34] If some British officers did try to rein in excesses, the danger remained that civilians often were at risk in the presence of the King's regulars.

To be clear: What we have described thus far was not yet "existential warfare." But the New Jersey experience through late 1776 had produced all of the ingredients. Among many residents calls for independence were unable to overcome old attachments to a generally benevolent empire. Loyalists and patriots then confronted one another in a cyclical pattern of action, reaction, and still subsequent reactions as levels of animosity and violence ratcheted upward. In some areas old religious schisms merged with political divisions. Slaves broke for possible freedom amid the turmoil, and many of them would take up arms. There was little political stability as fighting flared at the local level with scant regard for the "rules of war." The hard line emerged quickly. British regulars often showed little restraint in dealing with civilians, and rebels and tories found leaders willing to go to extremes. William Franklin would attract followers who fought literally with a vengeance, and "Devil David" Forman would relish his role as the terror of Monmouth County loyalists. What remained was for all of these factors to come together.

Into the Maelstrom

The British occupation was violent enough to trigger a popular insurrection. New Jersey militia, recovering from its early shock, began an effective campaign of sniping and harassment. Even before Washington's Trenton counterattack (December 26), the British were feeling the pressure and pain of rebel skirmishing. There were no fewer than 18 clashes between December 13 and 26, and after Princeton (January 3) there were 16 more over the rest of January.[35] The result was dramatic: The British, on the verge of crushing the rebellion in late 1776, had lost the initiative. This pattern continued over 1777 and into 1778. While regular troops were involved, usually in small units, the fighting evolved as part of a civil war, with most of the combat borne by local forces, patriot and tory. At least on the American side there was little or no central political direction behind the combat. Militia responded independently to British and loyalist incursions. On their part, tory bands frequently picked targets often in their old neighborhoods and singled out their own neighbors. Thus this personal civil war gave little thought to restraint, mercy, or compromise. It came to represent the kind of uncontrolled warfare that Vattel and other proponents of *jus in bello* had feared.

It might be pointless to offer an incident-by-incident account of events, but we need to look at least in broad strokes of how the fighting developed. Combat ranged across the state, but most of the action occurred in those regions contiguous to British garrisons in New York and, after Howe's invasion of Pennsylvania in 1777, his target Philadelphia. In the east, rebel authorities found the turmoil in the "Neutral Ground" of Bergen County's Hackensack Valley especially vexing. The troubles that swept the area in 1776 had only intensified as tory gangs, British probes and raids, and incursions by loyalist provincial units – often comprised of former residents – plagued the valley and neighboring regions. The rebel government and militia forces were unable to establish firm political control or guarantee local security, and Washington was unable to divert Continentals to protect the county.[36]

So the local war continued without the restraining hand Continental officers might have provided. The tit-for-tat local combat ground relentlessly on; raids and counter-raids, kidnappings, and reprisals became a regional commonplace by the spring of 1777. "Residing in the midst of enemies," recalled one Bergen County resident, "the Refugees and Tories on every side ... there was no safety for any male person competent to bear arms to stay at home in the night, and they were obliged, when not on actual duty, to collect together for ... common safety or to sleep in the woods or some place of safety."[37]

There was little defense against such irregular warfare. Who could predict where or when a raid would strike? Local militia usually could react only after a bloody incident had occurred. Even later in the war, when some American regulars were posted in the county and in nearby New York State, they could do next to nothing. Continental major general Alexander McDougall could only vent his frustration. The American regulars generally were too far from most locales "to give succour in time," he lamented to Washington. "The Inhabitants call upon Me for aid, but before it can be sent ... the mischief is done, and the Enemy move off."[38]

Monmouth County remained in turmoil as well. In January 1777 patriots finally broke the loyalist grip in a brief engagement at the village of Monmouth Courthouse (also called Freehold). It wasn't pretty. Rebel militia backed by over a hundred Continentals scattered about 200 poorly organized tories. Whig forces then moved through the county cleaning up remaining pockets of loyalist resistance. Hardly a conclusive victory, this rebel activity drove at least 500 Monmouth loyalists to arms in tory regiments – notably the 1st and 2nd New Jersey Volunteers, units that served the Crown throughout the war. Others fled to British-occupied Sandy Hook to become hit-and-run raiders whose ravages kept the county constantly on edge. Of course local patriots retaliated. In October 1777 the state government voiced no objection when Monmouth whigs drew upon vigilante tactics of their own, including the hanging of an especially active loyalist, Stephan Edwards, after a drumhead trial.[39] It is worth noting that *jus in bello* did recognize the legitimacy of measured retaliation for acts of violence, but only on the part of duly constituted authorities. Events in Monmouth County, however, were now driven by local passions and local actors. For patriots and loyalists retribution became a brutal norm, and amid the mayhem throughout 1777 the county had no effective government.

The man driving this havoc was David – "Devil David" – Forman. He had returned with a vengeance as the rebels swept through the county. Forman boasted a Continental colonel's commission while simultaneously serving as a New Jersey militia brigadier. A charismatic figure, he rallied county patriots and, dubiously claiming authority under martial law, instituted a virtual reign of terror. His men had hanged Stephan Edwards, harried tories wherever they could find them, exiled loyalist families, and coerced voters in a rigged election in an attempt to consolidate political control (the state legislature voided the poll). Forman himself quarreled with state authorities as his extra-legal brutalities finally alarmed moderate whigs. George Washington feared Forman was driving people to loyalist ranks, and he relieved Forman of his Continental command. Forman's gloves-off activities, however, were forcefully effective, and he prevented any tory resurgence in this area. But Washington was correct; Forman's uncompromising repression engendered a measure of sympathy for the royal cause.[40] Yet "Devil David" never wavered from his hard line.

Conditions were no better west of Monmouth County. During the British occupation of Philadelphia, violence plagued New Jersey's Delaware River counties opposite the city. Tories and patriots went at one another with abandon, with clashes mounting over late 1777 and into early 1778. Emboldened by the British in Philadelphia, furious loyalists generally held the initiative, and they wanted redcoat assistance. "Having long labored under the most cruel persecution & tyranny of Congresses Committees & other usurped powers of Independence & Rebellion," they petitioned General Howe, they wanted British assistance in organizing in their defense.[41] Their fury knew no limits in February when a Continental foraging expedition into the region paid particular attention to loyalist forage, comestibles, and livestock.[42] For many tories this was the last straw. Hundreds who had hitherto laid low now elected to fight. As loyalists took up arms there were around 25 engagements between February and June 1, 1778, in Burlington, Salem, Gloucester, and Cumberland Counties.[43] And by June the level of action had become a *de facto* loyalist rising. This aggressive tory activity generally was uncoordinated, but its frequency broke down militia morale to the point of causing rebel defections to the royal cause. Any number of former patriots began trading with the British, braving whig laws threating dire consequences for anyone caught so doing.[44]

Redcoat incursions from Philadelphia, usually with tory support, led to some particularly vicious incidents. In early March 1778 a British foraging expedition from British-occupied Philadelphia under Lieutenant Colonel Charles Mawhood crossed the Delaware River into Salem County, New Jersey. Mawhood was a man with a grudge. On January 3, 1777 he had commanded at Princeton, where Washington's force had defeated him. The lieutenant colonel escaped, but he detested the rebels, and his animosity showed. In command of some 1,300 men, including redcoats, New Jersey tory volunteers, and the crack loyalist Queen's American Rangers, on March 18 he ambushed 200 to 300 state militia near Quinton's Bridge, killing 30 to 40 of them. Then, on the 21st, one of Mawhood's subordinates, the able Lieutenant Colonel John Graves Simcoe, led the Queen's Rangers in a surprise assault on militia at nearby Hancock's Bridge. Simcoe's men bayonetted two sentries, then stormed into a home sheltering the rest of the militia and quickly dispatched them with cold steel. The Americans decried a "massacre," claiming some of the militiamen had died trying to surrender. Perhaps. But surrender in the midst of a lightning assault is difficult, and throughout the war Simcoe had no reputation for wanton cruelty. Quite the contrary. The truth was that the actions at Quinton's and Hancock's Bridges were brilliantly executed operations, and brutal as they were, they did not necessarily exceed the canonic bounds of "civilized warfare."[45]

Then Mawhood allegedly went further. Having shown what his command could do, he supposedly threatened considerably more. Unless local militia laid down its arms, he announced, he intended to "attack the militia wearing arms ... and reduce them, their unfortunate wives, and their children to beggary and distress." Under the rules of *jus in bello*, this kind of action was problematic – but it also revealed Mawhood's understanding that the militia was embedded in the civilian population. Mawhood was certainly a hard-line man, but he was a realist in knowing what his force was up against. The local fighting truly had blurred distinctions between soldiers and civilians – the rebels even employed women as spies – and royal forces simply had to be suspicious of virtually everyone.[46] Who were the combatants? Who were the noncombatants? No redcoat could ever be sure.

The local New Jersey militia commander, Colonel Elijah Hand, was quick to exploit the situation. Hand certainly believed Mawhood would follow through on his threat, and he was prepared to retaliate in kind against regional loyalists. But first the militia colonel seized the chance for a propaganda coup. He supposedly retorted that "[y]our threat to burn and destroy, induces me to imagine that I am reading the orders of a barbarous Attila, and not of a gentleman, brave, generous, and polished."[47] Here was another use for *jus in bello*: Like Colonel Hand, the rebels flogged the British in the public prints for their "barbarous" conduct. In the battle for hearts and minds, patriots consistently used reports – actual or elaborated – of enemy violations of the rules of war to prevent the British as far as possible from claiming the high moral ground.

Mawhood, of course, had plenty of company on the hard line. In June 1778, as they crossed into New Jersey after evacuating Philadelphia, junior officers in Lieutenant General Clinton's retreating army looked the other way when soldiers actually did much of what Mawhood had earlier threatened. They torched the homes, shops, and farms of known patriots while sparing those of loyalists. The town of Freehold was sacked in an overtly political act. An outraged Clinton offered rewards for information on looters and arsonists, but no soldier informed on a comrade. There was real tension between senior commanders trying to maintain order and the lower ranks, including junior officers, bearing the brunt of tough duty in the midst of a hostile populace.[48] Thus if ideals of humanity in war sought to spare civilians the cruelties of martial abuse, there is reason to question how commonly such notions prevailed among many (if not most) British regulars. There was equally little evidence that patriot civilians observed Vattel's warning to remain aloof from military affairs. What were the King's troops to think when they found a Freehold blacksmith crafting gun carriages for rebel artillery?[49] Angry redcoats and loyalist troops fully believed that local whigs deserved all merciless punishments they got.

Of course, patriots returned the feelings, and they were keen practitioners of the retaliation game. At one point rebel militia arrested 15 Salem County men for trading with the British in Philadelphia – with orders to shoot them all if redcoats tried to free them. In Penn's Neck, also in Salem County, the Swedish Lutheran reverend Nicholas Collin grieved as civil strife tore apart his congregation; raids, counter-raids, pillage, and murder were all too common. On Easter Sunday 1778 Collin was horrified to see patriots tie a man – caught illegally trading – to a tree and flog him until his flesh was "entirely crushed." "Some days later he died." "Everywhere," the distraught pastor lamented, "distrust, fear, hatred, and abominable selfishness were met with. Parents and children, brothers and sisters, wife and husband were enemies to one another."[50]

Patriots eventually won their regional civil war. The loyalist collapse came with the British withdrawal from Philadelphia in June 1778. Bereft of redcoat support, regional tories were not strong enough to hold their ground, and everyone knew it. Thus, as Sir Henry Clinton's army began its trek across New Jersey toward New York, at least some tory families joined his march, abandoning homes, farms, and livelihoods. The state would confiscate most of their properties, their estates passing to rebels with the wherewithal and political connections to purchase them at auction. Active loyalism in the river counties vanished; there would be no significant disturbances in the region for the rest of the war, and anyone still holding tory sympathies wisely kept quiet.[51]

The Long War

The violence had crossed a line, and any remaining restraint resulted largely from practical rather than moral or philosophical motives. This pattern emerged clearly in the conduct of New Jersey's first elected governor, William Livingston. The scion of an influential New York political family, Livingston, an attorney, had moved to New Jersey shortly before the war, seeking the quiet life of a country gentleman. He joined the Revolution as a moderate seeking redress of grievances rather than independence; indeed, he was wary of calls to leave the empire. Early in the war he shied away from draconian treatment of accused tories, even after a loyalist party had plundered his home. He willingly saw suspected tories rounded up, but as a lawyer, Livingston wanted legal proof before proceeding against them, and he allowed whig authorities to parole or to grant bail to non-violent royalists. He was also willing to forgive tories who swore oaths of allegiance to the new state government.[52] The new governor was anything but a fire-breathing, bloodthirsty radical patriot.

"EXPOSED TO BOTH INTERNAL AND EXTERNAL ENEMIES"

But as he settled into his governorship, his stance hardened. The scope of active loyalism in New Jersey appalled Livingston, and he resolved that halfway dealings would never win the war. The times called for sterner measures. In April 1777 he received a long letter from young Alexander Hamilton, then one of Washington's staff aides. The commander-in-chief, Hamilton informed the governor, was concerned at the extent of the "spirit of disaffection" in the state. The general hoped New Jersey would make "examples of some of the most atrocious offenders." If not, he feared active loyalism could erode popular support for the revolutionary cause. "Tories, emboldened by impunity, will be encouraged to proceed to the most daring and pernicious lengths."[53]

Livingston could not have agreed more, and he acted accordingly. He successively supported enactment of a treason act – for he now considered loyalists traitors, just as the Crown considered him a traitor – calling for harsh penalties, including capital punishment. He chaired a Council of Safety intended to "strike a Terror into the disaffected" – an echo of Hamilton's message – and traveled the state rooting out internal enemies. He urged the confiscation of tory estates. Livingston objected when Congress suggested offering amnesty to loyalists. New Jersey, he retorted, had suffered too much at loyalist hands.[54] By late 1777 he considered loyalists irredeemable: "a Tory," he told Washington, "is an incorrigible Animal: And nothing but the Extinction of Life, will extinguish his Malevolence against Liberty."[55] He wrote New York governor George Clinton in a similar vein: "we shall make rough work with them [loyalists], as soon as the state is reduced to a little more tranquility."[56]

This was brutal talk, and Livingston actually made it official policy. In an address to the assembly in May 1778 he spelled out New Jersey's posture toward loyalists going forward. Tories had no place in the state and could never be forgiven. They were "Men arrived at the highest possible Pitch of Degeneracy... They have, by a Kind of gigantic Effort of Villany, astonished the World, even that of transcending in the Enormities of

Desolation and Bloodshed a Race of Murderers before unequalled and without Competitor." The British were cruel enough, he proclaimed, but the loyalists were far worse. At tory hands, "Numbers of our most useful and meritorious Citizens have been ambushed, hunted down, pillaged, unhoused, stolen or butchered." Livingston went on and on, heaping obloquy on Jerseymen who had declared for the King, before concluding that "The Disgrace they have brought upon their native Country can never be expunged but by expunging them." If tories were to survive at all, the governor urged them to "Voluntary Banishment" to some place where they could enjoy "Vassalage" and the "Assassination of Liberty." Or they could go to Great Britain, "where the Massacre and Famishing of Thousands has been rewarded with a Peerage; and where no Man need to despair of Promotion for being a Rascal."[57] This was now unmistakably the language of existential warfare.

The British and loyalists reacted with stunned amazement to Livingston's extraordinary – indeed, savage – jeremiad. From London, a British correspondent to the *Royal Gazette* in New York excoriated the governor as "the NERO of New Jersey."[58] A commentator in the *Royal American Gazette*, also of New York, ranked the governor as "one of the greatest curses that can possibly fall upon a country," and lamented that New Jersey was "governed by one, who employs all of his ingenuity in improving the wickedness to the highest pitch; in which infernal art ... has arrived at such diabolical perfection, that even the Paramount of Hell must confess himself inferior."[59] Outraged at Livingston's speech, Ambrose Serle, secretary to Admiral Lord Richard Howe, snarled that he had "never read a more virulent or indecent Performance."[60] If the tories hated the governor, they obviously believed he was not "just talking"; they rightly believed he was in dead earnest.

The question became: Did New Jersey patriots preside over a reign of terror? It depends on whom you ask. New Jersey's loyalists certainly thought so, and they could point to thousands of their numbers fined, jailed, exiled, and fleeing from harassment and physical violence – even death – as well as hundreds of their properties confiscated. There is no credible record of tory women facing widespread sexual assaults, but more radical patriots were not above abusing and threatening loyalist women and families. Rebel diarist Thomas Olden of Princeton was especially ashamed of one incident. A local farmer had run off to join the British, after which "some over Zealous Whigs abused his wife and Plundered his house to a great degree" – even though the wife was sympathetic to the American cause.[61] Authorities rounded up scores of tories suspected of trying to join the Crown, clapped them in irons and jailed them. They escaped trials for treason and possible death sentences only because they could be useful in prisoner exchanges to recover valued rebels in British hands.[62]

And there were executions. The Council of Safety, county courts, and (with less formality) the occasional militia unit hanged any number of tories, usually those taken in arms against the patriot government. Livingston was particularly anxious to make examples. He especially wanted to hang loyalist lieutenant colonel Joseph Barton of the 5th (later the 1st) Battalion, New Jersey Volunteers. Barton, of Sussex County, was a controversial figure in tory circles – he was not above using his position to further private business dealings – but he was an able Volunteer recruiter and brought hundreds of Jerseymen into their green-coated ranks. Rebel forces did capture him at one point, but as a senior officer he was exchanged rather than hanged.[63]

Other tory officers were not so lucky. In November 1777 the governor informed Washington that Morristown jails held "seventy odd" New Jersey Volunteers (or intended Volunteers) facing trial for high treason. In December 35 received death sentences, although 30 were pardoned on condition of enlisting with the New Jersey Continentals (many of these promptly deserted and rejoined the Volunteers). Two officers, however – Livingston called them "Ring Leaders" – James Iliff and John Mee, were duly hanged. Livingston sent three additional condemned men to General Washington, who held them for prisoner exchanges.[64]

In June 1778, in the aftermath of the Battle of Monmouth, Dr. Samuel Adams, Jr. – son of firebrand Massachusetts radical Samuel Adams – arrived in Freehold too late to witness the hanging of two tories. He was disappointed; he had hoped to be there on time.[65] There is no official tally of executions, let alone of extra-legal killings or of tories killed during the brutal realities of irregular warfare.[66] But New Jersey was a small state, and even scores of deaths – and certainly loyalist fatalities from all reasons must have numbered in the hundreds – were enough to enrage those who remained loyal to King and Parliament.

As an attorney, however, Livingston insisted that all proceedings take place under the cover of law. This was not a matter of mercy or legal nicety; it was practical politics. The governor wanted to establish the legality of the new whig regime, and in his view any appearance of vigilante justice would only harm the quest for legitimacy. This does nothing to alter the fact that he went after the loyalists with a genuine hatred. Nor should we forget that modern revolutions, at least in the West, also covered some of their most drastic measures with a cloak of legality. Even Robespierre professed to worship the laws of revolutionary France, and if New Jersey town squares never ran red with tory blood, patriots fully succeeded in striking "a Terror into the disaffected."

The "disaffected," however, made repayment in kind. They hit back whenever they could, and the "Nero" of New Jersey was one of their prime targets. Loyalist and British attempts – or rumors of such attempts – kept Livingston on the move. His home, Liberty Hall, in Elizabethtown, was too close to British-occupied Staten Island. As a result, the governor spent much of the war in the New Jersey interior. In February 1779 his luck almost ran out. Word leaked of an ill-advised visit to Liberty Hall, and a large British and loyalist raiding force struck from Staten Island. Livingston escaped with only some 20 minutes to spare.[67]

The raid on Livingston was part of a larger picture as the tit-for-tat local combat ground on relentlessly. By 1779 loyalists in northern New Jersey were as active and bold as ever. The northeastern sections of the state alone saw 33 documented engagements of various degrees of severity (the actual number may well have been higher), while 1780 and 1781 saw a combined total of at least 85.[68] Bergen County and neighboring areas were particularly hard-hit. Relentless loyalist raiders, bent on plunder and revenge, struck again and again, sometimes with redcoat assistance.[69] In an especially gruesome episode, on April 21, 1779, a tory band surprised militia captain Jonathan Hopper on his farm in Wagaraw (close to modern Paterson) – a farm confiscated from a dispossessed loyalist. The "party of ruffians" broke through a stable door, wounded Hopper with gunfire, chased him into his house, and killed him with "upwards of twenty" bayonet wounds. One of the raiders, a Stephen Rider, was Hopper's former neighbor.[70] In New York, Hopper's ghastly fate was hailed as an object lesson to anyone purchasing confiscated loyalist estates. Learning of the murder (as patriots saw it), another purchaser declined to take possession of a tory property, "declaring that in the night he dreaded his throat also would be cut ... [like] that poor Devil Hopper."[71]

Matters remained just as fraught in Monmouth County. On Sandy Hook, white and black exiles or refugees established an operational base known as "Refugee Town" (sometimes "Refugeetown") not far from the Sandy Hook lighthouse. Tory bases on Staten Island also supported operations against Monmouth. Raiders, including James Moody, now with a loyalist commission, harried coastal and inland towns. These incursions, sometimes with the support of British regulars, captured leading patriots, plundered and burned whig homes, and destroyed public buildings. In early 1778 large raids destroyed a major rebel salt works owned by "Devil David" Forman at Manasquan. Some of these incursions met bitter resistance, but most of the time militia, unable to predict when loyalists would strike, offered only ineffectual opposition. This at least limited the number of fatalities on both sides. In response to the attacks, however, furious rebel authorities "issued a string of capital convictions against imprisoned Loyalists in early June."[72] This was now war in a style the *jus in bello* philosophers would have deplored.

Refugee Town also further illustrated the racial dimension of the contest. Many of its residents were escaped New Jersey slaves, and some of these former bondsmen became active counter-revolutionaries. The best of them was Titus Cornelius – better known under his *nom de guerre*, Colonel Tye (sometimes Ty). Until escaping in November 1775, he was the slave of John Corlies of Monmouth County, one of the last Monmouth Quakers to defy the Quaker ban against slave-holding. Accounts of Tye's early activities are clouded with misinformation; but by 1778 he was an active partisan, often fighting alongside white loyalists (including James Moody). In 1779 black loyalists on the hook coalesced into the Black Brigade, with Tye commanding. The brigade mustered only some 25 to 50 men, sometimes with white tories participating. Tye proved a talented guerilla, and his attacks raised hackles in coastal Monmouth County.[73] Tye's reputation grew exponentially; patriots feared him and the British respected him.

Tye never held a formal commission, but the honorific title of "colonel" came in recognition of his service. In September 1780 Tye received a wrist wound during a botched raid on the home of Monmouth militia captain Joshua Huddy. The wound festered, and Tye succumbed to tetanus and gangrene. He was among the most effective partisans, white or black, to emerge in the Middle States, a point on which even his bitterest enemies agreed. "The famous negro Tye," a Monmouth correspondent to the *New Jersey Gazette* moaned, "[was] justly much more to be feared and respected than any of his brethren of a fairer complexion."[74] After his death, "the Black Brigade carried on (although less active) until the end of the war when the British evacuated its members and their families to Nova Scotia."[75]

New Jersey's war had run in unexpected directions. The continuing civil strife was traumatic enough, but the active participation of black raiders on the imperial side left patriots

"EXPOSED TO BOTH INTERNAL AND EXTERNAL ENEMIES"

utterly perplexed. What in 1776 had been rumors and fears of black revolts, or at least of slaves turning on white masters, had now become a reality. Tye was not alone in his operations, as there were other black partisans in Monmouth County and elsewhere, and they mixed freely with white tories in a semblance of military equality.[76] This was significant: For white loyalists to overcome the era's racial prejudices and serve with black irregulars – let alone that some actually served under Tye's command – was yet another measure of tory hatred of the "unnatural" patriot rebellion.

Existential War

Given the new government's inability to establish firm authority over much of the state, thousands of state residents lived, in effect, in no-man's-land. Control of vast areas depended solely on who occupied a region at a given time, and often no one dominated an area for long. The state of flux gave rise to a development eerily reminiscent of events in the Thirty Years War that so troubled the Enlightenment writers: the growth of widespread banditry. Nominally loyalist, these were men "bound by no military discipline and restrained by no officers."[77] They pillaged for loot, engaged in the so-called "London Trade" – illegal commerce with the British in New York City, often with the connivance of New Jersey tories and even economically desperate whigs – and often intimidated rebel militia. The gangs had considerable reach. They infested northern and southern New Jersey, operated along coastal Connecticut, sallied from hideouts in the Hudson River Highlands of southern New York State, and were active north of New York City. While redcoat officers frowned on their freebooting, the brigands had plenty of loyalist support. These included former New York governor William Tryon, New Jersey's William Franklin, and New York mayor David Matthews. Tory leadership was willing to give the gangs a free hand as long as they confined depredations to patriot targets – nothing was too abominable if it contributed to rebel defeat.[78]

North Jersey banditti were brutal. Especially notorious was Claudius Smith, who led a gang that infested the rugged New York–New Jersey border. His reputation for pillage and murder terrified regional patriots, although he also had a bit of Robin Hood in him – there were instances in which he shared his pillage with the poor. He was finally run to earth on Long Island and hanged in January 1779.[79]

Smith's execution did nothing to stop the irregular marauding. Whig militiamen in Bergen County were favorite targets, and some were killed in their homes in the dead of night. In January 1779, William Cole and Thomas Welcher, in company with other banditti – and operating with the approval of senior tory officials – descended on the home of one John Clark, a Bergen militiaman. They plundered his house and shot him to death, stating they had done so to avenge Smith. Then, in a printed broadside, they threatened considerably more. If patriots hanged any additional tories – "friends to government" – the irregulars promised "to hang six for one" in retaliation. Their "Companies," composed of Indian as well as white individuals, promised "to be revenged on you for your cruelty & Murders. We are to remind you that you are the beginners & agressors, for by your cruel oppressions & bloody actions [you] drive us to it ... & we are determined to pursue it on your Heads & Leaders to the last till the whole of you is Massacred."[80] There was plenty of subsequent violence, but not by Cole and Welcher – they were caught and hanged.[81]

Banditti plagued southern New Jersey as well. Generally known as "pine robbers," they were true outlaws who operated from the vast Monmouth County Pine Barrens, although gang activity also affected parts of Burlington and Gloucester Counties. Altogether they terrorized a substantial part of the state. While claiming tory allegiance, they were often indiscriminate in their raiding and pillaging; but they mostly operated in the Pine Barrens as irregular loyalist guerilla robbers.[82] They were indeed interested in plunder, but they also cooperated with anyone in the London Trade. And they were formidable. Many were veterans of the New Jersey Volunteers, from which they deserted to become irregulars.[83] While the barrens were not impenetrable, they were highly defensible for those who knew the terrain – which the Pine Robbers did – and they generally made short work of any patriot militia who ventured too deeply into the pines. Militiamen dreaded the region.

Some of the Pine Robbers were truly notorious. Jacob Fagan was a Volunteer deserter who was obnoxious enough as a raider and London Trader for Livingston to put a price on his head. Patriots went to great lengths to end Fagan's career. In 1778 they successfully infiltrated a spy into his gang who tipped off Monmouth militia on the robber's whereabouts. Fagan, along with three of his men, then died in a shoot-out – cause for patriot rejoicing.[84]

A more celebrated (if that is the word) Pine Robber was "Captain" John Bacon (the title was unofficial), another former Volunteer. On occasion he commanded a gang of some 30 to 40 men, and he was involved in several serious armed confrontations with patriot forces. The worst was the so-called "Long Beach Island [or Barnegat] Massacre." On October 25, 1782, Bacon's men caught a rebel camp by surprise – the whigs were asleep – killing and wounding up to 19 men. The attack had come after peace talks with the Crown had commenced, and a furious Livingston offered a £50 reward for Bacon, dead or alive. He carried on until a militia officer surprised and killed him near Long Beach Island in March 1783. Bacon had the dubious distinction of being New Jersey's last fatality of the war. Vengeful patriots wanted to bury him in the middle of a road – a mark of contempt – but relented when a relative asked to inter his remains in a local cemetery.[85]

Irregular activity took an even more ominous turn in 1780. Acting on urgent pleas from senior loyalists in America, the Crown approved the establishment of a paramilitary organization: the Board of Associated Loyalists. Founded for the "Purpose of employing the Zeal of ... faithful Subjects in North America," Associators would prey upon "the revolted Provinces" independently or in conjunction with regular British forces. Not enlisted soldiers, Associators were civilians serving as "adventurers" only when they felt like it; their pay would come from the "equitable Distribution" of spoils taken in raids. The Board's "Articles" stipulated that operations would target only the rebellious and would avoid "Excesses, Barbarities or Irregularities, contrary to the acknowledged Laws of War as practiced by civilized Nations." In a technical sense, the new Board would operate, as it insisted, within the bounds of *jus in bello* – at least as defined in Vattel. *The Law of Nations* recognized maritime privateers if they sailed under a government letter of marque, and the situation of loyalist adventurers was analogous. The Board had formal royal sanction, and in effect the Associated Loyalists were privateers, albeit not on the high seas. At the organization's head was none other than "William Franklin, Esquire, Governor of New Jersey."[86] And Franklin was in a vengeful mood.

None of this activity pleased Sir Henry Clinton. As British commander-in-chief, he was skeptical of operations conducted outside of his overall command authority. Nor did he appreciate the fact that he was expected to provide the adventurers with resources he thought his redcoats could put to better use. Clinton also looked askance at the Board's privateering nature, which seemed an invitation to unrestrained freebooting. Sir Henry was aware that many tories, including Franklin, thought his conduct of the war was timorous and that they wanted action – whatever methods it took to break the rebels. This was too much for Clinton, who feared the hard line would drive neutrals and less-committed loyalists into the rebel camp. In reverse, it was the dilemma William Livingston faced – the chance that draconian measures would drive neutrals and lukewarm patriots to the royal fold. But the Board had a royal imprimatur, and the general felt he had no choice but to give Franklin and the Board their wings — although he took care to distance himself from responsibility "for any of its [the Board's] transactions."[87]

The Associated Loyalists enthusiastically went to work. At peak strength they were likely no more than 500 armed Associators, and they usually operated only in small bands. But with many members from Monmouth County, they knew how to take advantage of porous militia defenses. There is no question that the Board's irregulars were effective. They kept Monmouth whigs on edge and often in a state of panic. To be fair, they do seem to have honored the promise to restrict depredations to patriot targets; but they engendered considerable popular hatred, and while they did real damage, there is little indication that they seriously impeded the rebel war effort.

Indeed, as Clinton had feared, the Board's raids further embittered many Monmouth residents and created some major complications for the British high command. Relations between the British commander and Franklin were never cordial, and Associated Loyalist adventurers did the tory cause no good in southern New Jersey by cooperating with the Pine Robbers. British commanders really had no idea regarding what operations the Associated Loyalists would mount or what their repercussions might be.

Redcoat generals were hardly pleased when a party of adventurers carried out an execution (or murder, depending upon one's perspective) that actually embroiled the royal high command in an international incident. This was the "Asgill affair." In early 1782 Monmouth whigs captured loyalist Philip White, who then died in mysterious circumstances — certainly murdered. In retaliation, Franklin signed a summary death warrant for a militia captain, Joshua Huddy, captured in a British–loyalist raid. Unaware of Franklin's action, the British released Huddy to the loyalists, presuming Huddy would be used in a prisoner exchange. Instead, Franklin's men promptly hanged him. A placard attached to Huddy's body warned of further revenge — they would "hang man for man" — and proclaimed that "Up goes Huddy for Philip White."

Rebels exploded with demands for retribution. Political pressure was such that a reluctant Washington felt compelled to approve the hanging of a captured British officer of Huddy's rank. The lot fell to 19-year-old Captain Charles Asgill, who was spared the gallows only after considerable legal wrangling, the arguments of Continental officers who pointed out that Asgill had surrendered honorably with Cornwallis at Yorktown, and the pleas of the French court on Asgill's behalf (Asgill's mother was of French descent and had written personally to Louis XVI).[88] The new British commander-in-chief, Lieutenant General Guy Carleton (Clinton had resigned), was furious with Franklin. With the war all but over (at least in terms of major offensive operations), the last thing he needed was a hanging contest with the Americans, and he used the Asgill affair to effectively reel in the Board's operations – despite plaintive loyalist objections.

While they lasted, however, the Board's operations drew a desperate patriot response. And it was not only the Associated Loyalists; by mid-1780 the Pine Robbers, the Black Brigade, and British and other loyalist raiders had seized the initiative in Monmouth County. Rebels repeatedly petitioned the state for permission to do legally what they already were undertaking – a campaign of retaliation. But with the governor and legislature trying to establish formal law and order, they hesitated to approve extra-legal measures. Furious patriots then took matters into their own hands and inaugurated the Association for Retaliation. The Association was a mirror image of the Board of Associated Loyalists. Both organizations reflected the desperation of their respective partisans, both were disappointed in what they considered the ineffectual conduct of legal authorities, and both considered that personal survival lay in waging war by any means necessary, no matter what anyone else thought. The articles of the Association for Retaliation represented a statement of existential warfare. They bluntly stated that the organizers were "actuated solely by the principle of self-preservation," and they swore revenge for each and every tory act of violence. Moreover, knowing that it would be almost impossible to catch marauders in the act, they promised to wreak vengeance on any known "relations and friends" of tory partisans – "Black or White." Predictably, the Retaliators elected "Devil David" Forman as their chairman.[89]

Forman prosecuted the local war ruthlessly. He combined his Retaliator campaign with coastal scouting for General Washington; and if earlier in the war the commander-in-chief had looked askance at Forman's zealotry, after 1780, appreciating Forman's intelligence reports, he never inquired too deeply into the colonel's extra-legal activities. And Washington certainly was aware of them – Forman made sure of that. In a telling incident, the colonel informed Washington of the capture of one of the Associated Loyalists. The man confessed, Forman explained, that he was "not a Soldier – Neither was he to receive any pay." Their purpose was to plunder, with the "plunder to be divided amongst them." This, of course, was exactly what the Board's articles provided. "The fact is," Forman continued, the Associators were "a Marauding Gang." He then recalled that in 1776 "Genl Sir William How[e] ... published an order declaring all persons Not uniformed & Acting without a Commissioned Officer if Taken Should be hang'd Immediately As Marauders." Forman was all for doing just that as necessary "to deter that Class of People." He wanted to know if Washington felt that under "the rules of War prisoners Taken in that way sho[uld] be Executed."[90] Washington's response, if any, has not survived. But Forman's thoughts were clear enough; and while there is no record of the captured tory's fate, it probably did not end well for him.

The state never did grant legitimacy to the Retaliators, although Forman and other "hot" whigs repeatedly asked the legislature for a formal blessing. It didn't matter. They went about their business with enthusiasm that eventually did alienate some moderate whigs. Henry Clinton had distanced himself from William Franklin and the Associated Loyalists; similarly, Livingston and more moderate patriots winced at the

Retaliators' campaign of vigilante terrorism. Forman's adherents, they complained, had become "a combination to trample all law underfoot."[91] They had a point: The Retaliators were no more careful about whom they "trampled" than the Pine Robbers or the Associated Loyalists. But it is noteworthy that the Retaliators carried on despite any and all official disapproval. It is also notable that Livingston and the legislature, while never condoning Forman's activities, *never* tried to stop the Retaliators. They were powerless to do so, and one suspects they were having it both ways – bemoaning vigilantism in the name of legitimate government while being just as glad that Forman was rooting out the Revolution's enemies by any means possible.

There is little overestimating the hatreds unleashed in southern New Jersey. Indeed, the surrender of Cornwallis at Yorktown failed to contain animosities unleashed in New Jersey's civil war. Fueled by desperate patriots and loyalists, as well as freebooting brigands, the cycle of violence continued unabated through 1782 – and occasionally beyond. The Retaliators remained active at least through mid-1783, and they dissolved only by joining a new organization – the Association to Oppose the Return of Tories. As in desolated Bergen County, where postwar feelings against loyalists also ran high, many Monmouth County residents had no use for talk of reintegrating tories into society after the Revolution.

In Retrospect

In a state that saw so much fighting, it is little wonder that the conflict steadily took on an existential dimension. Recall our definition of existential warfare: a contest "for existence ... as a nation, as a people, and ultimately as an individual. When human beings fight for those stakes, there are no limits." In much of New Jersey this reality was clearly the case. Not all of the time and not everywhere – but at any given moment, thousands of state residents saw the war as a "choice of survival or extermination," and they put little faith in reaching any sort of accommodation with their opponents. And so – and continuing with the Mackenzie Institute's observation – as the civil conflict intensified, they fought "with all the ferocity, cunning and strength" they could command.[92]

Here we should recall the scale and scope of the fighting: New Jersey saw some 600 military and naval engagements in the state and off of its immediate coasts; and of these only 14 were larger actions pitting the regular armies against one another.[93] Trenton (First and Second), Princeton, and Monmouth, of course, involved larger-scale combat, and the numbers of killed, wounded, and missing were serious. But these battles were exceptions. The vast majority of combat took place at the local level, pitting local forces against one another. Rather than casualties mounting suddenly by the hundreds in the occasional major battle, they more often accrued over the war in ones, twos, dozens, and occasionally in scores. Revolutionary New Jersey bled slowly but steadily in small numbers.

But what were those numbers? We simply don't know with any certainty – but what we do know is certainly a serious undercount. New Jersey archivist David Munn listed about 1,000 casualties statewide in killed, wounded, captured, and missing; but for most of the listed actions he could find no casualty reports, and we can only (but reasonably) assume that the real toll was much higher.[94] Historian Michael Adelberg is sure of this. In his careful tabulation of casualties in Monmouth County alone, he found the war had significantly impacted 1,303 individuals: 143 dead, 77 wounded, 332 captured, 372 "plundered of property," and 379 punished under county or state laws. Such was a heavy toll for a single county, but Adelberg further concluded that gaps in the historical record likely meant that actual casualty figures were some 50 percent higher.[95] There are no comparable figures for the rest of the state, but the scope of local combat in Bergen County and other areas across the Hudson River from British-occupied New York suggest that casualties of all categories must have been similar in scale to those in Monmouth.[96]

None of these estimates take into account casualties, property losses, and dispossession among loyalists who actively opposed the revolutionary cause. Given the incomplete historical record, most historians have shied away from firm numbers; but there is a general consensus that some 5,000 Jerseymen at one time or another took an active role against the Revolution. Of these about 2,450 served in one of the six Volunteer regiments (reduced to three by the end of the war).[97] How many of these 5,000 fell dead, wounded, missing, or captured? We simply don't know – certainly there were hundreds of casualties in skirmishes and major battles on fields from the Middle States to the South. We do know that most Jerseymen in arms for the Crown became exiles. After the war New Jersey eventually reintegrated neutrals – including pacifist Quakers, many of whom were passive loyalists – and a fair number of the less prominent civilian tories who had caused no offense. Most of all, however, the state wanted no part of tory combatants.

The case of John Smith Hatfield told the tale. Smith was a carpenter who joined the British as soon as they landed on Staten Island in 1776. He became a harbor pilot for the Royal Navy and a guide for the British army, as a well as a successful raider. On one occasion he hanged a New Jersey rebel named Ball in retaliation for the hanging of a tory spy. The state confiscated his estate in 1779, and Hatfield led his family into exile in Canada. After the war, however, he came back to the state seeking to recover his property. As Hatfield was then a foreign citizen, New Jersey couldn't hang him – but did jail him for eight months. He never recovered his estate, and he never returned to New Jersey.[98] Like John Hatfield, over 650 active loyalists lost their estates to patriot confiscations, and after the war over 1,720 petitioned the Crown for relief and compensation for their losses.[99]

Any estimate of New Jersey's military and civilian casualties, including exiles (and bear in mind that hundreds of families followed parents and spouses into exile) can only be an educated guess. But a total of some 10,000 individuals, patriot and loyalist, would not be out of line – a substantial number considering the

"EXPOSED TO BOTH INTERNAL AND EXTERNAL ENEMIES"

state population of only 120,000. It should surprise no one that such dislocations, physical suffering – including combat deaths, murders, and executions – engendered hatreds to the point of existential fury.

This, of course, was a psychological dimension to the war that is difficult to assess. But consider the chronology of conflict: While there were incidents in New Jersey during 1775, the struggle gripped the state with greatest intensity between mid-1776 and late 1782 – a period of some 78 months. Based on Munn's research, this meant that New Jersey experienced an average of at least seven clashes per month. With violence so frequent, New Jersey civilians, patriot or tory, could hardly predict when or where the next raid or enemy incursion would come. "Self-preservation," as a Monmouth County Retaliator put it, was something no one took for granted. This was not an existence conducive to martial restraint; no matter what senior military or political figures may have wanted, at the local level, where most of the war was fought, *jus in bello* was virtually akin to a dead letter.

New Jersey's revolutionary experience was tragic; the dogs of war had pounced with a fury. The catastrophe was all the more extraordinary inasmuch as it played out in a small, long-settled state that had not been a hotbed of anti-imperial sentiments. The province had been relatively happy as a royal colony and had come a little late – and in many respects even reluctantly – to the revolutionary cause. Yet the conflict in New Jersey devolved into an existential war. And if such a war could overwhelm such a state, was anywhere else safe from a similar fate?

3

Theater of Fear: Existential War in the West

The West was the largest theater of the war. It encompassed the farthest backcountries of the Carolinas, Virginia, Georgia, Pennsylvania, and Trans-Appalachia out to the Mississippi River, including the old Northwest and Southwest. It was also the most complex theater. The region gave full play to the almost kaleidoscopic elements of the conflict: the patriot–tory civil war, imperial rivalries, the colonial rebellion against Britain, internecine struggles among Native Americans, the freelance schemes of land speculators, and – most significant of all – the clash between Indians and expansionist land-hungry Americans. All of these factors would contribute to an especially brutal war – Indians and white settlers would see the struggle in existential terms, and they would fight accordingly.

A Precarious Peace

By 1763 a century of Indian wars, imperial conflicts, trading ventures, and settlement attempts (usually illegal) had seen thousands of Europeans cross the Appalachians. After the French and Indian War (also known as the Seven Years War, 1756–63), scattered French and Spanish trading posts remained in the Ohio and Mississippi River Valleys, with British traders and Indian agents (often one and the same) also pressing into the interior. Colonial governments and speculative land

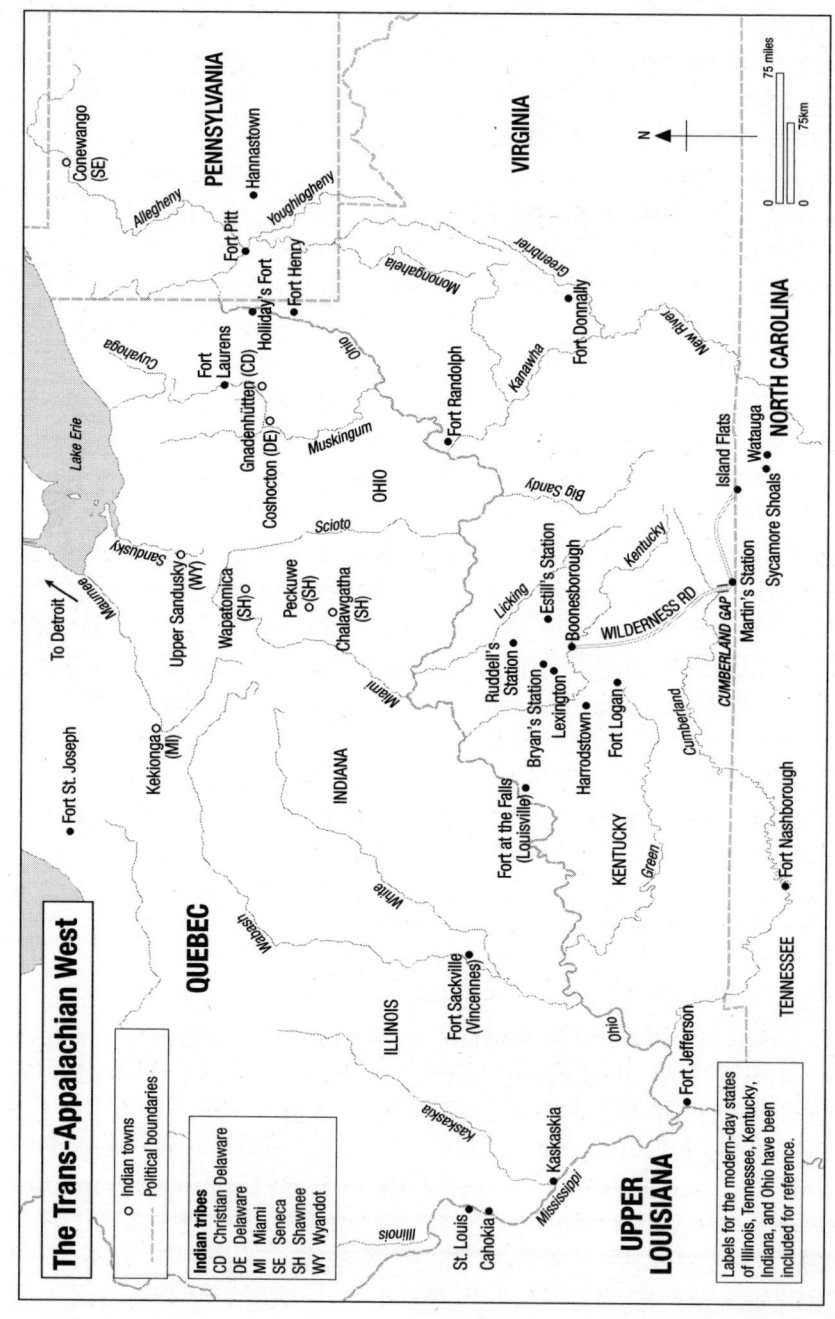

MAP 2

companies sent exploratory and surveying parties – including a young George Washington – into the Ohio Valley and beyond. Spain and Britain, who had inherited enormous western territories from the defeated French, were well aware of the commercial potential of East–West trade links via the Ohio and Mississippi Rivers.

Among most colonists, however, it was land hunger – the quest for free or cheap farmlands – that drove interest in the West. For thousands of white people who could not afford farms in the relatively populated East, western lands held the promise of a future they could not hope to find closer to the Atlantic seaboard. Following the French and Indian War, that land hunger was never more intense, while at the same time British efforts to control white western expansion were crumbling. Wishing to avoid hostilities with the Indians and to bring order to the frontiers (among other wide-ranging objectives), George III signed the Proclamation of 1763. The proclamation "established, for an indefinite period, a line along the watershed of the Alleghany Mountains as the western limit of British settlement." Territories west of the line were to remain in Native American hands.[1] The restriction on white expansion, however, caused widespread and bitter colonial resentment. Bowing to colonial protests, the British negotiated several treaties with the Cherokees and the Iroquois that moved settlement boundaries west. White settlers surged into western Pennsylvania, Virginia, Kentucky, and through the Carolina backcountries into modern Tennessee.

These treaties, however, were fraught with controversy. Among the Cherokees, heavily defeated by colonial forces in the Anglo-Cherokee War (1758–61), factions disagreed with the Treaties of Hard Labor (1768) and Lochaber (1770) that pushed the tribe west of the Alleghenies. Angry Cherokees sporadically harassed settlers on the Virginia and Carolina frontiers. The Treaty of Fort Stanwix (also 1768) was equally problematic. At Stanwix the Iroquois ceded claims to lands south of the Ohio – that is, to most of Kentucky – claims never accepted by the numerous

Shawnees, who saw the region as one of their traditional hunting grounds.² In 1774 Shawnee resistance culminated in Dunmore's War, in which Virginian forces defeated the Shawnees and allied Mingos. ("Mingos" was an Anglo term denoting an Indian people mostly from the Seneca and Cayuga tribes – members of the Iroquois Confederacy – who settled in the Ohio Country. There they assimilated many Susquehannocks and members of other regional tribes. Some white settlers used the term Mingos very loosely in reference to Iroquoian peoples generally.)³ But Indian resentments remained. They were rightly alarmed when settlers ignored even the new treaty boundaries, establishing farms and small communities on illegal plots or settling with dubious titles from speculative land companies. The Indian tribes saw this for what it was: a threat to their independence, and thus to their cultural and even physical survival. That is, they saw an existential threat.

Many tribes or factions of tribes were willing to act on their resentments – it was just a matter of when. In fact, low-level hostilities never completely stopped, although the occasional raid or violent incident failed to deter settlers. The Kentucky region saw a steady stream of immigrants. In 1771 Daniel Boone helped plant the first white settlement in modern Tennessee at Watauga (now Elizabethton); and in 1775 he blazed the Wilderness Road through the Cumberland Gap from Tennessee into Kentucky. There he established Boone's Station (which became Boonesborough). Another pioneer, James Harrod, founded Harrodstown (now Harrodsburg, Kentucky) in 1774, while a year later another party planted a large camp they called Lexington, in honor of the recently famous Massachusetts town.⁴

Boone, Harrod, and the Lexington settlers were private adventurers out to make fortunes in real estate. Their settlements, and most others that followed in the mid-1770s, consisted of a dozen or fewer cabins with a stockade or blockhouse, and all were illegal in that residents held no recognized land titles. Nevertheless they formed extra-legal militias to defend themselves and even to attack local Indians. Indeed, white immigration was quasi-military – a process of "clearing and holding." While there was no general Indian war, by 1775 sporadic tribal resistance forced early colonists to abandon some of their Kentucky outposts – Lexington, for example, would not be permanently settled until 1779. But the trend was clear: Land hunger was driving Anglo-Americans west despite any dangers or dubious land claims.

The West was clearly on edge. Indian resistance to Anglo-European expansion infuriated many settlers or would-be settlers. Hatreds stemmed, however, from more than land hunger. Prospects of Indian attacks were genuinely terrifying. American Indians usually struck by surprise at "soft" targets – individuals, small groups, or isolated farms were typical victims – and they frequently offered little quarter. White communities heard stories of the scalping knife and tomahawk with horror. Interwoven with such fears was an intense racism that ran far deeper than skin color. Most settlers saw their Indian antagonists as racially inferior "savages," almost inhuman and beyond hope of attaining any civilized status as Europeans understood it.[5] This was a racial hatred sometimes reinforced by religious convictions that Indians were literally in league with the devil; and white settlers on the frontier – especially those who had encroached on lands beyond treaty boundaries – were largely incapable of envisioning peaceful coexistence with any of the tribes. Horrified by Indian raids, many settlers saw little difference between peaceful tribes and those on the warpath; and they considered "all natives, regardless of behavior, as violent brutes best exterminated."[6]

Anglo-Europeans fought the tribes accordingly, and by the 1770s they had done so for well over a century. Indeed, there was a virtual relapse into the horrors of the Thirty Years War. This was, as historian John Grenier has called it, "extirpative" warfare in which colonists "accepted, legitimized, and encouraged attacks upon and the destruction of noncombatants, villages, and agricultural resources ... in shocking violent campaigns to achieve their goals of conquest."[7] Those locked in such struggles found scant use for mercy, and Indian and white populations drew few distinctions between combatants and noncombatants. The brutalized and terrified villagers of 17th-century Germany would have recognized the tragic circumstances. *Jus in bello* counted for nothing.

Two examples will establish the point: The New England war against the Pequot Indians during the 1630s was virtually a war of deliberate annihilation. The New England colonies and allied Indians fought to cleanse the region of the powerful and hated Pequots, and only remnants survived the killing to be enslaved. Frontier violence did not temper over time. In 1763, in the aftermath of Pontiac's "rebellion," a group of Pennsylvania settlers launched a murderous rampage against local Indians. Upset with what they considered the Quaker-dominated colonial government's neglect of frontier defenses, an extra-legal militia, the Paxton Boys, attacked unoffending Native Americans in Conestoga (near modern Millersville) and Lancaster. In two assaults they wantonly slaughtered 20 helpless men, women, and children. While many in the East blanched at the vicious cruelty, no one held the Paxton Boys to account.[8] It was yet another example of a tragic frontier norm; there were few thoughts of mercy on either side, and little enough was shown. Such were the expectations of frontier warfare as the War for American Independence loomed.

Yet the coming of the Revolution did not immediately trigger a general frontier war. Senior Indian leaders, especially among the numerous Cherokees and Shawnees, reacted cautiously to the rebellion and urged neutrality. They worried that an alliance with the wrong side could endanger trade with white settlers who supplied them with vital access to arms, munitions, and manufactured goods. Farther south the powerful Creeks agreed. Why rush to war on behalf of either side in a struggle among the settlers?

Voices of moderation, however, did not go unchallenged. Councils divided as younger Native Americans, raised as warriors, chafed at the quiescence of their seniors in the face of white land-grabbing. They saw the situation in stark terms:

THEATER OF FEAR

White expansion was a virtual invasion and an existential threat to Indian survival. There was no better example of this generational divide than the Cherokee experience. In March 1775, at Sycamore Shoals (in modern Tennessee), Cherokee chiefs met with representatives of the Transylvania Land Company – a group of private adventurers with no legal right to deal with the Indians. Senior chiefs, including the respected Attakullakulla (Little Carpenter), who had tasted defeat in the Anglo-Cherokee War, sold over 20,000,000 acres of Cherokee territory in Tennessee and Kentucky for about £10,000 in trade goods. The transaction outraged competing land companies and colonial governments, which refused to recognize the sale. But these reactions paled before the fury of younger Cherokees. Their spokesman was Dragging Canoe, the son of Little Carpenter, and his furious rejection of the treaty (as recorded by British Indian agent Alexander Cameron) merits quoting in full:

> Whole Indian Nations have melted away like snowballs in the sun before the white man's advance. They leave scarcely a name of our people except those wrongly recorded by their destroyers. Where are the Delawares? They have been reduced to a mere shadow of their former greatness. We had hoped that the white men would not be willing to travel beyond the mountains. Now that hope is gone. They have passed the mountains, and have settled upon Tsalagi [Cherokee] land. They wish to have that usurpation sanctioned by treaty. When that is gained, the same encroaching spirit will lead them upon other lands of the Tsalagi. New cessions will be asked. Finally the whole country, which the Tsalagi and their fathers have so long occupied, will be demanded, and the remnant of the Ani Yvwiya, The Real People, once so great and formidable, will be compelled to seek refuge in some distant wilderness. There they will be permitted to stay only a short while, until they again behold the advancing banners of the same greedy host. Not being able to point out any further retreat for the miserable Tsalagi, the extinction of the whole race will be

proclaimed. Should we not therefore run all risks, and incur all consequences, rather than to submit to further loss of our country? Such treaties may be alright for men who are too old to hunt or fight. As for me, I have my young warriors about me. We will hold our land.[9]

The chasm between younger and older Cherokees could not have been more graphic. Dragging Canoe was no lone wolf. His defiance eventually resonated with thousands of Native Americans who saw no other alternative to such piecemeal dispossession but to fight. Representatives of several northern tribes later endorsed the militancy of the younger Cherokees: "Better to die like men," a British Indian agent recorded them as saying, "than to diminish away by inches."[10]

Events took an unsettling turn shortly after Sycamore Shoals. When word of Lexington and Concord reached Kentucky, settlers saw an opportunity to link illegal land claims to the Revolution. They persuaded Virginia to make Kentucky a county and to legitimize regional land titles. Again, many Indians objected. In November 1775, Cornstalk, a Shawnee chief who had fought Virginians in Dunmore's War, minced no words in a message to the Continental Congress: "Our lands are covered by the white people," he wrote, "& we are jealous that you still intend to make larger strides. We never sold you our Lands which you now possess on the Ohio [River] ... & which you are settling without ever asking our leave or obtaining our consent." He pleaded with Congress to halt illegal land seizures, but to no avail.[11] Cornstalk wanted no more fighting, but he could not control the passions of a younger generation. The stream of immigrants from Virginia, Pennsylvania, and the Carolinas "created a generational divide among Ohio Valley Indians quite similar to that among the Cherokees."[12]

A number of tribes or factions of tribes clung to neutrality, including many Cherokees, Creeks, and the Delawares. But for most Indians neutrality gave way with the realization that standing aloof from the eastern struggle offered no protection from continued American westward migration. They realized that a rebel victory would lead to a tsunami of white settlement; the only real alternatives were – as Dragging Canoe had insisted – Indian retreats to the point of total dispossession or the defense of Indian lands through force of arms. War would lead to Indian alliances with the British; but it is important to note that Native Americans made these alliances for their own reasons and in their own interests, not out of any particular regard for King George III. Indian resistance to American expansion would have flared with or without the patriot independence movement.

Hostilities

Major hostilities began between the Cherokees and white settlers in the Carolinas and Virginia. This was the Cherokee War of 1776, and it was a continuation of the Anglo-Indian war that preceded it. In July, Dragging Canoe launched a typical guerilla campaign against isolated farms and settlements, and the attacks spread terror along the Carolina frontiers. The Cherokees killed some 60 South Carolinians and devastated nearly 50 miles of the North Carolina frontier. Dragging Canoe had acted unilaterally, and the British were not enthusiastic at the news. Unsure of Indian loyalties (many tribes, after all, previously had fought alongside the French against the British) and equally unsure of the consequences of an Indian war, Britain had not decided to actively enlist Indian allies. The Cherokee assaults struck indiscriminately at white settlers of all political persuasions, and the British feared the violence would drive neutral or even loyalist-leaning colonials into the rebel camp desperately seeking protection.

With Continental troops unavailable, retaliation fell to Virginia and the Carolinas. Some 6,000 state troops moved against *all* Cherokees, even those who had stood aloof from Dragging Canoe. Patriot tactics were typical of the period and resembled a medieval "chevaunche" – a large-scale plundering of enemy territory to demoralize an opponent, strip them of food and supplies, and kill anyone who showed any resistance. They worked. We "marched to the Cherokee nation to suppress the Indians," a North Carolina officer explained, "burnt their town, killed and destroyed as many of the Indians as we could get hold of."[13] By November most Cherokees were finished. They signed treaties relinquishing some 5,000,000 acres of homelands, including virtually all that remained in South Carolina. Only Dragging Canoe held out. The young chief led his followers south to found new towns on the Chickamauga Creek near modern Chattanooga, Tennessee. Henceforth they were the Chickamauga Indians, and they became the scourge of the southeastern frontier.

Shawnee neutrality died as well. By early 1777 Cornstalk and other senior chiefs could no longer restrain younger Shawnees. Americans were hardly surprised, as raiding bands had been taking scalps for months. They also knew most Shawnees had allied with the British. The architect of the alliance was Quebec lieutenant governor Henry Hamilton. Stationed at Detroit, Hamilton achieved a rapport with regional tribes, including those in the Ohio River Valley. Hamilton's early instructions forbade encouraging Indian attacks. But when efforts to crush the rebellion failed, and with Indian resistance to white encroachments stiffening anyway, in 1777 London finally decided to court Native Americans as combatants. Hamilton was to assist Indian forays against rebel settlements, and to that end he offered ceremonial war belts to Indian leaders with promises of material aid, including the support of loyalist militia and British officers. Tribes, including the Wyandots, some previously neutral Delawares, and (to Cornstalk's distress) the majority of Shawnees, jumped at Hamilton's offer. Although Hamilton denied it, patriots widely believed he offered bounties for white prisoners and scalps (Americans called him "Hair-buyer"). As a former regular officer with a regard for "civilized" war, Hamilton sincerely regretted the loss of civilian lives; but he understood that the Indian campaign would inevitably cause noncombatant deaths.¹⁴ Supported by Detroit, war parties prepared to win control of Trans-Appalachia.

Learning of Hamilton's initiative, Americans planned a preemptive strike into the Ohio Valley. Rumors of the expedition prompted Cornstalk and a small party to travel to Fort Randolph (modern Point Pleasant, West Virginia) to discuss the deteriorating situation. The rebels canceled the operation after recruiting efforts failed; but at Fort Randolph local militiamen murdered the Indians in cold blood. The killers escaped punishment when white witnesses refused to testify – a normal response when white individuals murdered Indians. Cornstalk's death meant all-out war with the Shawnees, and Virginia governor Patrick Henry warned frontier communities to look to their defenses.¹⁵

Once the Indians decided on war, no frontier settlement was safe. Patriots were unprepared for a major frontier war, especially one with effective imperial support. The West hosted a network of British agents and traders, many of whom had lived for years among various tribes. They served as intermediaries between the Native Americans and royal officials, and almost to a man they declared for the Crown. As "embedded" personnel among the Indians, they played active roles in military operations, and they gave the British considerable reach across the entire West. Along the Mississippi, James Colbert was a zealous loyalist and campaigned with the Chickasaws. Alexander McKee and the Girty brothers, Simon, James, and George – raised among the Indians – were active in the Ohio Valley. Alexander Cameron advised Dragging Canoe; and among the Creeks, the mixed-blood Alexander McGillivray was a prominent chief.¹⁶ There were others, and they proved capable leaders. Their names became anathema to American patriots.

Initial rebel defenses centered on three main forts: Pitt (modern Pittsburgh), a Continental post; Patrick Henry (now Wheeling, West Virginia); and Randolph. There were smaller posts as well, many of them private affairs, such as "John Holliday's Fort," also in western Virginia, and "Martin's Station" in Kentucky (more on these later). Indian raiders, however, easily slipped past the forts, and individual farms and travelers were vulnerable. Frontier militias were little match for the Indian offensive, and Shawnees drove off livestock, destroyed crops, burned cabins, and sent captives and scalps to Detroit. Nor were the forts immune to assault. Militia suffered casualties holding Fort Henry against parties of Mingos, Wyandots, Shawnees, and Delawares; and patriots abandoned beleaguered Fort Randolph in 1778. The Indians burned it to the ground.[17] Boonesborough held out under sporadic attacks, and there were innumerable skirmishes outside the smaller stockades — which at times were little more than prisons for those sheltering inside. White casualties mounted, and by the end of 1777 the only settlements left in Kentucky were Boonesborough and the posts of Harrodstown (or Harrod's Fort) and Fort Logan (modern Stanford). In 1784 John Filson (Kentucky's first historian and an enthusiastic development "booster") put it mildly when he wrote that the Indians "have continued ever ... troublesome neighbors to the new settlers." [18]

Things were no better for patriots farther south. Operating from their new towns in southeastern Tennessee, Dragging Canoe's Chickamaugas and Muscogees (Upper Creeks) repeatedly ambushed those on the rivers of Kentucky and Tennessee and in the backcountries of Georgia and South Carolina. They killed the grandparents of frontiersman and future congressman David ("Davey") Crockett.[19] The Choctaws generally favored the Crown but participated only sparingly in the fighting, although they scouted the Mississippi River for the British and over 1779 and 1780 helped them defend West Florida. The Chickasaws stood firmly with Britain, patrolling the Mississippi and joining in the fight against American incursions into the Illinois country. Only the small Catawbas in South Carolina (traditional enemies of the Cherokees) sided with the patriots, for which they suffered at the hands of the British and other Indians.[20] Even if all the Indians did not commit wholeheartedly to the imperial cause, from 1777 onward western settlements were subject to virtually constant threats. Ultimately, most of the western tribes, or at least factions of them, were drawn into the conflict; and to this point in the war the Indians held the initiative – and they were winning.

The West at Bay

Rebel responses to the offensive were problematic. It seemed as though they were facing a massive and coordinated Native American onslaught, actively assisted by British matériel and often with white loyalists as allied combatants. If the nature of the fighting was terrifying, however, there was another dimension to the Indian war that patriots found especially disturbing. While racial hatreds were in full play among white frontier settlers, ideological concerns also stoked their fears – at least among rebels of a more thoughtful bent. The full nature of republicanism, the political creed so many Americans shared and which lay at the root of much of the resistance to the Crown, is beyond our ken here. The zeitgeist, however, is crucial: Whatever else it was, republicanism was an ideology of *fear*. It dwelt on fears of conspiracies against liberty, of plots by tyrants to "enslave" the citizenry, and of machinations by a corrupt Britain to subvert the virtue of liberty-loving free peoples in America. In this regard, recall the warnings of James Lovell's "Massacre Day" oration. London, of course, was plotting no such thing; but much of the colonial mind was sure of it.[21]

Those who believed in British conspiracies had no trouble believing in other plots, and there seemed ample evidence that Indians were scheming grand alliances. Colonists recalled that Pontiac had done so (1763–66), and in the North the Iroquois Confederacy was a standing example of Indian political and military potential. Such fears were "white nightmares," and recent western events seemed to give white fears real substance.[22] Illegal settlers in Kentucky caused near hysteria when they circulated a specious letter supposedly proving a

Cherokee–British alliance. In response, Thomas Jefferson called on Congress to drive the Cherokees beyond the Mississippi.[23] With or without such deception, however, realities were serious enough. Dragging Canoe not only remained on the warpath, but he sent emissaries to the Creeks and the Ohio Valley tribes proposing a united Indian front. The Shawnees were cooperating with the Delawares, Wyandots, and other tribes in their attacks in Kentucky; and with Hamilton and various British agents offering Indians imperial support, frontier patriots envisioned a vast conspiracy at work.

Frantic western settlers appealed desperately to patriot authorities for help. But the Continental Army could do little; American regulars would be a rarity in Trans-Appalachia. Headquartered at Fort Pitt, at peak strength the patriot Western Department never mustered more than 953 troops, and of these only some 600 were actually "Present Fit for Duty." Usually effective strength was far less, and supplying the department was difficult.[24] The various department commanders were diligent officers, but with so few Continentals at hand they had to rely on militia for any sizeable effort, and many of the militia proved ill-disposed toward respecting the authority of regular officers.[25] Thus early rebel offensives came to little; indeed, the first was an abject failure. In February 1778 Brigadier General Edward Hand led 500 militia out of Fort Pitt, striking toward British-supported Mingo (Seneca) towns in the Ohio country. But foul weather forced a withdrawal to Fort Pitt, and the militia proved undisciplined. They caught no warriors and murdered some neutral Delawares, including three women. Mocked as the "squaw campaign," the expedition further incensed the Indians.[26] Hand succeeded only in proving that patriot forces in the West were too few and of insufficient quality to conduct operations far beyond Fort Pitt – and that the fort itself was too far from the Ohio Country to adequately support major operations there. The situation called for forts farther west and for regular troops.

Later in the year Brigadier Lachlan McIntosh, Hand's replacement, did little better, although he tried to extend the frontier and made the attempt with Continental regulars. No fool, McIntosh understood that the strategic target was Detroit. Taking Detroit would knock out British logistical support for Indian operations and greatly disrupt any direct military cooperation with the tribes. The brigadier pushed a small Continental and militia detachment as far west as modern Bolivar, Ohio. The troops built Fort Laurens (after congressional president Henry Laurens), about 106 miles from Fort Pitt and intended as a staging base for a march on Detroit. But the British spoiled the plan. Sallying from Detroit in February 1779, Captain Henry Bird besieged Fort Laurens with a large force of redcoats and Indians. The Americans held out but were reduced to eating their own moccasins. Bird eventually withdrew, but Colonel Daniel Brodhead, who had succeeded McIntosh, ordered the fort abandoned in the summer.[27] Laurens was a fruitless venture, proof that Trans-Appalachian expeditions faced exceedingly difficult logistical problems. It was the farthest west any Continental Army detachment moved during the war – for all the good it did – and the Americans never did take Detroit. Thus, at least through the first half of 1779, patriots in the West remained mostly on the defensive. With blunt realism, General Washington concluded that the West would have to look largely to taking care of itself.

Counterattack

If the Continental Army was unavailable, however, Virginia marshaled an effort to defend Kentucky. The impetus came from Kentucky leaders, with George Rogers Clark prominently among them. Clark was a surveyor and militia officer, and he had played a central role in persuading Virginia to organize Kentucky as a county and to recognize settlers' land claims. After privately dispatching spies into the Illinois country – roughly today's Illinois and Indiana – he concluded the best way to fight the tribes below the Ohio River was to knock out the British support structure above that waterway. This meant taking the Illinois settlements planted by the French before the Seven Years War, which now served as trading centers and British staging and supply bases. Targets included Kaskaskia, Cahokia (both in modern Illinois), Vincennes (Indiana), and smaller villages along the way. Clark's intelligence also indicated the loyalties of the region's French *habitants* to the British were ambivalent, and that the towns were virtually undefended. In December 1777 Clark sold an initially skeptical Virginia governor Patrick Henry on his plan. Commissioned a lieutenant colonel, he was to raise an "Illinois Regiment" of 350 men, take Kaskaskia, and then pursue other opportunities he thought of as promising. Thus began the best-known American military operation in the western theater.

Clark's expedition was not without its doubters. Some Kentuckians preferred to defend south of the Ohio rather than moving north, while many Virginians thought the deteriorating military situation dictated abandoning most of Kentucky until after the war.[28] Overall, the operation never proved popular enough to recruit over 200 men. In any case, the expedition sallied forth on May 12, 1778 and reached the Falls of the Ohio on May 27. Clark established an island camp in the middle of the rapids, safe from attacks from either shore.

The island encampment produced an unsung development that Native Americans might have found more alarming than Clark's small expeditionary force. Twenty families had accompanied Clark, demonstrating that American immigration would continue despite the Indian war. They planted corn on the island – thus "Corn Island" – and the following year moved to the south shore of the Ohio to found what became Louisville, named in honor of Louis XVI and the Franco-American alliance. Like other settlers, the Corn Island transplants built blockhouses and defensive stockades.

Louisville represented a strategic point. The Falls of the Ohio constituted the only barrier to navigation between Fort Pitt and New Orleans; and the nascent town soon prospered as a portage around the Falls for trade moving north and south, including covert Spanish aid to the patriots. Control of the Ohio would prove crucial to commercial links with the Mississippi Valley and the port of New Orleans. As early as summer 1776 Virginia had sent a mission downriver to New Orleans to explore military and commercial contacts with the Spanish.[29] For the moment that was a longer-term issue, but in the short term the new town promised an outlet for Kentucky produce, thus encouraging even more white settlers – an Indian nightmare. In the West, fear worked both ways.

Clark moved downriver and into Illinois in July. He encountered no opposition as he took Kaskaskia and smaller outposts all the way to the banks of the Mississippi River at Cahokia. Backtracking, Clark then moved on Fort Sackville at Vincennes. The local militia, mostly French *habitants*, surrendered without firing a shot. Clark's intelligence of the previous year had been correct: Former French subjects felt little empathy for George III. Neither did some Indians who, impressed with Clark, declared for the Americans.

In Detroit, Lieutenant Governor Hamilton was appalled. The loss of a few outposts was the least of his worries; his chief concern was the British ability to hold American Indians for the imperial cause. Hamilton knew that most tribes were fighting for reasons of their own and that their support for Britain was an ancillary consideration – a force-multiplier against American expansion. Indians repeatedly made clear their expectation of material aid and promises of direct military support in return for their service. Failing that, they made it equally clear that they could end cooperation with the Crown. Clark's unopposed march to the Mississippi left many Indians perplexed, and tribes as distant as the Odawa (Ottawa) from Michilimackinac (in today's upper Michigan) sent delegations to meet with the curious Virginian. Most remained committed to the British after speaking with Clark, but they demanded more from the British in gifts and supplies in return for continued loyalty.[30] And why not? If a small American force could march across the West with impunity, tribes could reasonably question the worth of British promises. For that matter, now that France was in the war, why should French *habitants*, some of whom hoped for a French return to Trans-Appalachia, not go over to the rebels?

Hamilton *had* to act. He did, and in a campaign as striking as Clark's. The lieutenant governor assembled a force of some 30 regulars, 145 Canadien (French Canadian) militia, and 60 Indians, and marched south from Detroit on October 7, 1778.[31] Hamilton gathered volunteers on the way, including some Indians who had just pledged loyalty to Clark; and he reached Vincennes on December 17 with over 500 men. The Canadien militia at Fort Sackville that had gone over to Clark promptly switched sides again. Western loyalties were nothing if not malleable.[32] Thinking he had done enough for the time being, Hamilton decided to winter in the village and take the other Illinois outposts in the spring.

Now Clark faced the task of reversing the fortunes of war. He was in Kaskaskia in late January 1779 when he learned of Hamilton's counter-stroke. He quickly gathered some 170 men, and in a truly epic march over three weeks he slogged 180 miles through freezing weather and across swollen rivers to reach Vincennes. On the evening of February 23, Clark easily took the town and opened fire on the fort; inside Sackville, the surprised Hamilton refused an initial surrender demand and a subsequent truce offer. Confronted with the lieutenant governor's intransigence, Clark decided on a grisly warning to the besieged garrison. The lieutenant colonel had four captured Indians tomahawked to death in cold blood in front of the fort. Clark made no apology for the murders, seeing them as payback for white casualties. The slaughter of helpless prisoners was a threat of no quarter, and Hamilton conceded the hopelessness of his position. He surrendered on February 25, and Clark had him sent to Virginia, where he was imprisoned, much of the time in irons, until exchanged in 1781.

Hamilton's surrender sent shock waves across the West. The chief problem for the British lay with the northern tribes – the Odawas, Ojibwas, and others from the Great Lakes region. Unlike the Native Americans in the Southeast and Ohio Valley, they were not facing the immediate brunt of American immigration. Thus, while allied with the British and sending warriors into the fray, they felt less compulsion to be active combatants on any terms but their own. They had "renegotiated" their loyalty to the British cause after Clark's initial invasion, and after the second fall of Vincennes – with the loss of a lieutenant governor and his detachment of regulars – the Great Lakes Indians expressed reservations about the royal cause.

Their alarm increased exponentially in the summer of 1779 when George Washington agreed to go on the offensive against the Indians. The general finally decided he could divert Continentals from the eastern theater; but instead of striking into Trans-Appalachia, the regulars drove into the heart of Iroquois country in central and western New York State. The invasion – the Sullivan Expedition – came after the Iroquois and tory allies had won a series of brutal regional victories. Local militias simply couldn't cope. Sullivan's task, discussed at greater length in Chapter 4, was to hit the Iroquois hard and take the pressure off the frontier.[33] While not directly threatened by Sullivan, the western tribes saw the expedition as a sign patriots were taking the western war with greater seriousness.

And so it seemed. As Sullivan campaigned, the Western Department came alive. Daniel Brodhead had long itched to strike at the Senecas – the colonel called them Mingos – of the Iroquois Confederacy in northwestern Pennsylvania and southwestern New York. In April 1779 Brodhead was positively breathing fire: "I will soon strike a Blow," he promised one of his officers, "that will convince the Villains of their errors. The woods will soon swarm with men, and I have every thing on the way for making my route with the Sloughter of Victims. Mingoes," he predicted, "will die first and then our enemies at Detroit and [Fort] Niagara. The scene will be closed with the remaining Rascals that may be found in arms against us."[34] It was brave talk, but Brodhead lacked the "swarms" of soldiers and resources necessary to support a major operation.

In the summer, however, the colonel got his chance. Thinking Brodhead could provide a diversion in favor of Sullivan, Washington allowed the colonel to proceed. On August 11 Brodhead moved north from Fort Pitt with a mixed force of some 600 Continentals, militia, and allied Delawares. It was the only time during the war that the Western Department moved in support of an operation from the East. But aside from a minutes-long skirmish at Thompson's Island on August 18 or 19, Brodhead met little resistance. Many Senecas had gone east to oppose Sullivan, and Brodhead's troops found only deserted villages. After a pillaging sweep of Indian territory — another "chevaunche" — the expedition returned to Fort Pitt with ample stores of plundered corn, livestock, and other goods.[35] Washington heartily congratulated the colonel.[36]

Viewed from Detroit, the activities of Sullivan and Brodhead were alarming. How far west would the Americans go? It was all the British could do to maintain the allegiance of the worried Lakes tribes. Credit for maintaining ties with the northwestern Indians went to Arent De Peyster, an American-born British regular who had replaced Hamilton. He convinced most Indians that their best chance for an independent future lay in the Anglo-Indian alliance. What would happen to the Indians, he asked, if they had to face victorious Americans alone? Fears among the tribes also subsided when it became clear that neither Sullivan nor Brodhead was moving west. But De Peyster never took the Native Americans for granted, and he repeatedly importuned Governor Sir Frederick Haldimand at Quebec City for funds to keep the Indians supplied with gifts — that is, to keep buying Native American cooperation.[37] De Peyster also wanted troop reinforcements in case some of the Indians actually turned on the British and in the event Clark marched against Detroit. Haldimand had no troops to send and grumbled at the mounting expenses, but he sent the money. If he hadn't, he was certain the Spanish would have.

Haldimand was right. In 1779 Spain declared war on Great Britain and entered the western conflict. Not that the Spanish had been bystanders. Spain was no friend to the rebels, but it was happy to discomfort its former enemy. In fact, since 1776 the Spanish had been sending covert financial and material aid to the Americans. Much of this aid wound its way up the Mississippi to the Ohio and on to Fort Pitt, a difficult upstream journey. It could also be dangerous. In October 1779, on the shores of the Ohio near modern Dayton, Kentucky, a large Indian–loyalist party ambushed camping American boatmen. A few rebels got away, but some 70 were wiped out.[38] The Spanish, while still technically at peace with Britain, also had given cover to American traders who plied the Mississippi under the Spanish flag. Spain even sheltered combatants. In January 1778 American navy captain James Willing led 29 men down the Ohio River; reaching the Mississippi, they raided, burned, and plundered the Natchez region in a fashion that would have embarrassed common banditti. They then found refuge in Spanish Louisiana.[39] In nearby West Florida, the British were livid; they eventually reestablished control of their posts, but tension ran high between the rival imperial powers.

The Indian-Anglo Offensive Renewed

Thus, by early 1780 the imperial cause in the West was at a crossroads. The Spanish were threatening along the Gulf Coast; Clark was still in the field and looking for a way to move against Detroit; and Native Americans were exasperated by continuing American immigration and the seeming British inability to react effectively. At best the western war was now a stalemate. At Detroit, the Shawnees and other northwestern tribes saw the situation as critical, and now they demanded more than logistical support: They wanted the direct support of British regulars. They told De Peyster the British had to commit troops to turn the tide – either that or the Indians would be "under the disagreeable necessity of falling back … or else quit the ground & go to the Southward."[40] De Peyster commanded only a limited number of regulars, but again fearful of wavering Indian commitments to the war, he nevertheless agreed to organize an expedition in support of a renewed Native American offensive.

In reality, De Peyster was doing exactly what London wanted. Alarmed at the wider scope of the conflict – it was now a world war – and at the lack of any military decision, Lord North's ministry concluded a serious western initiative was in order. The plan was threefold. A force from Fort Michilimackinac under Lieutenant Governor Patrick Sinclair would sweep the Americans and Spanish out of the Illinois country. Troops from West Florida would counter the Spanish in the Mississippi Valley and capture New Orleans. Finally, forces out of Detroit would take the Falls of the Ohio and Fort Pitt, thus regaining the initiative in Kentucky.[41] Details were left to local commanders, however, and as a result the various British operations received minimal coordination. Indeed, poor planning, lack of resources, tactical differences between the British and Native Americans, and enemy action frustrated the grand design (and it is charitable to call it that).

Spanish operations defeated two elements of the plan. In West Florida, Brigadier General John Campbell was to advance on the Mississippi – but the Spanish moved first. Louisiana governor Bernardo de Gálvez quickly swept the British out of the lower Mississippi and then turned east. In 1780 Gálvez took Mobile, and on May 10, 1781, Campbell surrendered at Pensacola. The Spanish also defeated Sinclair's expedition from Michilimackinac. In May 1780 they successfully held St. Louis against an attack by tory-led Indians, while directly across the Mississippi Clark beat off a simultaneous assault on Cahokia. Thus ended British efforts to control the Mississippi Valley, and in December the Spanish moved north. In February 1781 Captain Don Eugenio Pouré, with 60 Spaniards and an Indian contingent, took Fort St. Joseph near the southern tip of Lake Michigan. Pouré grandly claimed the fort and surrounding territory for Spain, although he withdrew after a stay of several hours.[42] Nevertheless, the raid was an expression of Spanish interest in the West – and of how the western theater had become part of the wider world war raging between Europe's imperial powers.

The only British initiative to produce any success was De Peyster's, and even it proved indecisive. The lieutenant governor tasked Captain Henry Bird – the nemesis of the patriots at Fort Laurens – with an expedition of 150 redcoats, tory militia, and approximately 1,000 Indians.[43] Bird marched on May 25, 1780, with the intention of seizing the Falls of the Ohio. Other than Fort Pitt, if any one western target could be described as strategically important it was the Falls and the new town of Louisville. An Anglo-Indian force there could cut river navigation that brought new settlers and supplies into the region from the East, block Spanish aid moving up the Ohio from the West, and raid into the Kentucky interior. Alexander McKee, longtime British Indian agent and Bird's second-in-command, felt sure the seizure of the Falls "would have been a fatal stroke to the enemies settlements."[44] Patriots fully appreciated the strategic importance of the location – its loss would have undone most of Clark's work – and in 1778 Clark ordered construction of a post, Fort-on-Shore, to guard it. (The post was subsequently enlarged and renamed Fort Nelson, in honor of Virginia governor Thomas Nelson, Jr. – another reminder that the chief effort in the West was Virginian, not Continental.) The Falls was a logical target.

Yet Bird never made the attempt. Despite his pleas, he was unable to convince the Native American contingent of the wisdom of the move. They feared that Clark, then near the junction of the Ohio and Mississippi Rivers, would march against them. The fear was groundless. Clark would have faced moving against the current coming up the Ohio and could not have stopped Bird from reaching the Falls. In any case, Clark had only some 200 men, far fewer than Bird's command. But such was Clark's reputation that the Indians were adamant; they preferred not to fight him and instead insisted on an expedition up the Licking River, an Ohio tributary, to attack the small Kentucky outposts at Ruddell's (also Ruddle's) Station and Martin's Station. Bird had no choice but to agree.

These posts stood no chance against Bird's advance. At Ruddell's, the residents initially refused to surrender, but when Bird brought up a 6-pounder the rebels gave in with the understanding their lives would be spared. The captain, however, was unable to restrain the Indians, who killed about 20 surrendered Americans before plundering and taking the rest prisoner. Bird was disgusted, but he was able to maintain order when Martin's Station surrendered shortly thereafter. In August the expedition returned to Detroit with some 300 prisoners. During the march the Indians killed prisoners unable to keep up (mercy killings from the Indian perspective).[45] Following tradition, the Indians also kept some white children to adopt into their tribes. At Detroit the prisoners revealed that many were not committed patriots. Some had gone west in search of cheap lands and to escape the war in the East, and a number even agreed to serve in tory militia in exchange for British protection.

Bird's expedition did restore some Native American faith in the British. Five years into the war, Bird had demonstrated how vulnerable the Kentucky settlements remained; and some alarmed Kentuckians pulled up stakes and headed back east. Clark was furious. Arriving at the Falls later in August, the Virginian briefly tried to block the main routes to Virginia in an effort to stem the reverse tide.[46] He had no luck. The best he was able to do was mount an ineffectual raid against several Shawnee towns — another "chevaunche" that burned villages, killed few warriors, and produced nothing of strategic value.

While the British were defeated (or facing defeat) along the Mississippi River or in Florida, elsewhere the Anglo-Indian effort had regained the initiative in the Northwest. Events later in 1780 underscored this fact. In perhaps the most curious episode in the western theater, a former French officer, Augustin de La Balme, entered the Illinois country and raised the French standard. He had volunteered his services to the Continental Army and had served briefly as Inspector of Cavalry, but he resigned in 1777 and went west under circumstances never fully explained.[47]

In any case, lacking any official authority, de La Balme launched a freelance operation. At Kaskaskia he rallied several hundred French Canadians, who may have believed his arrival signaled a French return to Trans-Appalachia. Under the French flag, de La Balme headed for Detroit, evidently seeking to replicate Clark's success against Vincennes. It was not to be. In early November, Miami Indians under Little Turtle virtually wiped out de La Balme's party at the village of Kekionga and on the Eel River in Indiana (modern Whitley County). It was a resounding Indian victory, and it made Little Turtle's reputation.[48] Except for Vincennes, Cahokia, and Kaskaskia, de La Balme's defeat left the vast balance of the Illinois country in Native American hands.

With Detroit secure, the Indian offensive continued with neither side wasting compassion on opponents. In April 1781, Brodhead sallied from Pittsburgh with 150 Continentals, linked up with 134 militia at Fort Henry, and then pillaged the Delaware hamlets of Lichtenau and Coshocton in Ohio. The rebels torched Coshocton, slaughtered livestock, and then murdered 15 captured warriors in cold blood.[49] Coshocton reflected white hatreds of the Indians, but the murders did nothing to alter the regional military balance. A few Delawares adhered to the Americans, but Brodhead's expedition succeeded only in driving most of the tribe firmly into the anti-patriot camp; and the war with the Ohio Valley tribes only intensified.

As the war wound to its climax in the East, Native Americans maintained the upper hand in much of the West. Shawnees and allied tribes, determined to defend the Ohio Valley or at least to keep settlers south of the river, hit almost constantly at settlements in Kentucky, northeastern Tennessee, and southwestern Virginia. They even helped foil a Clark plan for a descent on Detroit. In August 1781 at Laughery Creek (near present-day Aurora, Indiana), Indians and loyalists under the Mohawk Joseph Brant (who fortuitously happened to be west consulting with De Peyster) decimated a contingent of Pennsylvania militia under Archibald Lochry on their way to join Clark. Clark could never replace the lost Pennsylvanians. Farther west the Chickasaws proved equally capable. They shook off Spanish and American peace overtures and raided along the Mississippi, Ohio, and Tennessee Rivers. In June 1781 they forced patriots to abandon Fort Jefferson, which Clark had planted just below the junction of the Ohio and Mississippi. As late as April 1783 James Colbert, the longtime British agent among the Chickasaws, led a band of tories and Indians across the Mississippi in an ill-fated raid on the Spanish at Fort Carlos (modern Gillett), Arkansas.[50] Thus, while not always successful tactically, various tribes nevertheless held the strategic initiative in the defense of the Mississippi, the Ohio River Valley, and the Northwest through 1783 and beyond.

While other tribes campaigned, the Chickamaugas marshaled their greatest effort of the war. During the summer of 1781, Dragging Canoe raided settlements along the Cumberland River in Tennessee, forcing white settlers to evacuate all but three regional outposts until 1785. Although attacked, Fort Nashborough, forerunner of modern Nashville, was one of the hold-outs. Twice, in 1781 and 1782, Cherokees, sometimes with Creek and loyalist allies, also struck into northeastern Georgia and western South Carolina, devastating much of Wilkes County and raiding settlements along the Oconee River.

Cries for vengeance rang throughout the Carolina backcountry, and the attacks provoked strong responses. In Georgia, Andrew Pickens and other militia leaders led South Carolina and Georgia troops against Indian towns, burning and taking prisoners – a replay of the events of 1776. In Tennessee, Colonel John Sevier moved against other Cherokee bands, including the Chickamaugas. Sevier was a hard man. A veteran of Kings Mountain, he had led a sweep of Cherokee towns in 1780; he did the same in 1781 and 1782 in response to Dragging Canoe. These were "search-and-destroy" missions – the "chevaunches" we have seen repeatedly – that destroyed towns and crops and spread hardship among the Cherokees. They also spread further resentment. Although many Cherokees sued for peace, many others, as in 1776, joined Dragging Canoe. They again built new towns in remote areas of Tennessee and Georgia and fought on. Dragging Canoe continued diplomatic efforts with other tribes. In November 1782 he met with a delegation of Great Lakes tribes seeking help for operations in Kentucky, the Illinois country, and even for an assault on Fort Pitt (that never took place). The chief's brother, Turtle-at-Home, then led 70 Chickamaugas north to fight alongside the Shawnees.

Yet throughout the mayhem neither side could land anything approaching a knock-out blow. There is not much point in cataloguing the litany of raids and counter-raids; it is enough to note that they kept Trans-Appalachia in a perpetual state of anxiety, if not terror. It was a brave – even foolish – settler or family that traveled alone or beyond a defended village or outpost. And as the fate of Ruddell's and Martin's Stations proved, even defended positions were not always safe. But neither side could hold ground. Patriot and Indian raids, as the operations of Dragging Canoe, Brodhead, Clark, and Sevier demonstrated, were followed by withdrawals. Both sides pillaged and burned, killed, and took prisoners (whose fate could be worse than death) without doing anything decisive. All the while "incidents of bloodshed and atrocity became the norm throughout the west"; and if Indian and white communities feared the norm, they were also inured to it.[51]

Some incidents, however, still had the power to shock. In an example of hideous cruelty, on November 3, 1781, only weeks after Cornwallis had capitulated at Yorktown, defenders of Gowen's Fort in northern South Carolina (near modern Landrum) surrendered to a party of Dragging Canoe's Chickamaugas and loyalists under Captain William ("Bloody Bill") Bates. Bates had promised quarter, but when patriots gave up Bates ordered the massacre of men, women, and children. At least ten Americans died on the spot while others were later tortured to death. A lucky few escaped to spread the news to a terrified and infuriated countryside.[52]

Atrocity followed atrocity. In early March 1782, at Gnadenhütten, a Moravian mission on the Muskingum River in the Ohio Country, Pennsylvania militia under Colonel

David Williamson in cold blood slaughtered 96 pacifist Lenape Indians, including 29 women and 39 children. It was an act of pure savagery that appalled even some (but by no means all) patriots. But those who were appalled did nothing, cowed by a political and racial context of Indian hatred and not risking the censure that might result from demanding justice for the murdered Lenape.[53]

Outrage hardly described Native American reactions, and there was retribution. Three months later Indians overwhelmed 480 Virginia militia near modern Sandusky, Ohio. They captured Colonel William Crawford, a friend of Washington's, and in retaliation for Gnadenhütten they tortured and burned him at the stake.[54] The news stunned the commander-in-chief: "I am particularly affected with the disastrous fate of Colo. Crawford." He wrote grimly that "no other than the extremest Tortures which could be inflicted by Savages could, I think, have been expected, by those who were unhappy eno' to fall into their Hands; especially under the present Exasperation of their Minds for the treatment given their Moravian friends [at Gnadenhütten]. For this reason, no person should at this Time, suffer himself to fall alive into the hands of the Indians."[55] Here, indeed, was fear at its deepest. And, of course, the cycle of violent retribution continued as Clark once more (November 1782) swept through Ohio Valley Indian towns — yet another raid with little military effect.[56]

Crawford was not alone in defeat. In March 1782, Wyandots won the so-called Battle of the Clouds (or Estill's Defeat) in eastern Kentucky, killing most of the small militia of Estill's Station, not far from Boonesborough. On August 19, Wyandots and tories ambushed an ineptly led militia force, killing and capturing over 80 rebels in the Battle of Blue Licks, Kentucky, the last major engagement west of the Appalachians. Daniel Boone barely escaped, while a shot through the neck killed his son, Israel.[57] If any further evidence was needed, Blue Licks amply demonstrated the continuing Indian–British ability to strike hard in the West, even as the war wound down in the East.

End Game

By 1783 the military situation in the western theater had again stabilized.[58] The Indians still held the initiative; patriots could overrun defenseless Indian towns, but to little effect. As long as warrior casualties remained low – and Indian raiding tactics usually prevented the losses inherent in stand-up battles – the tribes and loyalist allies could regroup and continue the fight with British logistical support. Well after Yorktown, Clark still feared an attack from Detroit and even considered the destruction of the Kentucky settlements possible. Settlers "have been obliged to keep close in Forts," he reported to Fort Pitt, and the Indians were "so numerous" that Clark could not muster the manpower to fight them.[59] Patriots could march into the Trans-Appalachian countryside but they could never hold or secure it. The Ohio and Mississippi Valleys and the Northwest and Southwest remained largely "Indian Country."

Yet even while losing individual battles, white settlers were gradually winning the long war. Since Indian dominance of the countryside made American efforts to settle on widely separated individual farms virtually suicidal, circumstances compelled settlers to live near fortified posts, most of which gradually offered effective defenses against all but the largest (or luckiest) enemy operations. As new immigrants arrived in Tennessee and Kentucky, they lived, in effect, in military colonies; and if smaller forts remained vulnerable, larger towns proved able to withstand Native American threats. Booneborough's stockade held off and then discouraged repeated attacks; and at the Falls of the Ohio, Louisville, buttressed by newly built Fort Nelson's large stockade and full moat, was impervious to assault. Lexington expanded quickly and was able to defend itself after 1779, and nearby Bryan's Station proved too hard a nut for Native American raids to crack. The expanding white frontier was thus a region of fortified points, often in supporting distance, each with its own militia. That is, the colonists had continued and perfected their *de facto* "clear and hold" policy. In Detroit, De Peyster had identified the pattern but was unable to counter it.[60] Thus, if the tribes largely controlled the countryside, except at limited times and under limited circumstances (as in the aftermath of Bird's expedition), they were never able to drive the white settlers out or to prevent continuing immigration.[61] It was immigration, backed by arms, that was the making of an eventual Native American defeat.

The emphasis, however, is properly on "eventual." For in the short run, Yorktown and the subsequent Treaty of Paris (1783), in which Britain recognized American independence and formally concluded the war, meant little west of the Appalachians. The treaty had conceded Trans-Appalachia, including the Northwest and territories out to the Mississippi, to the new republic. The military situation in the West, and Clark's exploits in particular, had little (probably *nothing*) to do with the territorial settlement.[62] Rather, Britain gave up the West for diplomatic and economic reasons; there were no patriot troops above the Ohio River, and the Americans had not secured the area militarily. The peace agreement left the Indians perplexed; it included no mention of Native Americans. Indeed, the British had never consulted them before signing the treaty, and most tribes justly felt betrayed by the Crown. The peace ended overt British support to the tribes. Yet the Anglo-Indian connection was never fully severed. Citing American treaty violations, the British refused to evacuate Detroit and other Northwest forts; and clandestine aid continued to flow to the tribes in the form of trade – weapons and supplies for furs.[63]

In many respects, the war in the West had been a war unto itself. Military operations in Trans-Appalachia often (in fact, *usually*) had little bearing on events in the East; the conflicts on the western frontiers hardly influenced the British decision to seek peace after Yorktown. With or without the British, many Native Americans remained at war. Little Turtle and Blue Jacket (who had fought at Blue Licks) refused to recognize American sovereignty; and Dragging Canoe never gave up. The Chickamauga chief continued to seek Indian allies, and one of his young warriors, Tecumseh, would later succeed in assembling one of the most powerful Indian confederacies ever to confront American expansion. The Chickamaugas continued hostilities into the 1790s, and in the Ohio Valley the Indian wars never really stopped. The Shawnees and Miamis (under Little Turtle) were actively resisting white encroachments as early as 1784, and what became known as the Northwest Indian War dragged on for another decade. By then white pressure was building on the Creeks in Georgia and in what would become Alabama, and ferocious warfare erupted in the early 1800s. From the Native American perspective, the War for Independence was merely another chapter in the continuing war for *their* independence. The West remained a battlefield.

The West had seen war at its most brutal, with little to prevent martial excesses. The Enlightenment ideals of *jus in bello* simply did not fit the context of American frontier warfare, which was an all-or-nothing business – a continuation of the "extirpative" warfare of the early colonial period, which itself was reminiscent of the horrors of the Thirty Years War. Vattel would have shuddered. Only total victory would secure the futures of the rival combatants. Access to Indian lands meant prosperity and security for would-be American settlers; preventing any such access meant survival for the tribes. With racism, imperial rivalries, and ideology in the mix, fighting in anything less than an all-out fashion made little sense to anyone. Here we should recall the warning of the Mackenzie Institute: "Existential war is a war … for existence itself – as a nation, as a people, and ultimately as an individual. When human beings fight for those stakes, there are no limits."[64] This was all too true on the western frontiers of the Revolution. The western war was an existential contest, and the West functioned as the theater of fear.

4

"A Contagion of Violence": The New York Frontier

Like the war in the West, New York State's frontier war was a civil, racial, and imperial war. There were Continentals and redcoats in action (many more than in the West), and both sides saw success on the frontier as essential to overall victory. But for the British, the chief burdens of the frontier conflict fell to loyalist partisan bands and American Indians. As with the tribes in Trans-Appalachia, the New York tribes, who were mostly members of the Iroquois Confederacy, justifiably viewed the colonists as land-grabbing adversaries determined to drive them from ancient homelands. In turn, the rebels looked on the Indians and the style of war they waged with utter horror; and they felt nothing but loathing for the tories, many of whom were former neighbors. In addition, patriots happily accepted an alliance with the Oneida and Tuscarora Indians, who waged a civil conflict against the other Iroquois. With stakes high, ferocious acts of violence were commonplace, with little regard for the canons of *jus in bello*.

The Mohawk Valley

The key to the New York frontier lay in the river valleys west of Albany. They were fertile, boasting some of the best agricultural soil in the East; and during the Revolution they were one of the breadbaskets of the civilian economy and of the Continental

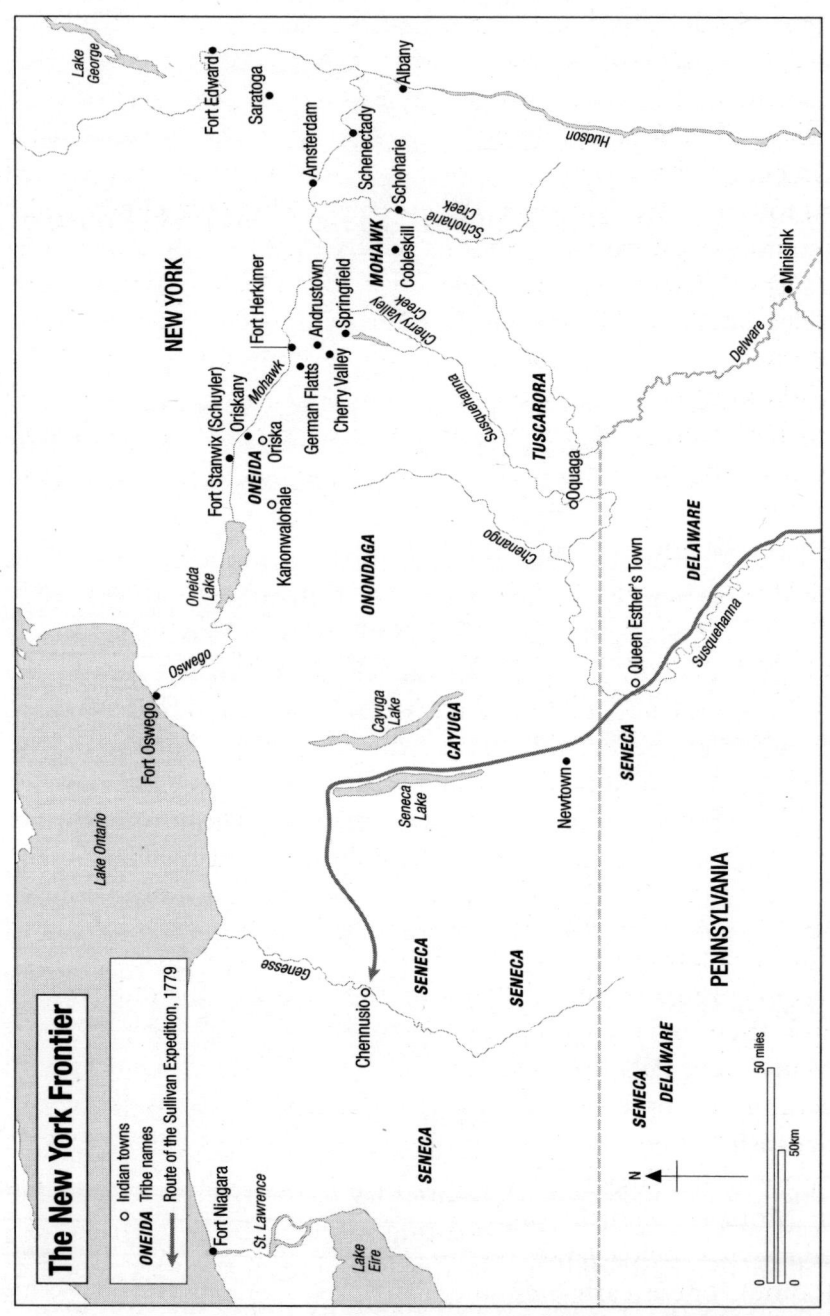

MAP 3

Army. Settlers lived on scattered valley farms and in small villages such as Cherry Valley, which lay on the Cherry Valley Creek that drained into the Susquehanna River. Also typical was the village of Schoharie, situated in its own valley on the Schoharie Creek, a tributary of the Mohawk River. But the truly critical region was the Mohawk River Valley, which extended some 150 miles west from Albany. The Mohawk River was an essential transportation artery. It flowed into the Hudson River a few miles north of Albany, and it offered the best route from the Hudson and points south into the central and western New York frontiers. The Mohawk allowed access to many of the smaller river valley systems; and its headwaters connected with well-established trails, waterways, and portages to Lake Ontario and from there to Canada. By any measure, the Mohawk Valley was a strategic prize of the first order.

The valley represented a volatile mix of conflicting human interests. The original settlers were the Six Nations of the Iroquois Confederacy; and the region took its name from the Mohawks, one of the confederacy's largest and most powerful tribes. Long before the appearance of European colonists, the Haudenosaunee people – the People of the Longhouse – had ended generations of inter-tribal warfare and established a formal league of political and military power. The Iroquois Confederacy stood united against external enemies, and Iroquois sachems and warriors understood that strife within Iroquoia would only aid outside aggressors, whether other Indians or Europeans.[1]

European outsiders first came in trickles during the 17th century and then in increasing numbers by the mid-18th century. Many were Palatine Germans fleeing Old World religious and economic oppression; along with them came Scots-Irish[2] and Scottish settlers also looking for greater freedom and economic opportunity. They migrated westward from Albany, first locating in Mohawk territory and then, by the 1760s, pushing into the edges of Oneida lands (in the vicinity of modern Utica and Rome). These early migrants often got along fairly well with their Indian neighbors. Some purchased land; others rented on the vast holdings of Sir William Johnson, a major cultural broker who served as the British Superintendent of Indian Affairs while having especially close ties with the Mohawks.[3]

Sir William, Irish by birth, was not universally beloved throughout Iroquoia. The Oneidas, neighbors of the Mohawks, were indifferent if not negative toward him. They had much closer ties with the likes of Palatine leaders George Klock and Nicholas Herkimer, aggrandizing landowners and traders with little regard for Johnson. The Oneidas, moreover, were unhappy about the construction of Fort Stanwix in the middle of their territory during the French and Indian War. They were no happier when Johnson, who enjoyed considerable influence with imperial officials, later maneuvered to have the fort and valued Oneida lands placed in territory outside the boundaries of the Proclamation of 1763. Johnson's action delighted white farmers and land speculators but left the Oneidas deeply aggrieved.[4]

In addition, many Oneidas felt a special bond with the Reverend Samuel Kirkland, a Presbyterian missionary from Connecticut and cultural broker in his own right. He lived in their villages beginning in the mid-1760s and won numbers of them over to the precepts of New Birth Christianity. Kirkland and Johnson disliked one another. Johnson stood with the Church of England, firmly attached to the Crown; but as tensions mounted between the colonies and the Mother Country, Kirkland preached the virtue of American resistance. Both men were planting seeds of discord that in time would ignite a civil war among the Haudenosaunee peoples.[5]

Johnson died in the summer of 1774, a few months before Lexington and Concord. Virtually everyone now had to reckon with the matter of allegiance. Guy Johnson, who replaced his uncle as Indian Superintendent, knew where he stood. During July 1775 he fled to Canada from his palatial Mohawk Valley residence, Guy Park, near the small town of Amsterdam. He did so amid rumors that New York rebels — striking first, as they did so often in other colonies — were about to arrest him to prevent his encouraging loyalist sympathies. He did not travel alone. Some 90 to 100 Mohawks and 120 loyalists, many of them Scots-Irish, fled with him. Once in Montreal he linked up with the charismatic Mohawk Joseph Brant (Thayendanegea), whose older sister Molly had been Sir William's longtime consort. At a conference attended by several hundred Canadian Indians as well as numbers of young Mohawk warriors, Brant and Johnson invited all to join in crushing the rebels. Johnson gave each of the attending Nations a war belt committing them to the British. Then he offered a feast of oxen and wine meant to symbolize the bodies and blood of the rebels. Thus, from the start there was bloodlust in the air.[6]

Not so fast was the reaction of the Oneidas and others in the Six Nations. Like the Trans-Appalachian Indians, they initially preferred a policy of neutrality. In August 1775, patriot major general Philip Schuyler, a wealthy trader-landowner in the Albany area and now commanding the Continental Army's Northern Department, urged the Iroquois to stay out of the imperial civil war. Speaking for the Continental Congress, Schuyler explained that "this is a family quarrel between us and Old England… We don't wish you to take up the hatchet against the King's troops. We desire you to remain at home, and not join on either side."[7] Aware that Brant and Johnson were urging Mohawks to side with the Crown, a Grand Council of Iroquois sachems, meeting in the heart of Onondaga territory (modern Syracuse, New York), admonished potential warriors against hostilities. They advised them to take the war belt they had accepted from Johnson and hand it over to Schuyler and other patriot Indian commissioners in Albany.[8] The seeds of inter-Iroquois civil strife were sprouting.

The year 1776 was a decisive one in the Mohawk Valley. The Oneidas confirmed their commitment to neutrality; but many valley loyalists, quite often Scots and Scots-Irish, rallied to the banner of Sir John Johnson, son of the late Sir William and heir to his father's massive property holdings and baronet's title. Pressured by rebel militia, including many Palatines, Sir John fled to Canada in May with about 200 of his followers. There he organized the King's Royal Regiment of New York, commonly known as the Royal Greens. The regiment was comprised mainly of aggrieved loyalists determined to get back at rebel partisans who had chastised, threatened, and even driven them from their property.[9]

Brant's Volunteers

While Johnson organized his Royal Greens, Joseph Brant was rallying Iroquois villagers to the British side. He was an inspirational leader who argued an Indian agenda. A British alliance, he pointed out, offered the best chance to protect Iroquoia. On the other hand, an American victory would doom the tribes to dispossession amid a torrent of white settlers. In early 1777, Brant returned to his home at Oquaga along the Susquehanna River, where he organized his own partisans from disgruntled Indians and loyalists – Brant's Volunteers. Over the course of the war, Volunteers joined from other areas as well.[10]

As in the West, it was no novelty to find white loyalists serving alongside Indian warriors. But the appearance of Brant's Volunteers was something genuinely novel. In this case, white men chose to serve *under* a Native American commander. They had other choices. They could just as easily have enlisted with Johnson's Royal Greens or with Lieutenant Colonel John Butler's Rangers, also recruited in northern New York. Both the Greens and the Rangers were formally organized and on the official provincial roster.[11] While Brant held an authorized commission as a captain, his Volunteers were unofficial combatants. They received no pay or government recognition, although after 1778 authorities in Quebec Province did provision them. Their pay was plunder, and until they received government provisions they lived off the land and what they could pillage. One can safely assume they had never read Emer de Vattel.

Who were these men and what motivated them? In fact, we know relatively little about them. Originally there were about 100 Volunteers, perhaps 20 Mohawk and 80 white. At peak strength later in the war there were some 300 of them, with a higher proportion of Indians, probably because some white men eventually transferred to Butler's and Johnson's corps. Still, white Volunteers served with Brant until the end of the war. The tory Volunteers were mostly Scots, Irish, and English from central and upper New York State and the upper Delaware River Valley, and they probably came from the margins of colonial society. They had little to lose in going to war. As irregulars, unlike Johnson's Greens, the Volunteers were not uniformed. Many of Brant's loyalists also adopted Indian dress and even war paint. We might consider them cultural hybrids – patriots saw them as race traitors.

Brant's Volunteers were not wealthy men by any stretch of the imagination. And if, as seems to be the case, they were just trying to survive and be left alone in marginal socio-economic circumstances, demands and intimidation from seemingly fanatical republicans could well have driven them to the Crown. But whatever their motives, they were angry enough to transcend normal frontier racism and to volunteer to serve under an Indian commander. There was no greater statement of the depth of loyalist hatreds of patriot Americans.

Brant was also a factor in their decision. The Mohawk was a magnetic leader, but he was a controversial man as well. He straddled two cultures – Iroquois and British – and neither the Indian nor white populations knew fully what to make of him. Some of the more traditional Iroquois, leery of Brant's close ties to the British, his white education, and his genteel polish, never fully trusted him. The British winced at his insistence in pursuing an Indian agenda, including independent military operations, even as he allied with the imperial war effort. But Brant was brave and a capable combat commander – by any measure, he was one of the best light tactical leaders of the war – and he did his best for his followers. On occasion he even supplied them with his own credit when provisions were otherwise unavailable. Men followed him.

The Volunteers would prove no more or less brutal than other partisan groups, although they adopted Indian practices that appalled the white inhabitants on the frontier. In the heat of battle the Volunteers seldom took prisoners, and when they did, as in the West, captives unable to keep up with Volunteers on the march could expect to be tomahawked and scalped. On the other hand, Brant did not condone torture, and he discouraged violence against women and children. And in a reflection of his engagement with European ideas and culture, he was conversant with the rules of "civilized warfare." At one point, offended at the treatment of Indian prisoners in rebel hands, he dispatched an astringent letter to whig authorities in the frontier settlements. "It is a shame to destroy those who are defenceless," he wrote. "This has been uniformly my conduct during the War. I have always been for saving and releasing [prisoners]. These being my sentiments, you have exceedingly angered me by your threatening and distressing those who may be considered as prisoners. Let there be no more of this conduct. Ye are or once were brave Men. I shall certainly destroy without distinction does the like conduct take place in the future."[12]

Yet for all his expressed concern for what he considered reprehensible in war, Brant would not be above retaliating in kind for the destruction of Indian homes and the deaths of Indian noncombatants. His command also developed a reputation for free-booting and going its own way; and given the Volunteers' loyalty to Brant, they had little patience with the formal British chain of command. Indeed, British officers looked askance at them. A redcoat major complained that in his 30-year career he "never had so much trouble as with those fellows."[13]

If British regulars were dubious about Brant's men, patriots absolutely loathed them. To Americans the Volunteer tories were the worst of savages. In following an Iroquois leader, dressing like Indians, painting their faces like Indians, and fighting like Indians, they were alarming and hideous "others." Terrified of the Volunteers, patriots showed them no mercy. Writing to one of his colonels in Cherry Valley, Continental brigadier general John

Stark issued a revealing order regarding Volunteer prisoners: "If your scouts should be fortunate enough to fall in with anymore of those painted scoundrels, I think it not worth while to trouble themselves to send them to me. Your wisdom and your scouts may direct you in that matter." This passage, as Caleb Stark, the general's grandson and editor of his papers, explained, was code for "knock them on the head."[14] In other words: no prisoners.

Firestorm

Brant, Johnson, John Butler, and most of the entire British–Indian–loyalist northern alliance ranged freely over the New York frontier and occasionally into Pennsylvania, but the firestorm ignited in the Mohawk Valley. It sprang from Lieutenant General John Burgoyne's 1777 invasion of northern New York. British strategy focused on severing New England, the original center of the rebellion, from the rest of the colonies. The key was to take control of the Lake Champlain–Lake George–Hudson River water corridor; and the operational plan for 1777 had Burgoyne moving some 8,000 British and German soldiers, along with tory partisans and Indian auxiliaries, south from Montreal onto the lakes to reach the Hudson and Albany. Once there his army would link up with another major force theoretically moving up the Hudson River from the main British base of operations in and around New York City.[15]

As part of the plan, Burgoyne provided for a diversionary column that would approach Albany from the West. This force, under Brevet Brigadier Barrimore (Barry) St. Leger, was to proceed from Montreal along the St. Lawrence River, then onto Lake Ontario, and subsequently move down the Oswego River and into the Mohawk River Valley. St. Leger would drive down the valley toward Albany, forcing patriots to defend on two fronts.[16] The brigadier commanded a mixed group of about 1,800 troops. Brant was with him, leading some 300 Mohawk and loyalist partisans – the Volunteers – as was

Johnson and 500 Royal Greens. Butler's Rangers were there as well, and Butler was an angry (and soon to be notorious) man. A onetime confidant of Sir William Johnson, he was driven from his immense property holdings in the valley because of his outspoken loyalism. Operating out of Fort Niagara, Butler had rallied a substantial number of Senecas and Cayugas who had concluded that continued neutrality was foolhardy. St. Leger, who had supplied the tribes with critical weapons and supplies, completed his force with about 200 British regulars and a few Germans and Canadians. Thus his column was essentially an Indian–loyalist corps; regulars would play only a minority role in what was to come.[17]

Their immediate target was Fort Stanwix (called Fort Schuyler during the war), located at the western end of the Mohawk Valley. St. Leger planned to burn his way down the valley, but he couldn't do so while leaving the fort's 750 defenders (mostly New York Continentals) in his rear. If he did, the Continentals could harass his column every step of the way to Albany. Brant's scouts reached the fort by early August, and soon after St. Leger began siege operations and demanded the garrison's surrender. The rebels spurned the demand. But the brigadier had other problems. His march had taken him uninvited through Oneida territory, infuriating the tribe, which then cast its lot with the patriots. The elements were now in place for a full-scale civil war among the Iroquois – a complication St. Leger had not anticipated.

The situation spun out of control. Indeed, ugly incidents were afoot before the Stanwix siege began. In late July three young girls ventured from the fort without permission, hoping to pick raspberries. A party of St. Leger's Indians spied them and attacked. Soldiers rushed from the fort at the sound of musket fire but arrived too late: They found one girl shot, scalped and dead; the second girl shot, scalped, and dying; and the third, who survived, shot twice. Colonel Peter Gansevoort, in command of the 3rd New York Regiment, ordered all women and children at Stanwix to move down the valley to safer locations.

The Bloody Massacre by Paul Revere, showing the March 5, 1770 confrontation between British redcoats of the 29th Regiment and a Boston crowd. As a representation of reality, Revere's print was nonsense, but as anti-British propaganda it was brilliant. During the Revolution, patriots showed a real gift for portraying their opponents in the worst possible light. (Metropolitan Museum of Art, Gift of Mrs. Russell Sage, 1910)

As the author of *The Law of Nations*, Emer de Vattel (1714–67) was one of the key interpreters of *jus in bello*. (Photo by Fine Art Images/Heritage Images via Getty Images)

The illegitimate son of Benjamin Franklin, William Franklin (1730–1813) was a popular royal governor of New Jersey before the Revolution. Deeply embittered after his overthrow and arrest in 1776, he was a staunch loyalist and advocated a hard line against the patriot cause. He and his father were never reconciled. (From the New York Public Library, EM9850)

William Livingston (1723–90) was a moderate whig and not an early advocate of independence. But as governor of revolutionary New Jersey the experience of war radicalized him. Livingston became a ferocious enemy of loyalists and supported the harshest measures to suppress them.
(Photo by Hulton Archive/Getty Image)

George Rogers Clark and the surrender of Fort Sackville, Vincennes, on February 25, 1779. The fort surrendered to Clark after a brief siege and after Clark ordered the public murder of four Indian captives as an example of what awaited the British garrison if it did not capitulate. (Signal Photos/Alamy Stock Photo)

The Gnadenhütten Massacre, March 8, 1782. In one of the most heinous atrocities of the war, Pennsylvania militia massacred in cold blood 96 pacifist Moravian Lenape Indians, including 29 women and 39 children. While some patriots were aghast, no action was taken against the militia. Other Indians were enraged and swore vengeance. (Henry Howe, *Historical Collections of the Great West*, 1852)

Joseph Brant (Thayendanegea) by George Romney. Romney painted Brant while the Mohawk was visiting London in 1776. Brant returned to America to skillfully lead Native American forces allied to the British; he emerged as one of the best light infantry commanders of the war. (GL Archive/Alamy Stock Photo)

Incident in Cherry Valley – Fate of Jane Wells, engraving after painting by Alonzo Chappel. During the Cherry Valley massacre on November 11, 1778, a combined force of Indians, loyalists, and a detail of redcoats fell on the village by surprise. Lax patriot security left many civilians outside of a fortified post, and some thirty noncombatants died, as well as a smaller number of patriot troops. Joseph Brant and loyalist leader Major Walter Butler (son of John Butler) were unable to restrain some of the Iroquois. (Library of Congress)

Oneidas at the Battle of Oriskany by Don Troiani (2005). Fought on August 6, 1777, the Battle of Oriskany pitted Tryon County, New York, militia and Oneidas against a mixed force of loyalists and Indians (mostly Iroquois). While a bloody tactical patriot defeat, the battle marked the end of the British drive east toward Albany. It also saw the beginning of a fierce civil war among the Iroquois, as most Oneidas and Tuscaroras allied with the patriots while the rest of the Iroquois joined the British. (Private Collection © Don Troiani. All Rights Reserved 2025/Bridgeman Images)

Major General John Sullivan, leader of the 1779 Sullivan Expedition. Sullivan's forces – about a third of the Continental Army, plus attached militia and Oneida scouts – marched from Easton, Pennsylvania, into the heart of Iroquoia in central New York and back, between June 17 and October 3. The scorched-earth campaign devastated Iroquois towns, fields, and livestock, effectively knocking the Iroquois out of the war for the rest of the year. (Library of Congress)

Gathering of Overmountain Men at Sycamore Shoals by Lloyd Branson (1915). The rendezvous at Sycamore Shoals gathered frontier militia – the Overmountain Men – and some of their families in late September 1780 near today's Elizabethton, Tennessee. From Sycamore Shoals, some 1,100 militia set off to trap loyalist forces under British Major Patrick Ferguson at Kings Mountain, South Carolina, on October 7. (Tennessee State Museum)

Schooner Ajax leaving Delaware from the William H. Meyers diary. *Ajax* was one of thousands of privateers that preyed on British shipping and drove the Royal Navy to distraction. They came in all sizes, from open boats rowed in shallow waters to larger men-of-war that raided on the high seas. Whatever their sizes, the privateers vastly outnumbered the ships of the small Continental Navy. (From the New York Public Library, b16044202)

Nancy Hart (c.1735–1830). While much of Nancy Morgan Hart's story lacks firm corroboration in research, her experience was indicative of the dangerous conditions and violence prevalent on the revolutionary southern frontier. Her confrontation with loyalists, depicted here by an unknown artist, while blending with folklore, apparently had a basis in real events. Hart was a cousin of Continental brigadier general Daniel Morgan. (Photo by Fotosearch/Getty Images)

Escaping slaves armed in British service were a white patriot nightmare. This soldier, a former slave, served in the Ethiopian Regiment recruited in late 1775 under Virginia royal governor John Murray, Lord Dunmore. While the regiment disbanded in the summer of 1776, thousands of southern slaves escaped to the British over the course of the war, many of them to take up arms. But fears of black insurrections or alliances with the British were not confined to the South. A newspaper advertisement in the *Pennsylvania Gazette* in May 1780 reported on a runaway slave by the name of Michael Hoy and notes his probable flight with a white loyalist on a mission to carry intelligence to the British in New York. (Artwork by Gerry Embleton © Osprey Publishing Ltd)

Such incidents inflamed emotions of vengeance and retaliation. One angry soldier inside Fort Stanwix declared: "It is equally the same [to marauding Indians] if they can get a scalp, whether it is from a soldier or an innocent babe."[18] It was clear that civilians would not be spared in the fighting to come; there would be no distinctions between noncombatants and combatants, no regard for age or sex. Fighting would be to win or survive at all costs and without restraint.

Farther down the valley, militia general Nicholas Herkimer rallied a force of about 800 militiamen, mostly Palatines, to relieve Fort Stanwix. Joined by 60 to 100 Oneidas and a few Tuscaroras, early on August 6 Herkimer marched into a disastrous ambush six miles south of the fort. With about 500 Indians and loyalists, Sir John Johnson, John Butler, Joseph Brant, and Seneca leaders Old Smoke and Cornplanter unleashed a vicious surprise attack. The Battle of Oriskany was a civil war on two fronts: Americans versus Americans and Iroquois versus Iroquois. The regulars – British and Continental – were not there. But one did not need regulars for a desperate and grisly action. Oriskany represented a slaughter for the militiamen, who suffered approximately 500 casualties, including more than 350 killed. There was plenty of close-quarter combat. Blacksnake, a young Seneca warrior, recalled later in life that he saw that day "the most Dead Bodies ... I never [again] Did see, and never will again." Blood resembled "a Stream Running Down on the Descending ground During the afternoon."[19]

The end of the fighting did not end the dying. Some of the militiamen and Oneidas got home only to succumb to wounds. Herkimer himself was mortally wounded early in the engagement and bled to death a few days later after a botched amputation of his damaged leg. Several militiamen were taken prisoner and suffered brutal deaths at the hands of the enraged Senecas and other Indians, who were furious that more than three dozen of their brethren, including a few chiefs, had been killed in action. The Indians forced many of these unfortunates to run a gauntlet while they clubbed them to death. Perhaps the most horrific incident involved an exceptionally tall militiaman named Robert Crouse. To torture him his captives cut off his lower legs and ordered him to walk around as an average-sized person before they finally scalped him and stabbed him to death. Apparently only three or four captives escaped death. Taken to Canada, they were later exchanged for British prisoners held by Americans.[20]

The Battle of Oriskany is fraught with significance. Besides being one of the bloodiest battles during the war in terms of the nearly 60 percent casualty rate suffered by Herkimer's column, it signaled the end of Iroquois neutrality and the beginning of a civil war among the Six Nations. Not only had Senecas and Mohawks fallen that day, but so had Oneidas. Now drawn into the imperial "family quarrel," the Six Nations would continue fighting against each other, which meant the end of the ancient bonds of unity. Beyond the divide among the Iroquois, the bitterness spawned at Oriskany gave sustenance to seemingly endless scenes of retributive violence in the days ahead. Only very rarely would there be nods in the Mohawk Valley and adjacent regions to civilized, humane warfare in the spirit of *jus in bello*.

Oriskany, however, was a pyrrhic victory; it did nothing to save the overall British plan from ultimate frustration. A patriot force moving up the valley under Benedict Arnold helped scare off St. Leger's Indian allies and relieve Fort Stanwix. A perplexed St. Leger retraced his march to Canada. Next came Burgoyne's surrender on October 17 after two battles near Saratoga. A critical consequence was that in February 1778 American diplomats worked out a formal alliance agreement with the French, who would now openly provide invaluable military, naval, and material support to the Americans.[21] There is a good argument that with Burgoyne's defeat the British had lost their best opportunity to win the war. Such is a view based on hindsight, however, for as events in the Mohawk Valley and many other regions would amply demonstrate, the war in the North was far from over.

Merciless Retribution

Once unleashed, the contagion of violence resulted in merciless retribution and retaliation – over and over again – in the months ahead. The vicious cycle began only days after Oriskany. Brant led a war party against Oriska, a small Oneida village close to the battlefield and home to a few of those Oneida warriors who had joined Herkimer. According to one witness, Brant's Indians, likely Mohawks, "burnt their houses, destroyed their fields, crops, & killed and carried away their Cattle."[22] The village of Oriska, also home to noncombatant women, children, and elderly persons who had not fought in the battle, simply ceased to exist.

Blood-soaked hostilities continued into 1778. Operating out of Oquaga, on May 30, 1778, while pillaging and burning out rebel residents in the Schoharie Valley, Brant drew a small detachment of Continentals and a few militiamen into a firefight near the small hamlet of Cobleskill. Five of the rebels defended themselves in a house; they perished when the Indians burned it to the ground. More than a dozen other Continentals died, and their bodies were cut up and "Butchered in the most Inhuman manner." According to one survivor, one of the soldiers had "his body cut open and his intestines fastened around a tree several feet distant."[23]

New York State west of Albany was panic-stricken. In Albany, Brigadier John Stark scrambled to defend the town. The two Continental regiments in the area had been ordered away – they were needed badly to the west – but Stark detained one of them. The alternative was to defend Albany with militia; but in the aftermath of Brant's Cobleskill raid, the militiamen were terrified and Stark considered them worthless. "Such a set of poltroons," he fumed, "is not to be found on the face of the earth." Indeed, the brigadier accused the militia of failing to support the Continentals at Cobleskill. While the American regulars fought their losing battle, the militia supposedly had "coldly looked on, but did not go to their assistance." Albany's patriots took out their fears and frustrations on local tories.

"They [the people] do very well in the hanging way," Stark rather casually observed. "They hanged nine on the 16th of May; on the 5th of June, nine; and have one hundred and twenty in jail, of which, I believe, more than half will go the same way." In the meantime, he noted a deteriorating security situation and lamented his own circumstances. "Murder and robberies are committed every day in this neighborhood. So you may judge of my situation, with the enemy on my front, and the devil to my rear."[24]

Brant and his raiders kept up their damaging forays during the summer of 1778. The raids were large and small, but collectively they traumatized regional patriots. On June 2 Indians killed two militia officers near Cherry Valley. Then, in a larger operation, on July 18 Brant's command wiped out the small villages of Springfield and Andrustown (Andrew's Town), killing and capturing several men but, following Brant's orders, sparing women and children. Eighty refugees escaped Springfield to flee east, while most residents of Andrustown sheltered in Fort Herkimer on the Mohawk River. They returned to their village only sporadically to tend their crops, often with militia escorts. On September 18 the Volunteers attacked German Flatts, another hamlet along the Mohawk. Warned of the impending assault, most of the inhabitants escaped to local forts; but Brant and the raiders leveled virtually every home and barn in the area, besides killing or carrying off hundreds of farm animals.[25] Everywhere they went they destroyed crops. It was all undeniably gruesome. But mindless mayhem? No. Brant knew what he was doing. His aim was to instill massive fear in the local populace and thus weaken patriot resolve and military effectiveness. Equally important was his objective to destroy crops and livestock in this food-basket region which fed George Washington's often ill-supplied Continental forces.

The bloodletting in the Mohawk Valley was hideous, but it was matched by a slaughter along the banks of the Susquehanna River in Pennsylvania's Wyoming Valley (near modern

Wilkes-Barre). In recognition of John Butler's service during St. Leger's campaign, the British commissioned him a lieutenant colonel and asked him to enlist a full regiment of rangers. Butler did so enthusiastically. In June 1778 he linked about 130 of his rangers with some 450 Indians, mostly Senecas and Cayugas still furious over losses at Oriskany. Their leaders, Old Smoke and Cornplanter, thirsted for revenge. The Indians also wanted to drive away the hundreds of white settlers, many of them from Connecticut, who had moved onto the Wyoming lands, which they considered their own. They were spoiling for a fight as Butler swept into the valley.

The tory–Indian assault hit the rebels by surprise on July 3. In a tactical masterpiece, the attack virtually annihilated ineptly led militia and a few unfortunate Continentals. Tales of slaughter in battle and the subsequent torture of prisoners spread across the rebellious states, probably exaggerated but with a grisly basis in fact. Hessian captain Johann Ewald reported a conversation with one of Butler's Rangers who was in the Wyoming fighting. The ranger supposedly claimed "two whole brigades massacred [this was a gross exaggeration], of which the greater part were scalped half dead, and in such misery lost their lives." He continued that he had "worked so hard with my tomahawk and scalping knife that my arms were bloody above the elbows."[26] Exaggerated or not, the reality was bad enough. Butler reported 227 scalps as the trophies of war. Colonel Nathan Dennison, in charge of the Pennsylvania militia, estimated his overall casualties at 300; by comparison, Butler claimed to have suffered only 11 losses, including two dead rangers and one dead Indian.[27]

A human slaughter this battle was, but should we apply the term "massacre"? That charge revolves around a story (which some historians consider apocryphal) about a powerful mixed-blood Indian woman named Queen Esther Montour. She allegedly used a war club to crush the skulls of 16 captured militiamen after the battle. Recently it has become fashionable to dismiss this incident as pure fiction; however, the Wyoming settlers believed the incident to be true and spread the story far and wide.²⁸ Regardless of the preferred description, the Wyoming Valley was now defenseless.

The battle's aftermath was drawn out and indicative of the desperate outlook of all concerned. Some of the militia survived. They had remained inside Forty Fort, Wyoming's chief bastion, and had missed the fighting. But they were incapable of anything but awaiting their fate if Butler committed to a siege. Instead, the loyalists and Indians, who wanted to avoid a lengthy operation, agreed to a formal capitulation. Colonel Dennison pledged not to take up arms again during the war, and he agreed to dismantle Forty Fort and all other defensive works in the area. Butler promised to protect the property of local inhabitants.²⁹

Neither man kept his word. By the time Butler's raiders withdrew to New York, they had plundered and burned an estimated 1,000 dwellings, along with all local flour mills, while seizing or killing livestock numbering in the thousands. Local civilians had nothing left and they fled eastward in an understandable panic. They now demanded retribution – and got it. Dennison joined a detachment of Continentals who traveled up the Susquehanna River to wreak vengeance by wiping out Indian towns, among them a mostly Seneca village known as Queen Esther's Town. The Senecas, in turn, would use Dennison's perceived dishonesty about staying out of the war as justification for remaining on the warpath.³⁰ The cycle of violence and retribution was in full swing.

Brant Again

The War for Independence saw both sides produce partisan commanders of exceptional talent. Arguably, however, none was better than Joseph Brant. By 1778 he had won the admiration of the British, loyalists, and many Indians, while rebels shuddered at his name. He was continually on the move. While Butler was wreaking havoc in Pennsylvania, Brant kept busy in the Mohawk Valley, bringing devastation to lives and property wherever he went. Local militia couldn't stop him, and patriot residents cried out piteously for protection.

Washington was in no position to offer help. His army, having fought the Monmouth campaign in the early summer of 1778, was reorganizing and committed to monitoring the main British forces in and around New York City. Yet the American commander-in-chief realized he had to do something, if only with a nominal force. He ordered Lieutenant Colonel William Butler (no relation to John) and his 4th Pennsylvania Regiment to destroy Oquaga, Brant's primary base of operations. Moving in at night in early October, Butler's soldiers found the village abandoned. Word of Butler's mission had leaked, and noncombatant women, children, and the elderly had fled. Oquaga was, Butler stated, "the finest Indian town I ever saw"; but his men torched "forty good houses" and reduced the town to a pile of smoking rubble.[31]

Of course, Brant was furious about the loss of Oquaga – just as Seneca leaders were enraged at the devastating raids on Queen Esther's Town and other native habitations. Once again the contagion of vengeance-filled retribution came into play, and it resulted in one of the war's ugliest incidents. Because John Butler was ill, his son Walter took charge of the rangers during the autumn of 1778. A little over 300 Indians, primarily Senecas, likely again led by Old Smoke and Cornplanter, joined about 150 rangers and 50 British regulars, all nominally under Walter Butler's command. Brant brought along some 30 to 40 Indians, mostly Mohawks. Their target was the small, relatively isolated community of Cherry Valley.[32]

The inhabitants of Cherry Valley were sitting ducks. In reaction to Brant's earlier raids, they had constructed a stockaded fort around their church. Then Colonel Ichabod Alden appeared along with about 300 Continentals of the 7th Massachusetts. Over the villagers' protests, Alden excluded the locals and restricted the stockade – which he now immodestly called Fort Alden – to his Continentals. He and his officers chose to lodge in the spacious residence of Robert Wells, about a quarter of a mile away.

On November 8 Alden received intelligence that a large enemy party was moving in his direction. Inexplicably (and foolishly), he did nothing to prepare.[33] The assault came early on the morning of November 11. Escaping the Wells home, Alden was tomahawked and scalped less than halfway to the fort. Most of the officers – a few were taken prisoner – and the Wells family and their servants were literally ripped to pieces. Some of Butler's Rangers pinned down the Continentals inside the stockade, while most of the Indians and rangers began sacking the town. They slaughtered civilians indiscriminately. The final death toll that day was roughly 48 persons, including 32 settlers (mostly women and children) and 16 soldiers. Another 70 became captives, at least one of whom the Indians tomahawked because she lacked the energy to keep up as the raiders marched away. The next morning Brant and some rangers returned to destroy every building that they could find except Fort Alden, which was still defended by Continentals. Thanks to their incompetent and now dead colonel, they had done nothing to protect the community.[34]

If ever retaliation was an obvious motive, the massacre at Cherry Valley is a prime example. Brant and others said that the raid was revenge for the destruction of Oquaga: "[W]hen we Indians were gone from our place … you Burned our Houses, which makes us and our Brothers, the Seneca Indians angry, so that we destroyed men, women, and Children at Chervalle [Cherry Valley]."[35] In explaining their role, the Senecas claimed to be greatly disturbed by allegations that they had killed many noncombatants during the Wyoming Valley raid, and they expressed their wrath at Dennison's participation in attacks against their villages.

Rationalizations aside, Lieutenant General Frederick Haldimand, the new governor of Quebec Province, admonished John Butler for his son's inability to control the Indians under his command – as if the Native Americans were solely responsible for the devastation at Cherry Valley. "[I]ndiscriminate vengeance," Haldimand bitterly wrote, was "contrary to the disposition and maxims of their King, in whose cause they are fighting."[36]

"A CONTAGION OF VIOLENCE"

The governor was a decent man and as thorough a professional soldier as the British army could boast, and his censure of Butler is interesting on several counts. First, he was oblivious to the Iroquois agenda. As they had at Wyoming and elsewhere, the Native Americans fought without a particular interest in George III. Cherry Valley was about protecting Indian interests; that those interests coincided with imperial interests made only for an alliance of convenience. Haldimand's message, however, did represent a rare bow to the ideals of *jus in bello* in relation to the fighting on the New York and Pennsylvania frontiers. But it was also an exception that proved the rule. Haldimand admonished against excessive violence, tacitly pronouncing on "civilized war" as a senior officer far from the action, removed from the perspective of his subordinates in the field, and with no apparent understanding of the cultural norms of Indian warfare. Again it was a case of ideals contrasting with realities.

Joseph Brant was not done. A year later, in July 1779, he led his Indians and loyalists into the upper Delaware Valley. Looking for supplies, the Volunteers raided the small village of Minisink (now Port Jervis), New York. Brant destroyed the village but spared women and children; casualties on both sides were minimal. The aftermath, however, was far different. When militia gave chase to Brant, on July 22 he turned and trapped many of them on a hilltop near the Delaware River. After a vicious fight, the Iroquois and Volunteers overran the patriots, including many helplessly wounded. Survivors, their commander reported, were terrified of the "bloody monsters" and expected "nothing ... but the hatchet, spear, and scalping knife. The tremendous yells and whoops, all the fiends in the confines of the Infernal Regions with one united cry, could not exceed it. Add to this the cries and petitions of the wounded around me not to leave them, was beyond parallel or idea. My heart bleeds for the unfortunate wounded who fell into their hands." Of 120 or so militia engaged, over 40 died.[37] In proportion to the numbers involved, the Battle of Minisink was one of the worst patriot defeats of the war, and it left the region traumatized. Thus, at least through mid-1779 the British – mostly through loyalist and Indian proxies (the regulars of either side counted for relatively little) – were winning a particularly vicious frontier war.

Enter the Regulars

Even before the carnage at Cherry Valley, the Wyoming Valley disaster had prompted discussions among Washington and his advisers about a retaliatory strike. They agreed on launching a massive raid into western New York – into the heart of Iroquois country – with the British fortress at Niagara as an overall target. The Cherry Valley massacre clinched the decision to go after the Senecas, Cayugas, Onondagas, and other British-allied Indians. After Horatio Gates refused the assignment, Washington selected one of his less-inspiring major generals, John Sullivan, to head the expedition. The force totaled some 4,500 troops, an overwhelming number the Iroquois and allied loyalists could not hope to match. In late August 1779 they proceeded northward into southern New York toward Cayuga and Seneca territory. On the 29th at Newtown (near today's Elmira), Sullivan brushed aside some 500 Indians, including Brant, as well as John Butler's Rangers and a few British regulars. Resistance melted away as Sullivan's troops advanced all the way north to the major Seneca village of Chennusio on the Genesee River. Sullivan burned as he marched, and by the time his scorched-earth campaign ended in early October his troops had razed 41 villages and towns and had destroyed innumerable acres of Iroquois crops. Sullivan concluded that "we have not left a single settlement or field of Corn in the Country of the Five [Indian] Nations."[38]

The expedition's stated purpose was to lay waste to the land, not to maim and kill Indians, unless they offered combat. Acceding to Sullivan's superior numbers, the Indians did their best to keep out of the way, but ugly incidents still occurred. Near Chennusio Sullivan asked Lieutenant Thomas Boyd to scout the immediate area. The Oneida scout and warrior Han

Yost Thahoswagwat and about 25 soldiers joined in the sortie. Han Yost warned of a trap, but Boyd felt he knew better and led his detachment into an ambush set by John Butler and some Senecas. Fourteen soldiers were shot, scalped, and mutilated. Unfortunately for Boyd, he fell victim to horrific torture when captured. When some of Sullivan's soldiers found his almost unrecognizable remains, they reported that not only was his body mutilated, but that his eyes had been bored out and his head cut off and skinned. John Butler and his captors gave no thought to keeping Boyd alive as a prisoner for future exchange. As for Han Yost, his Iroquois brethren showed no respect. They killed him, lifted his scalp, and dismembered his body.[39]

Both sides committed atrocities. Lieutenant William Barton of the 1st New Jersey Regiment was hoping to bring home some sort of souvenir from the campaign. When his company found the lifeless bodies of a few Indians, his troops skinned the legs of two of them so that Barton and his major could each have a pair of leggings. Overall, however, such acts of disrespect for human life were rare during the expedition, but only because the combatants, with few exceptions, stayed clear of one another. When Sullivan turned his troops back south, the Indians and Butler's Rangers retreated to Fort Niagara. There they endured the harshest winter weather of the war, and many hundreds of them, facing clothing and food shortages, died during that dreadful season when supplies of every kind all but ran out. In this sense, Sullivan's expedition did take a heavy toll, not only on property but also on noncombatants, including Indian women and children and the elderly.[40]

Here was another lesson. Committed in numbers, disciplined and well-provisioned regular troops could be successful — at least in the short run. Washington never thought Sullivan and his Continentals (who also had militia reinforcements and Indian scouts) could knock the Iroquois completely out of the war. He did hope that Sullivan could take some pressure off of the frontiers for at least a season, if not longer, and the expedition did serve that purpose. Moreover, if Sullivan had pursued a scorched-earth policy, he had done so only after Americans had warned the Iroquois to give up their British alliance or face the consequences. Washington had authorized Sullivan to break off his assault if the Iroquois were willing to talk peace, and at least some of the expedition's troops hoped for just such a development. But that was not to be. It is not to mitigate the suffering of so many noncombatant Indians to note that patriots considered Sullivan's expedition as no more than justified retaliation in kind for the recent Indian–loyalist raids on Wyoming, Cherry Valley, and elsewhere. A century later, at New York's centennial celebration of the expedition, it was none other than William Tecumseh Sherman – who knew a thing or two about burning out an enemy's heartland – who conceded the grim nature of Sullivan's operation. But he noted that Sullivan did what he had to do; after all, there was a war to be won.[41]

Those Iroquois who survived the Continental onslaught, however, entered the 1780 campaign season with renewed vigor and with a commitment to revenge. With Sullivan's return to Washington's main army the frontiers were again open to attack. What followed were destructive raids, often referred to as the "Burning of the Valleys." No one seemed safe as Johnson's Royal Greens and Brant's Volunteers cut wide swaths of devastation through the Schoharie and Mohawk Valleys. Brant even drove a large number of Oneidas, still largely allied with the rebels, all the way east to the Schenectady area after his rangers destroyed their principal village of Kanonwalohale. Hundreds of farms went up in smoke and thousands of white settlers fled east. The raids destroyed crops and livestock to such an extent that feeding the region's civilian population, let alone Washington's half-hungry Continentals, became problematic.[42]

After the war, Mohawk Valley survivors – Indian and white, loyalist and patriot – had to deal with the realities of dispossession, a despoiled landscape, and thousands of damaged and wasted lives. Of some 10,000 white inhabitants living in the region before the war, nearly two-thirds had disappeared. Of the 3,500 remaining souls, about 300 were widows and 2,000 were orphaned children.[43] In effect, it was a variety of "ethnic cleansing," with the victims this time being Anglo-Europeans violently driven from their homes and lands.

Loyalists suffered as well. By 1784 some 10,000 loyalists had made their way to Quebec Province alone, many of them from the Mohawk Valley. The likes of Sir John Johnson, Guy Johnson, John Butler, and other well-to-due tories relatively easily reestablished themselves in Canada. But most tory exiles were small to middling farmers who brought little or nothing with them. Their New York homes were gone, burned out by patriot raids or confiscated by revolutionary authorities.

The case of Peter Fenny was fairly typical. He was a veteran of Johnson's Greens, and before the war had lived on "100 acres of Sir John Johnson's Land for 4 years." He had cleared eight acres and he "had a House & some Furniture. He had 4 Cows & had a Crop in the ground." Fenny lost everything. So did John McKay, who rented 150 acres in the valley, and he had a "House, Barn & Sable ... [and] a Horse & Cow & some grain, all taken by the rebels." The rebels had jailed him three times before "he was obliged to fly for furnishing Provisions to the Army under Sir John Johnson. He had a large family to support," so, exiled, in 1780 he enlisted with the Greens.[44] One can reasonably believe his family joined the ranks of camp followers. The Fenny and McKay stories of dispossession from the Mohawk Valley were repeated in their hundreds in postwar pension applications. Some of Brant's Volunteers followed their Iroquois commander to Canada as well and settled among the Indians. The vast majority of these exiles were dependent on government support as they started new lives, and to its credit the Crown resettled thousands of loyalists in Canada and elsewhere with land grants and, in many cases, with financial compensation for their losses. Unwelcome in the new republic, it was the rare tory who recovered property left behind on the New York frontier.

The divided survivors of the Six Nations now found themselves under relentless pressure to move elsewhere. Despite the urging of the British, most Iroquois had never moved back to their homelands after the Sullivan Expedition; instead, they remained dependent on the Crown for subsistence living on the fringes of the New York frontier and in Canada.

In the West, of course, the war went on; the tribes there were battered but not beaten, and they carried on with clandestine British assistance. But this was not the case in New York. The Iroquois had fought and lost. They had engaged in combat because everything that they had and knew was at risk, and they fought accordingly. They inflicted grievous wounds on rebel soldiers and civilians. Hundreds of warriors had died in combat, and many more – combatants and noncombatants alike – had succumbed to disease, exposure, and starvation. Of those who survived, many left with their leaders seeking shelter and new homes in Canada or elsewhere. Those who remained in the state received little sympathy from victorious Americans; the Indians had no choice but to give way in front of postwar demands for major land concessions. Their civil war had undercut their capacity to mount a united defense of their homeland; even the Oneidas faced the harsh reality of removal despite their costly support of the rebel cause. Thus, Iroquoia ceased being what it once was, the mighty home of the Haudenosaunee people.[45]

The Iroquois homeland was lost along with so much else amid an overwhelming tragedy. The New York frontier endured virtually all of the elements that made an existential struggle seemingly inevitable: Racial animosity, psychological trauma, cycles of revenge and retribution, and the continuation of "America's first way of war" (again to use John Grenier's phrase) led to horror after horror. While most fighting was between local combatants, often without the controlling hands of senior political or military authorities, with few exceptions regular troops had similarly few scruples about *jus in bello*. Sullivan's expedition, however justified in the eyes of patriots, was a deliberate effort to eradicate an Indian military threat by destroying an entire people's ability to feed, shelter, and protect itself – erasing any line between combatants and noncombatants. It was the essence of existential warfare.

5

Target New London: Benedict Arnold from Jus in Bello *to* "Hard Line"

Early in the Second World War, Bomber Command of the Royal Air Force arrived at a fateful decision. Unable to bomb German industrial targets accurately, the air officers chose to employ nighttime "area bombing" against the enemy. The new policy called for hitting wide swaths of German cities, including residential areas. The logic was that if it was impractical to destroy factories and other industrial facilities effectively, then killing or crippling the industrial workforce became necessary – however distasteful such warfare seemed from a humanitarian perspective. While the U.S. Army Air Force tried to pursue daylight "precision bombing," it often proved impossible to miss hitting civilian areas. After all, what was the difference between the soldier who fired the gun and the worker who manufactured it? Bombing in itself obliterated the distinction between soldiers and civilians as actual targets in war.

Making such a distinction, so important in the works of Vattel and other writers on just war, had been largely a fiction when it came to the realities of human conflict. The War for American Independence was no exception in this regard, as the fighting in New Jersey and on the western and New York frontiers made clear – and as we have argued from the beginning of this book. In this chapter we will look at a classic example of how patriot civilians engaged in occupations and economic activities linked to the war effort invited – at least from the British perspective – the hard hand of warfare. It is not the story of combat between the main armies but rather a deliberate and calculated strike by a desperate Britain at the civilian infrastructure that supported rebel military operations – and at any rebels, soldiers or civilians, who got in the way. RAF Bomber Command would have understood.

The Conundrum

On September 6, 1781, turncoat Brigadier General Benedict Arnold led a British raid against the Thames River port of New London, Connecticut. A Connecticut native, Arnold knew the region well. He had grown up less than 20 miles from New London, and his assault actually struck old business associates and Arnold family acquaintances. The attack was a tactical masterpiece, demonstrating Arnold had lost none of the verve he had shown as a Continental leader. The raid was unquestionably violent and saw the destruction of considerable public and private property, the defeat of militia resistance, and the costly storming of Fort Griswold at Groton, directly across the Thames from New London. The Fort Griswold fighting saw over 80 patriot troops killed – many of them "massacred" after they had surrendered, at least according to patriot accounts. The attack left the region traumatized and Arnold's reputation among patriots even darker than after his initial apostasy. Patriot newspapers decried "the monster Benedict Arnold," and an enraged Congress, denouncing British violations of "the benevolent rules by which civilized nations have tempered the severities and evils of war," considered hanging British officers in retaliation.[1]

Traitors do not fare well among historians, and Arnold is certainly no exception. Most histories have agreed with the damning patriot assessments of the raid, and especially of Arnold's role. In 1835 Harvard historian and president Jared Sparks set the tone, depicting Arnold as a virtual demon.

"It has been said," Sparks informed his readers, "that Arnold, while New London was in flames, stood in the belfry of a steeple, and witnessed the conflagration; thus, like Nero delighted with the ruin he had caused, the distresses he had inflicted, the blood of his slaughtered countrymen, the anguish of the expiring patriot, the widow's tears and orphan's cries. And what adds to the enormity is, that he stood almost in sight of the spot where he drew his first breath."[2]

More recent authors have moderated Sparks' tone but barely altered his conclusions. They have placed the onus for the violence that engulfed New London squarely on Arnold and the British, not on anything New Londoners might have done to invite the undoubted severity of the attack. Eric D. Lehman, who has told the story of the raid essentially from the New Londoners' point of view, captured their feelings when he termed Arnold's assault "Homegrown Terror."[3]

The persistent focus on Arnold is no surprise. The man is intrinsically interesting – arch villains usually are. But our interest in the New London operation goes beyond the turncoat general. The raid opens a window on *jus in bello* and the realities of the war that contrasts markedly with the struggles on the western and New York frontiers and the tit-for-tat raiding that plagued New Jersey.

New London was a coastal and not a frontier town; by 1781 it had been settled for well over 200 years. It was a well-established residential, mercantile, and political center with military defenses. It would take more than a frontier-style raid to strike the town effectively, so here we encounter regular troops as primary combatants, at least on the British side of the action. And in the worst of the fighting, patriots would deploy experienced militia fighting from fixed defenses – again a major difference from most of the action on the frontiers.

The New London raid also raised a profound moral question, and it was the same one Bomber Command faced a century and a half later: Who was the enemy? Was it the soldier or sailor who shot at you? Or the civilian who manufactured and supplied the ammunition or repaired equipment and ships? In New London, as in other American ports, private citizens were thoroughly integrated into the American war effort. They not only allowed rebel privateers safe haven, but they also provided an essential support network for the privateer fleet. The town's wharves, warehouses, rope works, shipwrights, coopers, and related businesses offered the repair, replenishment, maintenance, recruiting, and even armament facilities essential to keeping the privateers at sea. Moreover, New Londoners based much of their regional economy on the spoils of war – the enemy prizes brought into port. Local merchants bought and sold captured cargoes, often dealing from private offices and other buildings. Civilians worked on the docks and in the warehouses that supported this commerce. Militia and privateers rallied from private homes. Many local civilians from time to time doubled as privateers; merchant captains frequently sailed under letters of marque, and civilians who never set foot aboard a vessel invested in privateer ventures.

The case of New London resident Nathaniel Shaw, Jr., presents a classic illustration of the matter. Shaw was born into a mercantile family. He expanded his father's already prosperous business, trading locally and up and down the East Coast and with the West Indies; occasionally he sent his ships to European and Mediterranean ports. Shaw dealt in "molasses, flour, iron, paper, beaver hats, rum, coffee, and the occasional horse." His business acumen made him one of the richest merchants in Connecticut, and by the 1770s he was well-connected politically and was an ardent revolutionary. Shaw remained a keen businessman during the war, but he also owned some 13 ships, ten of them armed.[4] One of them, the 20-gun privateer *General Putnam*, took 14 prizes during the war.

Although never under arms himself, Shaw was a key figure in the naval war. In 1776 Congress appointed him Naval Agent in New London and tasked him with fitting out armed vessels; he was also responsible for housing British prisoners and assisting wounded American sailors. The patriot merchant arranged any number of privateering ventures, helped equip the defenses of New London Harbor, and gathered intelligence for General Washington. His fine stone mansion (although damaged, it was one of the few major structures to survive Arnold's raid) housed Connecticut's Naval Office and records.[5] For Shaw, civilian and military activities were inextricably intertwined. He and civilians like him in New London and other ports were hardly innocents.

Had Shaw and New London crossed a moral line – a line beyond which Shaw as an individual and the town generally could not reasonably expect anything but the harshest treatment at the hands of the enemy? Although civilians, had they become legitimate military targets? If so, then we must consider whether the conduct of Arnold and the British at New London was considerably less horrid than traditional accounts would have it – and that the circumstances of New London patriots were considerably less innocent.

The Military Context

Benedict Arnold's persona, of course, became inextricably connected with the controversies that followed the New London raid, particularly the widespread destruction and violence associated with the operation. However, we need to consider that given the opportunity most British officers would have welcomed command of the expedition, and for the same reasons as Arnold: In their eyes New London was a legitimate military objective, and New Londoners, in their support for and direct involvement in privateering operations, had all but invited everything they got.

Indeed, it is impossible to understand "why New London" outside the context of a war-long British struggle to contain American privateers. During the War for Independence, Britannia did not rule the waves uncontested. Although never a match for the Royal Navy, Americans nevertheless mounted a credible maritime threat. As a rule, the small Continental Navy, the various state navies, and the numerous privateers that swarmed American and foreign waters seldom pursued ship-to-ship duels with British men-of-war. Rather, their goal was to hit imperial merchant and military cargo shipping. Here Britain was vulnerable. The Royal Navy had global commitments, and with France in the war after 1778 (followed by Spain in 1779 and the Dutch in 1780) the imperial fleet was stretched thin. British men-of-war simply could not be everywhere. This reality allowed sea-faring rebels, as well as French, Spanish, and Dutch ships, to fight a maritime guerilla war, avoiding major actions and using their smaller forces to strike by surprise at vulnerable targets.

The impact on British shipping was stunning. Of some 6,000 British vessels engaged in overseas trade and supply operations, 3,386 fell into American, French, Spanish, or Dutch hands (albeit about 1,000 were recaptured or ransomed back to British owners). Of all captures by American ships, privateers bagged some 75 percent of the total, while Continental and state vessels accounted for the remaining 25 percent. Financially, privateer seizures garnered three times the prize money credited to government ships.[6] British citizens were outraged, and the 1778 edition of London's *Annual Register* aptly expressed the chorus of popular indignation:"It is true, that the coasts of Great Britain and Ireland were insulted by the American privateers, in a manner which our hardiest enemies had never ventured in our most arduous contentions with foreigners. Thus were the inmost and most domestic recesses of our trade rendered insecure."[7] It was "our trade" on which Britain's welfare and security depended, and much of the British public saw threats to that security in existential terms.

The Royal Navy simply could not ignore a threat of this magnitude, nor did it. The British chased American vessels with a vengeance, but also with difficulty. Given Britain's imperial commitments, it lacked the resources to wage a consistent war against such major privateer havens as New

London. When resources allowed, however, royal forces struck with fury at the privateer bases – "nest[s] of rebel pirates," General Clinton called them.[8]

These forays were destructive and violent, and fully reflective of the gravity of Britannia's fears for its security. On October 6, 1778, a raid under Captain Patrick Ferguson devastated the bustling New Jersey privateering center on the Little Egg Harbor River. The British destroyed supplies they could not carry off, leveled the hamlet of Chestnut Neck, and burned or scuttled any patriot vessels they could find. Nine days later, Ferguson wiped out part of Casimir Pulaski's Continental legion in a night bayonet assault. Patriots decried "the Little Egg Harbor Massacre," while the British were unrepentant.[9] In July 1779, Clinton sent Major General (and New York royal governor) William Tryon and 2,600 men to hit the Connecticut ports of New Haven, Fairfield, and Norwalk. The raiders seriously damaged patriot facilities and stores in all three towns, and Norwalk was virtually destroyed.[10]

Concerned about privateers operating off the coasts of northern New England and Nova Scotia, royal forces established a base on the mouth of the Penobscot River in the Maine district of Massachusetts (modern Castine, Maine). Over July and August 1779 the British demolished a Massachusetts-sponsored expedition against Penobscot, wiping out or capturing the entire American fleet (the worst American naval defeat until Pearl Harbor).[11] In early September British raids hit Martha's Vineyard, New Bedford, and Fairhaven, Massachusetts, burning ships, warehouses, public and private buildings, and wharves – "every thing that comes in their way" – and devastating the regional economies that had thrived on privateering.[12]

To put it mildly, the British took anti-privateer operations seriously; they also appreciated that such operations would involve brutal fighting and considerable material destruction. The entire point to these raids was to put the rebel privateers out of business, and to do that required inflicting maximum damage on the rebels' maritime support infrastructure.

In late 1781 there was every reason for the British to focus on New London. Of all losses to privateers, some 500 captures were attributed to Connecticut vessels alone.[13] Bear in mind that the privateer war involved American ships from most of the eastern seaboard as well as French, Spanish, and Dutch vessels. So 500 captures from a single small state was notable. Not all of these prizes were victims of privateers out of New London (we cannot be sure of the precise number), but the Thames port figured heavily in the calculation. New London's activities had annoyed the British from early in the war, and the Royal Navy kept a close watch on the town. British patrols, sometimes visible from the local shore, periodically had raised fears of invasion. The naval blockade was tight early in the conflict, and in 1777 the Royal Navy prevented any prizes from reaching New London. Thereafter, however, the pace of the maritime war quickened. The American privateer fleet counted some 73 ships in 1777, but the number had swollen to 228 by 1780, then surged to almost 450 by 1781.[14] During this time, New London had emerged as the state's leading privateer base. The port saw consistent traffic in prizes, including loyalist privateers captured sailing out of Long Island ports.[15]

The British hated the place. If Clinton eyed the town ominously, Admiral George Collier, commanding the Royal Navy squadron off New England between 1776 and 1779, was equally indignant. The Connecticut port "was a famous receptacle for Privateers," he complained, "and was thought on that account to injure the British trade as much as any harbor in America." If the British had done nothing directly about the town prior to 1781, they certainly had their eye on it.

New London authorities tried to maintain at least minimal local defenses.[16] Patriots built Fort Trumbull (named after Connecticut governor Jonathan Trumbull) on the west bank of the Thames, roughly two miles from the mouth of the river and about a mile south of the town. It was largely an earthwork meant to block incursions moving up the river; the fort mounted eight artillery pieces sighted on the Thames. But the post was vulnerable, virtually defenseless on its landward side. Just west of Fort Trumbull, southwest of the town proper, a small work dubiously called Fort Nonsense (or Fort Folly) lay on a rise beside the road immediately into New London. Fort Griswold was across the river on Groton Heights. It was a more substantial post with stone facing, a large defensive ditch, and several outworks; properly garrisoned, it would be difficult to take.[17] But in the late summer of 1781 neither Fort Trumbull nor Griswold was strongly held, a result of the state's precarious finances and war weariness.

In the meantime, New London was living dangerously. On the eve of Arnold's raid, and probably contributing to British resolve to hit New London, the large privateer *Minerva*, an 18-gun brig under Dudley Saltonstall, brought in the British merchantman *Hannah*. *Hannah*, out of London and bound for New York, was one of the most lucrative prizes of the war. Its loss, valued at £80,000, infuriated the British and illustrated New London's central role in the privateer war. The Crown saw New London as "a den of serpents"; and while the general Connecticut economy sagged under the burdens of a long and enervating war effort, the port's economy remained relatively buoyant. Captured shipping and the support services that kept the privateers operational maintained a semblance of prosperity. By 1781 New Londoners never had a greater stake in the war or had more at risk, their weak defenses notwithstanding.[18]

Benedict Arnold and His Raid

We do not know exactly who suggested the New London operation – it may have been commander-in-chief Henry Clinton's idea. Clinton's adjutant, Major Frederick Mackenzie of the Royal Welsh Fusiliers, noted only on September 1 that Arnold would lead an expedition against the Connecticut town, notorious as a privateer base.[19] But the British commander-in-chief already had expressed serious concern about New London's privateers, and as early as September 1778 he had planned to raid the port. Only poor weather kept Clinton from embarking an expedition.[20]

In 1781 the military situation had changed; the French were in the war, and the major theater of operations was the American South. These facts prompted Clinton to plan a joint army–navy strike against Rhode Island, hoping to disrupt privateer operations and destroy the small French fleet sheltering at Newport. Apparently – "apparently" because Clinton was never explicit on the point – he also hoped the Rhode Island venture would serve as a diversion in favor of the British forces operating in Virginia under Lieutenant General Charles Lord Cornwallis. Combat in Rhode Island, this line of thought went, might prevent Washington from concentrating against Cornwallis. But the French men-of-war slipped away, and with the main quarry gone, Clinton canceled the operation. However, having marshaled resources for the attack, he readily agreed to a new and *overdue* target – New London.[21]

If the mission was not Clinton's brainchild, we must look to Arnold. The former Continental general, anxious to get into action again after his return from Virginia in June, may well have suggested the target. Perhaps he did, but as we have seen, Clinton needed little persuading.[22] Arnold had wanted to lead a raid on New London, or even against Boston, as early as December 1780, only two months after his defection to the British.[23] Given Arnold's enthusiasm and intimate knowledge of the New London area, Clinton saw the logic of giving him the command. There was some irony in the decision: In late 1776, reacting to Connecticut's fear of a Royal Navy attack on the town, Washington had dispatched Arnold to the region to help bolster area defenses and oppose any assault.[24] Arnold's role now would be fully reversed.

The New London operation would be Arnold's second independent mission after donning a British uniform, and his conduct in Connecticut would reflect the experience of his

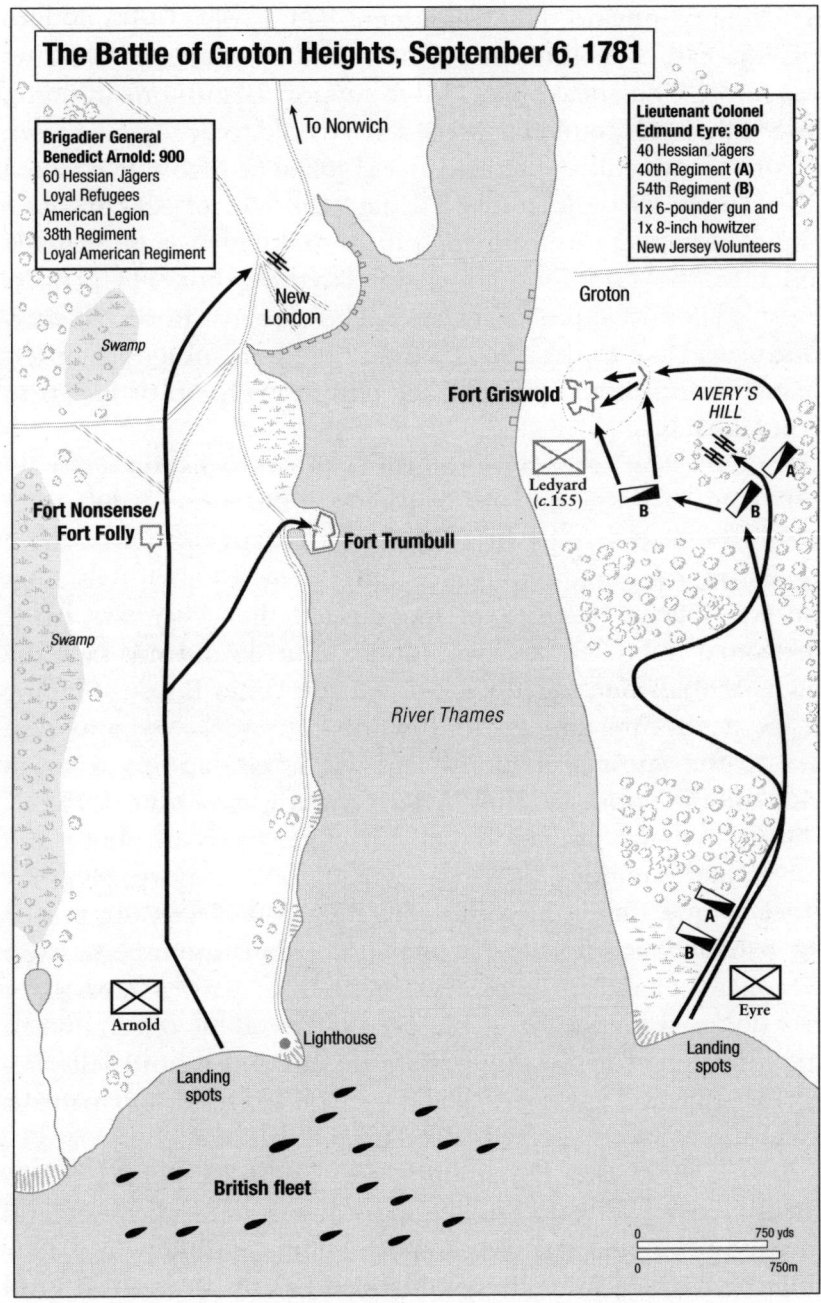

MAP 4

first royal command. This assignment had involved his raid into Virginia earlier in the year. Clinton had long wanted a secure base in the Chesapeake Bay area to support British operations in the South. In December 1780 he sent Arnold to occupy the town of Portsmouth and, if circumstances looked favorable, to strike at other targets of opportunity. Portrayed in patriot accounts as a rampaging operation featuring pillage and destruction, Arnold's raid into the Old Dominion was anything but. He actually displayed considerable forbearance. The turncoat hoped to draw Virginians back to the King, and he issued unambiguous orders against unauthorized plunder and gratuitous harm or insults to noncombatants.

Arnold's fleet arrived piecemeal (a storm had scattered it) in early January 1781, and over January 5–7 the turncoat brigadier raided the state capital in Richmond. His troops sent patriot legislators running, plundered and burned public buildings and war-related facilities in and outside the town, and made ineffectual militia forces look foolish. But he did not sack the town. Arnold then sailed back down the James River, stopping to hit economic targets (mostly tobacco stocks, which were vital to the Virginia economy and war effort) and to skirmish with militia before landing in Portsmouth, which he fortified. Throughout the operation, he restricted targets to public and war-related facilities, leaving civilians and private property largely alone unless in some way they had clearly supported the patriot war effort.[25] He made a serious attempt to woo Virginians, pledging to protect them from patriot reprisals if they declared for the King. He even chastised his officers when they threatened to destroy private homes and barns sheltering patriot snipers. It was a brilliant tactical exercise, and patriots across the colonies seethed at the traitor's success.[26]

Arnold held the Portsmouth area until May 1781 when Major General William Phillips arrived with reinforcements and assumed command. Arnold campaigned under Phillips and, after Phillips' death in June, he commanded briefly again until Lord Cornwallis marched north to unite British forces in Virginia.

Arnold then returned to New York. He had fought well in Virginia, and Clinton approved of his performance.

Yet Arnold had suffered a private disappointment. His hope was to use his name – formerly magical among patriot soldiers – to entice Virginians back to the royal standard. In the end, he had to concede the futility of overtures to reconcile Virginia to the Crown. Patriots there rejected him as a traitor, and loyalists failed to rally, having seen too many earlier, empty, promises of British protection.[27]

Arnold thus returned to Clinton with his warrior reputation intact but without laurels as a reconciling peacemaker. He had learned a bitter lesson: The charisma of the Arnold name was gone. In the future he would fight under no illusions of enticing patriots back to the British Crown. As such, New London would be different. Arnold had no thoughts of vengeance against old acquaintances, most of whom he knew reprobated his treason; but he would waste no time on overtures to locals to return their loyalty to the King. All evidence suggests Arnold's approach to his mission was strictly professional and that he had gone over to the hard line. For him, the raid would be a potent military strike – period.

With the decision to attack made, arrangements came together quickly. The organization of troops, equipment, and ships began late on September 2, and the flotilla of 24 sail departed Whitestone on Long Island (now the northernmost part of the Borough of Queens in New York City) on the 4th. Arnold's expeditionary force comprised some 1,732 troops, along with another 120 loyalists who sailed from Long Island to join the main force at sea. Most of the troops were redcoats of the 38th, 40th, and 54th Regiments; the balance were the experienced Hessian Jäger – some of the best light troops on either side during the war – and components of three veteran loyalist units. These included the American Legion, mostly Continental deserters that Arnold had raised himself; the Loyal Americans, who were New Yorkers; and a battalion of the veteran New Jersey Volunteers.[28]

They sailed under orders, suggesting the mission was never intended as "diversion" in favor of Cornwallis. Only a major offensive in, or an occupation of, the Thames River region would have served that purpose – that is, would have forced Washington to consider diverting significant forces from other operations (and Washington and his French allies were then well into planning their march to Virginia to trap and defeat Cornwallis). As it was, Arnold's troops carried only two days' worth of rations and no tents or horses.[29] They were to knock out the privateer base and pull out; their mission was a raid, *not* an invasion.[30]

The Royal Navy transported the expedition the 135 miles to New London without incident. Arnold personally led a column of over 900 men up the west bank of the Thames, chasing off the two dozen or so militia at Fort Trumbull, who fled across the river to the larger garrison at Fort Griswold. He then marched on New London as further militia opposition evaporated. Arnold had issued orders not to molest civilians or private property (reflecting his instructions from Clinton), but his command commenced a systematic destruction of wharves, warehouses, public buildings, stores, prize goods, and any ships that failed to escape upriver. Anything remotely connected – or *seemingly* connected – to military or economic activity and too big or inconvenient to carry off went up in flames or into the river. Many troops paid little attention to differences between public and private property and erred on the side of inflicting maximum damage. The raiders were nothing if not diligent in their work.

Acting on Arnold's orders, on the Groton side of the Thames some 800 rank-and-file soldiers led by Lieutenant Colonel Edmund Eyre assaulted Fort Griswold. The fort commanded the river, and Arnold wanted to prevent the escape of rebel shipping upriver and to suppress any fire from the fort in support of patriots in New London. Local tories had assured him the fort was thinly garrisoned, and he expected Eyre to have an easy victory. Standing on a rise above the town, however, Arnold witnessed that Fort Griswold was a stronger post than first supposed. When he saw some dozen rebel vessels already escaping upriver – his raiders had burned the rest – he dispatched orders to call off the Griswold attack, feeling there was no longer a point. It was too late. Eyre had already moved. Before the fighting commenced, however, the lieutenant colonel sent a flag to the fort, and the accompanying captain – after some stiff formalities over rank and who would speak to whom – asked for Griswold's surrender.

The post commander, Lieutenant Colonel William Ledyard, refused. Hoping for a substantial militia reinforcement, the colonel and his troops resolved to make a fight of it. Ledyard then declined a second surrender demand. This obstinacy, according to a militiaman who survived the battle, prompted Eyre to threaten the garrison with "martial law" – "that is, whom they did not kill with balls should be put to death with sword and bayonet." Barring the discovery of some new evidence, it is impossible to verify the truth of Eyre's threat. But if he did make such a threat, he did so in keeping with the rules of war. Garrisons in hopeless circumstances, offered terms of honorable surrender, could expect only the worst if they forced an enemy to expend needless blood in a final attack. Nevertheless, Ledyard supposedly replied he would resist "let the consequence be what it might."[31]

Eyre then assaulted the fort, but after a brutal half-hour of combat the bloodied redcoats made little headway. Eyre was hit and his men had suffered scores of casualties. Then, in a stroke of grim chance, a British shot severed the lanyard of the fort's colors; this development, as a militia survivor of the battle recalled, "proved fatal to us, as the enemy supposed it had been struck by its defenders." Although a militiaman quickly remounted the flag, some British soldiers apparently failed to notice and thought Ledyard had surrendered. According to one account, they left their cover and marched toward Fort Griswold thinking the battle was over – only to have rebel fire cut down more of them.[32]

Inside the fort, Ledyard assessed the situation. Confronted with a far superior British force and with expected reinforcements not arriving, Ledyard concluded that an honorable surrender was warranted. As the British assault pressed home, however, he was unable to communicate his decision to the British or to his own men. The redcoats, unexpectedly taking more casualties and thinking they were victims of a bad ruse – had not the Americans struck their colors? – were infuriated and stormed over the fort's walls and through the main gate "with redoubled impetuosity."[33]

Major William Montgomery, who had taken over from the wounded Eyre, fell dead as he entered the fort, speared by a maritime boarding-pike. According to patriot legend, his dying words (certainly apocryphal) were "Put every man to death."[34] Then the real killing began. New London lore has it that a British officer, having accepted Ledyard's sword in surrender, then ran the American through with it. The tale is a nice piece of patriot propaganda (more on this shortly), but the final butcher's bill was real enough. Royal bayonets killed the American commander and played havoc with patriot soldiers, some of whom went down fighting and others dying while trying to surrender.[35]

In 40 minutes of fighting both sides suffered cruelly. Eighty-six Americans lay dead. Of these, only three died in the early fighting while 83 were killed after the British broke into the fort; an additional 60 were wounded, some mortally. That is, some two-thirds of Ledyard's garrison had fallen dead or wounded, while still others were captured. Of the 600 or so attacking British soldiers (of Eyre's full contingent of 800 troops – the artillery and the New Jersey Volunteers arrived too late to engage), 48 were dead and 135 wounded – a casualty rate of over 30 percent.[36] In proportion to the numbers engaged, Fort Griswold was one of the costliest battles of the war for both sides.

Aftermath

The Battle of Groton Heights, as the fighting at the fort and the surrounding locale became known, was a blood-spattered, ghastly affair, with patriots thereafter accusing the British and less directly Arnold of perpetrating a deliberate massacre. The British, of course, denied any such characterization. They did, however, devastate New London and the smaller village of Groton. To his credit, in several instances Arnold personally enforced orders to avoid unnecessary damage to private property. But his mission was to put the privateer base out of action, and unlike in his Virginia expedition, he wasted little effort in restraining the conduct of his officers and men when many of them had needlessly pillaged the town. New London was sacked, and damage included 31 mercantile establishments and warehouses, 18 "mechanics shops," 20 barns, and nine public buildings "including the Episcopal church, courthouse, jail, market, custom-house, &c." The troops destroyed all wharves and, according to Arnold, ten to 12 ships and an "immense quantity of European and West India goods," including *Hannah*'s cargo.[37] Some of the destruction was unintentional, and the worst occurred when powder exploded on a burning ship and the wind blew the flames ashore. Amid the mayhem a few noncombatants were injured or killed, and a number of civilian freebooters took advantage of the confusion and plundered shamelessly.

The town never recovered its prominent role as a privateer haven. Later in 1781 a local newspaper (probably New London's *Connecticut Gazette*) reported a dismal prospect: "The little portion of this town that was preserved from fire on the 6th of September, is so crowded with those that have been burned out of house and home" that New London residents could offer little aid to refugees from other areas. "In short, if there is no redress of this intolerable evil, this town and Groton must be depopulated." Although New London was not "depopulated," Norwich, located about 15 miles upriver, replaced the former as the chief Thames River port of departure.[38] There was no questioning the success or brutality of Arnold's raid, both in relation to New London and Fort Griswold.

As the word of the raid spread beyond New London, patriots were genuinely shocked. Rebels quickly seized on the incident as an opportunity to flog the British as barbarians, and the American press had a field day. In a typical report, the *New-Jersey Gazette* carried a lengthy description of the raid, making the most of charges of unrestrained pillaging and of the destruction of private property: "Some ho[u]ses were plundered; the soldiery seemed to be under no regularity, and everyone at liberty to commit what devastation he thought proper. The party was headed by that *parricide* of his country Benedict Arnold." The *Gazette* continued with an account of Ledyard's supposed death by his own sword as he offered an honorable surrender of Fort Griswold. As for the rest of the garrison: "The enemy, with their usual barbarity, murdered all that came in their way; the groans and pains of the wounded were put an end to by being stabbed with bayonets."[39]

In Boston, the *Independent Chronicle*, looking for a silver lining in the clouds, insisted there was a lesson to be learned: Whatever Arnold did served only to demonstrate "the weakness and debasement into which Britain has fallen."[40] And in Philadelphia, the *Freeman's Journal* suggested "the incendiary general Arnold ... change his Christian name as soon as possible. Sir Harry [Henry Clinton] will supply him with a dispensation. As he cannot with any propriety call himself Benedict, i.e., the blessed; with a small alteration he may easily change it to Maledict, i.e., the accursed. We can inform the wretch that his wanton cruelties will not but hasten his own destruction. American liberty will flourish in spite of traitors, death and fire."[41] Thus, military defeat became a patriot propaganda victory.

Congress reacted with fury. Having received Connecticut governor Jonathan Trumbull's report, including the story of Ledyard's alleged murder, the delegates momentarily turned bloodthirsty in contemplated retaliation. Objecting not only to the New London raid but denouncing other destructive British strikes against privateer bases, on September 20 John Mathews of South Carolina, seconded by James Mitchell Varnum of Rhode Island, brought to the floor a startling motion: It called on Congress to order "the officers commanding our troops to put to death all persons found in arms against these United [States] without discrimination." Mathews and Varnum also wanted "to employ people to reduce to ashes the towns of Great Britain, as a just retaliation for the wanton acts of cruelty committed by the enemy."[42]

But cooler heads among the delegates prevailed, and after considering various amendments Congress backed off the most extreme proposals in the Mathews–Varnum motion. On October 1, guided by "respect due to the benevolent rules by which civilized nations have tempered the severities and evils of war," the delegates decided "remote and unoffending inhabitants of ... [British] towns and villages" were not fit targets for patriot "vengeance." Instead, they called for the execution of all captured British officers should the enemy continue with depredations "contrary to the laws of war among civilized nations."[43] However, with the surrender of Cornwallis only weeks later, and the subsequent end of major combat operations, the retaliatory measure was never put to the test.

While American patriots fumed, the British congratulated themselves on a job well done. Arnold had no regrets about the destruction inflicted on his home region, and he praised the conduct of his troops in his official report to Clinton. Clinton winced at the heavy redcoat losses at Fort Griswold, but he thought well of the raid's results.[44] Arnold's friend, royal governor of New York General James Robertson, groused about the casualties as well and complained that the raiders had failed to detonate Fort's Griswold's powder magazine; but he credited Arnold with a successful military operation.[45]

Tory reaction was positively gleeful. Loyalist lieutenant colonel Joshua Upham, a veteran officer with many successful operations to his credit – and an unapologetic advocate of the hard line – had commanded a tory contingent on the New London side of the Thames. He was proud of the action. He wrote William Franklin, former royal governor of New Jersey and president of the *very* hard-line Board of Associated Loyalists, that his men had brushed aside the rebels "cheerfully" and "spiritedly" and had soundly beaten the King's enemies.⁴⁶ Franklin was glad to learn it. Embittered by what he considered a pusillanimous British war effort, Franklin wanted a much tougher line against the rebels. Relying on men like Upham, he had sent tory raiders against any number of targets in coastal Connecticut and New Jersey.⁴⁷ The New London operation was precisely the kind of action Franklin had in mind.

In New York, Rivington's *Royal Gazette* reported the gallantry of Arnold's men and the success of the attack. "The breast of every honest loyalist can not help emotions of joy on finding that the most detestable nest of pirates on the continent have at last (the measure of their iniquity being full) attracted the notice of his Excellency the commander-in-chief." One can read a sense of "it's about time" between Rivington's lines, but there also was real satisfaction in concluding, "the blow now given will affect the sensitive nerves of every staunch rebel on the continent."⁴⁸ So ended the last major engagement of the War for Independence in the North.

An Assessment

New London paid the price for its leading hand in the privateer war. But here we come to the key questions: Was the price, as patriots insisted, too high? That is, did Arnold violate the accepted norms of *jus in bello* – the canons of "civilized warfare" – as he brought fire and sword to the port? Or, as the British felt, did the town only suffer its just deserts, with those deserts fully within the bounds of acceptable military action?

There is no question about the town's legitimacy as a military target. In attacking New London, the British certainly satisfied the *jus in bello* requirements of "distinction" and "necessity"; that is, they struck at an objective of unmistakable military value or, in the case of Fort Griswold, an actual enemy garrison. Arnold had issued orders to avoid non-military property if possible and to spare noncombatants. All told, there were few civilian casualties and no evidence that those few were other than inadvertent. In war, innocents suffer.

Property damage was another matter. Given the deep civilian involvement in support operations for the privateers, distinctions between civilian and military structures — wharves, warehouses, shops, and commercial offices — were hardly clear-cut. And in such circumstances *jus in bello*, while seeking to limit military excesses, did justify military discretion in undertaking actions necessary to secure legitimate military objectives. This discretion was not an invitation to wanton destruction. "The lawfulness of the end does not give us a real right to anything further than barely the means necessary for the attainment of that end," Vattel cautioned. "Whatever we do beyond that, is reprobated by the law of nature ... and condemnable at the tribunal of conscience." But there was no fixed definition of what was "reprobated." So Vattel went on: The justifiable use of violence "varies according to circumstances," he stated. "What is just and perfectly innocent in war in one particular situation, is not always so on other occasions."[49] In effect, military commanders had the right to make judgment calls on what was necessary "for overpowering the enemy's resistance, and attaining the end of a lawful war." Such actions, even when violent and destructive, were "by the law of nations, deemed lawful in war, and consistent with propriety."[50] In British eyes, and by any interpretation of *jus in bello*, neutralizing a chief enemy privateer base was fully "lawful in war, and consistent with propriety."

But what of the utter destruction of the town? Was devastation and pillage really "necessary for the attainment of that end," meaning an end to New London as a haven for predatory (in British eyes) rebel mariners? That is, did Arnold's expedition transgress the bounds of "proportionality" and go too far? Vattel answers with an emphatic "No." "Since the object of a just war is to repress injustice and violence, and forcibly to compel him [an enemy] who is deaf to the voice of justice," *The Laws* concluded, "we have a right to put in practice, against the enemy, every measure that is necessary in order to weaken him, and disable him from resisting us and supporting his injustice: and we may choose such methods as are the most efficacious and best calculated to attain the end in view, provided they be not of an odious kind, nor unjustifiable in themselves."[51] "Efficacious" methods included the pillage "of a town taken by assault." "It is lawful to take away the property of an unjust enemy in order to weaken or punish him, the same motives justify us in destroying what we cannot conveniently carry away."[52]

Vattel conceded that violence could get even worse. "On certain occasions … matters are carried still farther: A country is totally ravaged, towns and villages are sacked, and delivered up a prey to fire and sword. Dreadful extremities, even when we are forced into them! Savage and monstrous excesses, when committed without necessity!" But they were necessary when "checking" the brutality of "an unjust and barbarous nation" and "preserving ourselves from her depredations." Vattel then offered a striking example of when such dire measures were appropriate. "Who can doubt," he asked rhetorically, "that the king of Spain and the powers of Italy have a very good right utterly to destroy those maritime towns of Africa, those nests of pirates, that are continually molesting their commerce and ruining their subjects?" "Nests of pirates"? "Molesting their commerce"? Sir Henry Clinton could have written as much about New London's privateers.[53] It was all another affirmation that the rules of "civilized warfare" had *plenty* of room for the savagery of combat and its consequences, even for civilians.

There remains the troubling matter of Fort Griswold. The fighting there was as brutal as any in the war. No doubt most deaths occurred after Lieutenant Colonel Ledyard tried to surrender. Historians, however, have been less certain than contemporary patriots that the British perpetrated a deliberate, merciless massacre. In reality, no one actually saw Ledyard fall, much less did anyone view him murdered in cold blood with his own sword after surrendering. At least one eyewitness who originally alleged seeing a deliberate massacre later changed his story.[54]

The issue probably will never be settled to everyone's satisfaction. Yet a charge of "massacre" deserves a longer look. Massacre-oriented interpretations can obscure the nature of actual combat in any age, and such certainly was the case at Fort Griswold. The appalling death toll arose from a combination of British confusion over patriot intentions after the initial fighting at Fort Griswold (fight or surrender?), a collapse of command and control on both sides of the battle, and the proverbial "fog of war" – all of which may be lumped under the category of just plain bad luck.

A surrender in the heat of battle is one of the most difficult actions to conclude. Most garrisons or major troop concentrations would surrender after negotiations between the antagonists. During the War for Independence, the classic examples were John Burgoyne's surrender at Saratoga, Benjamin Lincoln's at Charleston, and Charles, Lord Cornwallis' at Yorktown. There were smaller examples as well, but the general outlines were the same: Victors had established a clearly dominant position (either slowly after extended operations or having quickly developed or exploited a favorable tactical situation), while their opponents, out of options, recognized the hopelessness of their positions. Negotiations, usually conducted under flags of truce – such as the flag Lieutenant Colonel Eyre sent to Fort Griswold – normally led to agreed-upon surrender terms (not always pleasant) and organized capitulations. Command and control among victors and vanquished remained intact throughout; there were supposed to be no excesses as defeated troops laid down arms and became prisoners of war (although there were examples of grim duplicity when surrendered troops were subsequently attacked and murdered).

Indeed, command and control was the key; the alternative was potential, if not actual, chaos. The example here was the Waxhaws, fought on May 29, 1780 in the aftermath of the patriot surrender at Charleston, South Carolina. Continental colonel Abraham Buford, marching to join the Charleston garrison, counter-marched his force northward when he learned of General Benjamin Lincoln's capitulation. Lord Cornwallis sent out Lieutenant Colonel Banastre Tarleton to intercept Buford, and the British dragoon caught the Americans unprepared and disorganized at the Waxhaws, north of Camden, South Carolina. Tarleton sent a flag to demand Buford's surrender, but the Continental elected to fight. The battle quickly became a rout, and Buford then tried to surrender. But command and control had disintegrated. Tarleton was wounded and never received Buford's message, and not all Buford's troops understood that they were to cease fire. Nor did Tarleton's men, most of whom were loyalists who continued to tear into their opponents. It took time for Tarleton to reestablish control, and in the meantime hundreds of patriots were wounded or killed. Americans decried the "Waxhaws Massacre" and afterwards threatened "Tarleton's Quarter" in revenge. The best evidence is that with fighting raging and command and control lost on both sides, an orderly surrender at the Waxhaws was all but impossible.[55]

Unfortunately, the circumstances at Fort Griswold were analogous to those at Waxhaws. Again, the key factor was the integrity of command and control. As patriot defenses at Griswold crumbled, officers on neither side knew fully where their troops were or what they were doing. Chains of command had fractured. With the wounding of Eyre, Montgomery dead, and other officers *hors de combat*, orders to cease fire either never reached the British rank and file or did so only piecemeal as junior officers sought to regain control of the situation. For all that, many British troops knew the fight was still on.

It was the same for the rebels. Ledyard's decision to surrender was never communicated to all American troops, many of whom kept fighting. With confusion gripping both sides, it is difficult to blame attacking troops for carrying on in the absence of orders to the contrary. Once inside the fort and faced with ineffectual American resistance, British officers acted directly to stop the killing – a fact some patriots acknowledged – saving some militia lives;[56] but they reestablished control of their men too late to save most. Unquestionably, there was a slaughter at Fort Griswold, but if the definition of "massacre" implies a deliberate or *de facto* decision not to take prisoners, then events at Groton, no matter how grisly, simply did not qualify.

At least some Americans understood the situation in this light. In Boston, Continental major general William Heath learned particulars of the New London raid on September 10. He shared his outrage over the event and reported the patriot version of Ledyard's treacherous murder. Heath also suspected that Arnold, whose fleet Heath mistakenly thought was still in the area, might strike again. And while shocked at the carnage at Fort Griswold, as a soldier he was not really surprised at the course of events; his observations on the tragedy bordered on the philosophical. He had no intention to "exculpate or to aggravate the conduct of the enemy on this occasion," he wrote, but he thought "two things are to be remembered: first, that in almost all cases the slaughter does but begin when the vanquished give way; and it has been said, that if this was fully considered, troops would never turn their backs, if it were possible to face the enemy: Secondly," the general continued, "in all attacks by assault, the assailants, by the feelings of danger on the one hand, and resolution to overcome it on the other, have their minds worked up almost to the point of fury and madness, which those who are assailed, from a confidence in their works, do not feel." Then came the critical loss of command and control: "Consequently when a place is carried, and the assailed submit, the assailants cannot instantaneously curb their fury to reason, and in this interval, many are slain in a way which a cool bystander would call wanton and barbarous, and even the perpetrators themselves, when their rage subsided, would condemn; but when the human passions remain as they are now, there is scarcely a remedy."[57] Heath recorded this in his journal (subsequently published in his memoirs), and his observations clearly were at variance with the patriot narrative of British barbarity. Nevertheless, General Heath had it right – tragic as it was.

There is another dimension to consider. Before the British stormed the fort, Ledyard had refused Eyre's summons to surrender. While undeniably gallant, Ledyard's rejection again raises questions of allowable conduct under the rules of war. Vattel is clear on one point: A stout and brave defense in the face of long odds was worthy of honorable treatment at the end of the fighting. Even a hopeless defense in one quarter could buy time for allied combatants elsewhere. But what of fighting on when resistance seemingly served no broader purpose? Here Vattel considered "the justice of the war to be problematical," and under such circumstances there were times when no quarter was understandable, if not sanctioned. "Resistance carried to extremity does not become punishable … except on those occasions only when it is evidently fruitless. It is then obstinacy, and not firmness or valour," he explained. When "no succour is to be expected from without," a garrison commander may be "summoned to surrender; and he may be threatened with death in case of his persisting in a defence which is absolutely fruitless, and which can only tend to the effusion of human blood. Should this make no impression on him, he deserves to suffer the punishment with which he has been justly threatened."[58]

The attacking British soldiers suffered casualties that a patriot surrender would have avoided, and they clearly were not in a charitable mood when they finally overran the Americans. What followed was undeniably brutal, but there is no evidence any British officer ever considered the redcoats had violated the canons of *jus in bello*. Explaining is not to excuse, but it helps to further our understanding what happened at Fort Griswold.

The same can be said of Arnold's New London raid generally. It was a brutal but effective strike at a legitimate target and conducted within the constraints of the canons of *jus in bello*. But as Benedict Arnold demonstrated in New London, those constraints could be quite liberal. The busy port town had done virtually everything it could to place itself in harm's way. As a privateer base – and a major one at that – New London had erased the distinctions between combatants and civilians. And in response, Arnold confirmed that waging "civilized war" never implied "going easy" on an enemy – and that, perhaps, "civilized war" is a truly hollow phrase indeed.

6

The South: Terror from the Start

In the absence of British troops or effective imperial authority, in 1775 patriots in Virginia, the Carolinas, and Georgia quickly replaced royal governments with new ones of their own. The rebels who engineered the overthrow of the colonial regimes did so through the unashamed use of intimidation and terror – including the use of physical violence. Most friends of the King – and there were thousands of them – faced with threats and virtual political pogroms, chose sullen subservience or flight. There were always exceptions, and some tories continued in arms. But they were too few to challenge the new political realities; by late 1775 active loyalism was essentially dead. During the two years following their rebuff at Charleston in 1776, the British attempted no major operations in the South and, in general, whig southerners went unchallenged.

In late 1778, however, the patriot ascendancy began to unravel. Successful as it initially was – and in many respects *because* of the brutal nature of early successes – the revolutionary grip on the South threatened to collapse. In their swift resort to intimidation and violence, southern patriots had made plenty of enemies. They had embittered legions of white southerners with sentiments favorable to the King. Many American Indians never forgot the humiliations of earlier defeats and of continuing white land-grabs, and black slaves chafed under the heel of patriot masters. The latent threat posed by any one of these groups was considerable; however, should they find common cause, their

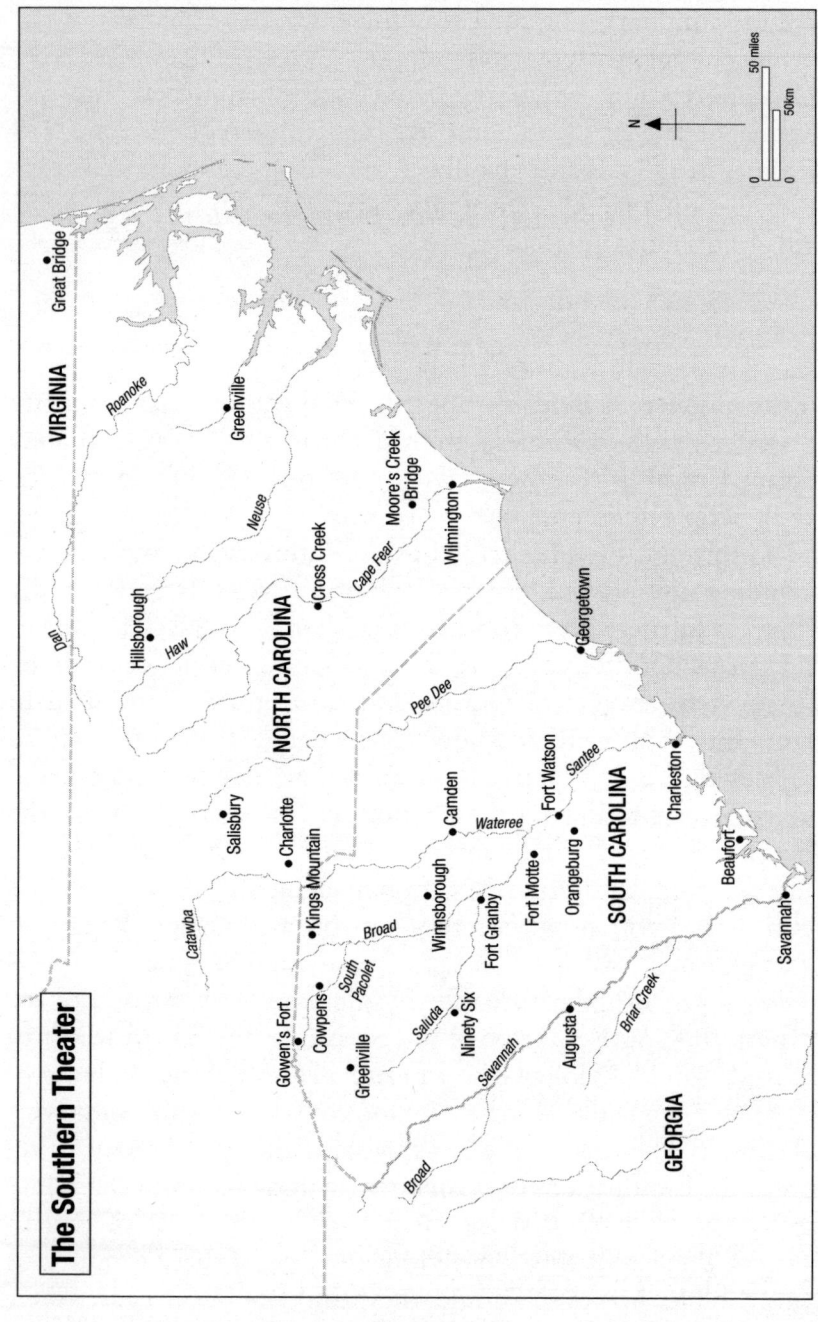

MAP 5

combined military potential was formidable – especially with British encouragement and support.[1] Such encouragement and support came when the King's troops returned, first in Georgia in late 1778 and into 1779, and subsequently in the Carolinas in 1780. Rebels had been sitting on a powder keg, and the long-simmering resentments exploded into an existential conflagration. In this chapter we examine how and why.

The Roots of Preemptive Tyranny

When southern patriots decided on resistance to the Crown, they moved quickly to scotch any notions of dissent among their fellow southerners. The groundwork for a whig tyranny – for it certainly was that – took shape with considerable popular support. As historian T. H. Breen has emphasized, local rebels were often more radical, and more willing to act on their passions, than patriot colonial elites – who often had to catch up with popular boldness. When angry colonials throughout the South formed the now familiar "associations" to enforce boycotts of trade with the Mother Country, efforts to suppress loyalists – suspected and actual – took on a momentum of their own despite the reticence of any moderates. Those who failed to join the boycotts risked ostracism at first, but soon after found themselves hailed (some even hauled) before whig committees to confess and repent their sins. After this came intimidation in the form of being disarmed, followed by threats of physical violence and mob justice, including tarring and feathering. These tactics successfully cowed most southerners who might have rallied to support royal authority.[2]

While details differed in the individual colonies, when resistance escalated to rebellion the results across the South were largely the same. In South Carolina whigs easily cast out the royal governor and quashed any royalist voices in the eastern Low Country. They went so far as to invade the sick chamber of a Charleston minister, forcing him to sign his loyalty to the association. They tarred and feathered other obstinate tories. In the backcountry, rebel militia made quick work of any armed tory resistance, even to the point of shamelessly breaking formal truces loyalist bands had negotiated in good faith.[3] By the end of the year, South Carolina was firmly in the grip of patriot authorities; loyalists were bullied into silence, or they fled as royal government crumbled. Some made their ways west to join with various American Indian tribes (mostly Cherokees) friendly to the Crown, or at least hostile to the rebels.[4] By early 1775 North Carolina governor Josiah Martin reported to London that royal authority in the colony was all but impotent.[5] In Georgia, aggressive patriots sent royal governor James Wright packing; and as we have seen, the fate of outspoken loyalist Thomas Brown – "Burntfoot Brown" – served as a grim warning to other Georgians who might espouse the royal cause.[6]

There was some real fighting, but it was brief. On December 9, 1775, Virginia militia needed only minutes to smash a loyalist force at Great Bridge, dashing Lord Dunmore's hopes of clinging to power. On February 27, 1776, a crushing loyalist defeat at Moore's Creek Bridge extinguished the last gasp of royal government in North Carolina.[7] The common thread in all of this was the unapologetic willingness of whigs to resort to violence – or, more precisely, to fully believable threats of violence – to secure their authority and suppress the voices of anyone with inclinations to the contrary.[8] By any other name, southern patriots, like their northern brethren, had employed terror tactics, and they had done so successfully. It is a trait of successful revolutionaries in any era.

There was a logic to the prompt whig resort to violence and tyranny – a logic rooted in several interrelated factors. The first factor was a simple matter of numbers: Southern patriots operated on the assumption that, despite all efforts to discourage loyalism, the King still enjoyed substantial popular support. In North Carolina, as late as 1776 Governor Martin was convinced the province could put up to 9,000 armed tories into the field. Governor Lord William Campbell thought South Carolina could count on another 4,000 loyalists. In Georgia, Governor Wright offered no numbers, but in June 1775 he assured London that even in the face of revolutionary intimidation there were "still many friends to government here," although British support would be necessary to rally them.[9]

But even if the claims of the royal governors involved a great deal of wishful thinking – and they did – patriots, who had no precise estimate of southern loyalist strength, feared the potential of tory ranks. It is generally the case that people react not so much to what is empirically true, but to what they believe to be true. And not unreasonably, patriots worried that given time and leadership – or British support – tories could pose a deadly threat to the Revolution. Therein lay the argument for the quick application of any and all measures to prevent tory strength, real or supposed, from coalescing into effective military or political opposition.

Then there were the slaves, and there is no question that they had a major impact on patriot calculations – and from the beginning. Fears of a black rising were visceral. There was a pervasive and longstanding dread of internal rebellion everywhere slavery existed. In November 1775, when Virginia's desperate royal governor John Murray (Lord Dunmore) famously offered to emancipate slaves willing to flee patriot masters and fight for the King, white people throughout the South reacted with consternation.[10] But patriot fears of British-inspired slave revolts predated Dunmore's proclamation. Months before the Virginia governor acted, white communities had feared royal officials were contemplating instigating a black rebellion. "We have reason to believe," warned the municipal council in Williamsburg, "that some wicked and designing persons have instilled the most diabolical notions into the minds of our slaves." Norfolk's white residents harbored the same misgivings, and in mid-1775 a young James Madison was warning friends of British designs to turn slaves against their masters.[11] Long after Dunmore's ouster, Virginians were still convinced that a British incursion into the state would result in slaves teaming with white loyalists to "be actively employed for her [Virginia's] destruction."[12] It was a terrifying prospect of race war.

White Virginians were hardly alone in their anxieties. There were similar fears in the Middle Colonies – recall the case of New Jersey – but the far larger black population of the South exacerbated tensions. Frenzied North Carolina whigs were convinced the British would turn their slaves against them, and Governor Martin gave them ample cause when he hinted he would arm the colony's slaves to defend royal authority.[13] Maryland whigs charged that Britain was waging war "with cruelty, outrageous violence, and perfidy; slaves, savages, and foreign mercenaries, have been meanly hired to rob a people of their property, liberties, and lives."[14] Archibald Bulloch informed John Adams that if the British sent as few as a thousand redcoats to Georgia, he feared that within two weeks perhaps 20,000 slaves in Georgia and South Carolina would flock to the King's standard.[15] We need to bear in mind that among white southerners concerns over slave resistance, if not actual rebellion, were a more-or-less constant fact of life.[16] But previously, such concerns had not been set in the context of what, in effect, was the real possibility of a multi-front war: The new states would have to confront not only the British and tories, but also their own slaves.

Southerners took no chances; they reacted savagely to signs of slave resistance. Slaves who rallied to Dunmore could expect the worst if recaptured. Punishments included floggings, cropped ears, and forced labor in Virginia's saltpeter works and lead mines – making munitions for those who would keep them enslaved. Some were sold to the brutal plantations of the West Indies. Those taken in arms were hanged, their heads placed on stakes at crossroads as warnings to others.[17] North Carolina patriots, every bit as alarmed as white Virginians, sent troops to aid the Old Dominion after learning of Dunmore's proclamation.[18] The guard against black insurrection never dropped. Georgians worried that "the vast number of Negroes we have, [are] perhaps of themselves sufficient to subdue us." And like South Carolina, Georgia would assign major contingents of its militia to local security; among other responsibilities, militiamen were to prevent slaves from decamping to the British and to nip any signs of rebellion in the bud. Such measures made sense to Continental major general Robert Howe of North Carolina, who thought 7,000–8,000 troops might be necessary just to keep them in check.[19]

American Indians constituted a third potential front. Frontier warfare, or the threat of warfare, was another more-or-less constant possibility in the backcountry. Southerners lived with it much as they did with the possibility of slave rebellion, and in 1775 memories of Indian conflicts were fresh. The Carolinas had fought a bitter conflict with the Cherokees in the 1760s, and Virginia had fought the Shawnees and allied tribes in Lord Dunmore's War as recently as 1774. For the tribes these were costly and embittering defeats. Even so, as historian Jim Piecuch has correctly observed, Native American military potential remained substantial. The Creeks, Cherokees, Choctaws, and Chickasaws alone could marshal on the order of 14,000 warriors[20] – a potential enhanced considerably if one considered the Shawnees and other Trans-Appalachian and Great Lakes tribes. And as the Revolution loomed, South Carolinians strongly suspected that British agents might incite the tribes against the frontiers.[21] Georgia was sure of it. Captured correspondence between British agents and the tribes seemingly confirmed the worst. "I am afraid the emissaries of Government have at last accomplished their hellish designs with the *Cherokees*," a backcountry whig informed Governor Bulloch; but he hoped that the powerful Creeks would remain friendly.[22] The southern atmosphere, to say the least, was charged with uncertainty.

The prevailing republican ideology of the day had predisposed whigs to see conspiracies, and white patriots dreaded the possibility of alliances between their various enemies. In fighting the Cherokees in 1776, South Carolina militia were appalled to find white South Carolinians dressed as Indians among their antagonists. If white renegades dressed as and fought alongside the Cherokees, patriots considered them no better than "savages" themselves – much as northerners saw Brant's Volunteers.[23] And it was seemingly evident that loyalists were conspiring with the tribes. When Cherokee attacks erupted within days of the British assault on Charleston, what were patriots supposed to think? It was easy to assume the attacks were coordinated – part of a British–Indian conspiracy. In Charleston the Reverend James Creswell pronounced it "quite evident" that the Indians were informed of the British assault on the city, "and that there was a concerted scheme between them against our country." Henry Laurens, a leading Carolina whig and future president of the Continental Congress, agreed. The Cherokees, he told his son, likely had "acted in a concerted Plan with" the British at Charleston.[24] Such were the opinions of well-informed patriots.

Across the South, rebels assumed they faced a perfect storm of threats. From southern Georgia a perplexed patriot spelled it out, adding black people to the list of antagonists: "The *Indians*, both south and northwestwardly," he warned, were "upon our backs," while nearby St. Augustine served as a rendezvous not only for British troops, but also for "our blacks and Tories." The situation had become desperate.[25] In the patriot view, their enemies had combined against them in a diabolical alliance. Fear was the order of the day, and fear is the parent of violence. In effect, over 1775 and into 1776 patriots launched preemptive strikes against all potential internal enemies, fighting when they had to. Only the most decisive measures would do. This was the context in which Governor Bulloch had proclaimed there could be no room for "moderation"[26] – a message southern patriots took fully to heart.

How well it all worked was notable. There was killing, yes, and southern patriots were unapologetic about it. However, aside from the Cherokee war, there was surprisingly little bloodshed outside of the few larger engagements (essentially those of Great Bridge in Virginia and Moore's Creek Bridge in North Carolina, followed by British failure at Charleston in June 1776).

But convincing intimidation and some vicious but targeted physical violence – terror, if you will – effectively cowed most opposition to the patriot takeover. In Charleston whig printer Peter Timothy coolly observed that the King's friends were frankly scared; he hardly knew anyone of royalist sympathies "who did not tremble."[27] And they did tremble. Looking back from the vantage of 1780, a Georgia tory recalled that "every man that was suspected of thinking" – that is, not espousing the anti-imperial line – "became a suspected person, and to think different from people that did not think at all was a crime which exposed to every species of insult, suffering, and injustice."[28] Counter-revolution never really stood a chance.

None of this is to argue that there were no southern moderates, individuals who balked at radical measures even as they espoused the patriot cause. At least initially, not all rebels were crying for blood. But the experience of one such patriot is instructive. North Carolina's William Hooper was a well-to-do attorney, legislator, and planter. An early patriot, he was a delegate to the First Continental Congress, and in April 1775 he was elected to the Second, during which he signed the Declaration. Patriot that he was, early on Hooper saw no reason to institute a reign of terror or to stifle loyalist opinion. It seemed a "Strange Infatuation," he wrote in late 1774, "that while we contend with enthusiastick [sic] ardor for liberty of the press ourselves that we should with such an intolerating spirit deny it to others." He saw no danger in the open exchange of ideas, believing the tory cause would fail in the forum of free discussion. Why worry?[29]

But Hooper's was a minority view – it appears he knew as much – and it was not destined to last. Events radically changed his outlook. A year later he was worried that patriots could expect assaults from "Indians, Negroes, Russians, Hanoverians & Hessians." By early 1776 he remained open to reconciliation with Britain, but thoroughly alarmed by tory activity in western North Carolina, he now wanted full military mobilization. Bid "adieu to plough shares & pruning hooks," he warned, "until the Sword can find its scabbard with safety & honor." The contest was now a matter of "Slavery or Liberty" – not Abigail Adams' or Patrick Henry's phrasing, but close enough.[30] Gone was toleration of tory opinions. As to Native Americans? Hooper understood there were sentiments "to extinguish the very race of them [in this case, the Cherokees]." Christian lenity, he hoped, would spare Indian women and children, "but mercy to their Warriors is cruelty to ourselves."[31] The course of the war only further hardened Hooper. Crown forces ravaged his estates near Wilmington and compelled him and his family to flee, literally hunted, to safety in the North Carolina interior. At war's end Hooper was as bitter a rebel as North Carolina produced. So much for patriot moderation.

The Patriot Unraveling

Despite patriot intimidation and violence, the tories, slaves, and Indians were still there; and they were angry. What would they do if they got the chance? There were hints, and the rebels saw them. The activity of the recovered Burntfoot Brown was a case in point. Brown initially fled to backcountry South Carolina, and when his wounds healed he recruited a sizeable loyalist band. He fully intended to take the war to regional patriots around Augusta, Georgia, in his (formerly) home territory. But before he fled the province, South Carolina royal governor Lord William Campbell warned Brown off, urging him to bide his time and to wait for the British to come back. Brown, unwilling to wait, instead made his way to East Florida where royal authorities in St. Augustine allowed him to recruit a unit of rangers and plan operations alongside Indian allies.[32] None of this was a secret, and no doubt there were patriots regretting not having killed Brown when they had the chance. They would try harder later.

To patriot dismay, the hints of trouble turned to full-blown loyalist resistance. After some three years without an effective challenge, the patriot ascendancy steadily collapsed with the return of the British. The redcoats landed unopposed near

Savannah, Georgia, in December 1778; and with British and loyalist reinforcements from Florida – including Thomas Brown's Rangers – they easily took the city in January 1779. There was some serious fighting inland. In February, Georgia and South Carolina militia cut up a large loyalist party at Kettle Creek in Georgia; but on March 3 the British returned the compliment at Briar Creek. The engagements left patriots in tenuous control of up-country Georgia, while the King's cause was strong enough in the East to restore royal government under Governor Wright.[33] A patriot siege of Savannah failed later in the year, and in 1780 they suffered a crushing defeat when the British took Charleston. Rebel efforts to retrieve the situation died with the defeat of Horatio Gates' army at the Battle of Camden in August 1780.

Loyalists rejoiced, and they hungered to settle scores. Their world had fallen apart in 1775, but with British protection they could at least restore a semblance of legitimate authority. Even better, perhaps, they could inflict a measure of retribution for several years of patriot tyranny. In Savannah, a letter to the *Royal Georgia Gazette* captured the raw loyalist emotions and their desire for a reckoning. "O!, Clintonians" – an appeal to the British commander-in-chief – "come, march far and wide ... consume with fire and every mode of destruction, houses, inclosures, and plantations, laying your hands only [that is, sparing] such things as are necessary for present subsistence! The soft reconciliatory measures are no more; violent exertions are necessary... Lenity has ever been construed [as] timidity by the American politician and his people believe him."[34] It was time for payback.

As the British and tory allies pushed up-country in Georgia and South Carolina, events seemed to bear out whig fears of a multi-threat war. The redcoat presence openly encouraged a tory revival; and from the first days of the British landing in Georgia, slaves indeed fled to British protection. The royal success also emboldened the tribes on the backcountry frontiers, who now – as in the West and on the New York frontier – saw alliances with the Crown as a means to protect their homelands from white encroachment. It was the patriot nightmare come true.

Trusting that imperial troops would protect them, thousands of tories revealed their true colors. Many took up arms. A few enlisted with the redcoats, while still others filled the ranks of British-sponsored provincial military units of various sizes. These were recruited on regular lines for long-term service, and they served under colonial as well as British officers. Beginning in 1778, North and South Carolina and Georgia each had at least one such tory organization. Some were small. The South Carolina Dragoons, for example, counted only 38 men; but the Royal North Carolina Regiment enlisted some 600, while the South Carolina Royalists had another 660. By the end of the war, over 2,100 loyalists had served in the ranks of units large and small as provincial regulars.[35] In many cases they proved excellent soldiers. But these troops were the tip of the proverbial (and very large) iceberg: Thousands more fought in loosely organized militias, as irregulars in small *ad hoc* bands, or even as individuals. We have no reliable estimates of the total number of loyalist combatants; but we can say that their military potential was considerable.

The British and allied tories, however, were never strong enough to crush rebel resistance. The South thus descended into the chaos of civil war. The violence unleashed beginning in late 1778 was on a scale the equal of anything the War for Independence would see, and it was a prime example of the consequences of political collapse. The canons of *jus in bello* envisioned war as the business of organized governments (even organized rebel governments), a context absent in much of the revolutionary South. Indeed, in the three Deep South states patriot military and political authority dissolved in whole or in part after the British returned. Over much of 1780 and 1781, there was virtually no effective rebel government in Georgia. Such as there were whig authorities, at times they sought shelter in the neighboring South Carolina backcountry.[36] And South Carolina was little safer for patriots; at one point the state government fled to North Carolina. The state was frequently without a functional legislature, and Governor John Rutledge was unable to return permanently until April 1781.[37]

The situation was little better in North Carolina. There, the death of William Hooper's moderation was part of a wider pattern. Wayne E. Lee's insightful study of violence in pre-revolutionary and revolutionary North Carolina illustrates the matter. If the initial years of the war saw virtually unrestrained violence against the Cherokees, the colony saw a relatively bloodless suppression of white individuals suspected of loyalist sympathies. Certainly there was plenty of intimidation. Militia policed and harassed those suspected of disaffection, and threats of violence – and occasional physical violence – generally kept tories fearful and in a state of political (let alone military) impotence through roughly 1779. But thereafter, pent-up loyalist frustrations boiled over with the return of the British to the Carolinas. Lee then sees a "paradigm" shift as North Carolinians came to accept brutal new realities; combat thereafter raged in a vicious "militia war" at the local level, mirroring the fighting in neighboring colonies.[38]

There were some especially grisly incidents. On February 24, 1781, near the Haw River in modern Alamance County (then Orange County), the mounted Legion of Lieutenant Colonel Henry Lee ("Light Horse Harry"), along with the militia of partisan brigadier general Andrew Pickens, surprised some 400 tories led by Dr. John Pyle. Pyle's men mistook the rebels for an expected column of Lieutenant Colonel Banastre Tarleton's British Legion – Tarleton's and Lee's uniforms were similar – and initially failed to fight back as rebel sabers and gunfire cut them down. It was a slaughter. "Pyle's Hacking Match" (or "Pyle's Massacre") resulted in 93 dead and another 250 wounded. While tory raiding would continue, Pyle's disaster spelled the virtual end to major organized loyalist activity in the state. It was a savage victory, but a battle fought fully within the bounds of *jus in bello*. There was nothing in Grotius or Vattel to discourage the use of a *ruse de guerre* or taking advantage of an enemy's mistake, no matter how gruesome the outcome.[39]

The battle's aftermath was every bit as ugly. A party of rebel-allied Catawba Indians walked the battlefield, reportedly spearing to death seven or eight of the tory wounded. Some of Lee's troops joined in the sordid affair. They slaughtered six prisoners with broadswords – retaliation, they claimed, for Tarleton's alleged excesses at the Waxhaws the previous year.[40] If Light Horse Harry was disturbed by these developments, he probably was not surprised; he already had noted that the war had become one of "extermination."[41]

Government in North Carolina was fragile as well. On September 12, 1781, loyalist colonel David Fanning captured Governor Thomas Burke, most of the legislature, and a host of ranking militia and Continental officers (among a total of some 200 prisoners) in a daring raid on the temporary capital of Hillsborough. Fanning had a reputation for daring and brutality, and his frequent raids – he fought in over 30 local engagements in 1781 alone – made him the terror of whigs in the Carolina countryside. He survived the war, but North Carolina refused to pardon him and he spent his remaining years in exile.[42] But that was in the future. In the meantime, Fanning's coup left patriot military leadership largely in local hands – and the cycles of revenge and retribution continued.

The Blame Game

Thus the ongoing struggle devolved on local forces who mostly fought local wars, and any notions of martial restraint depended largely on the whims of whigs who often saw no reason to restrain the violence born of unleashed hatreds. Historians of the revolutionary South have thoroughly documented the grisly litany of barbarity.[43] Yet they have disagreed on who was chiefly responsible for the greater part of the mayhem, with most American historians seeing the loyalists as the primary villains. The careful work of Jim Piecuch, however, has dispelled this longstanding misconception. Piecuch rightfully points out that patriots were the first to resort to violence and intimidation, and if they hoped to survive they could hardly quit when loyalists replied in kind after 1778.[44] In fact, neither side considered that it could quit without total defeat at the hands of the vengeful other – *the very definition of an existential struggle.*

One needs only to look at the career of South Carolina's Thomas Sumter ("the Gamecock") to see the patriot version of the hard-line outlook. Sumter, a planter, merchant, Indian fighter, and politico before independence, proved a magnetic recruiter and militia leader.[45] He could be utterly ruthless. Ian Saberton, a close student of the war in the South and editor of the *Cornwallis Papers*, has assessed the partisan commander in especially dark terms. Sumter, he found, "consistently displayed a marked streak of ruthlessness which did not scruple to employ measures such as cold-blooded murder on a grand scale."[46] If this was an exaggeration, it was not by much. Sumter was known to respect the rights of redcoat prisoners and (sometimes) those of captured loyalist regulars; but he allowed his men, who mostly received no official pay from barely functioning state authorities, to plunder with a free hand. He also condoned some ghastly violence. Upon capturing Orangeburg in May 1781, he did nothing to stop the cold-blooded murder of 13 captured tories; they were shot out of hand. And there is no question that he was responsible for the deaths of any number of other loyalists or suspected loyalists his partisans encountered during their various operations.[47] Of course the British responded in kind. "A few days ago," a redcoat subaltern wrote, "after Genl. Sumter had taken some wagons on the other side of the Santee [River], in South Carolina], and the escort of them had laid down their arms, a party of his horse who said they had not discharged their pieces came up, fired upon the prisoners and killed seven of them. A few days after we took six of his people. Enquire how they were treated."[48] Unsurprisingly, the murderous cycle of revenge and retribution continued.

None of this is to argue that *all* combatants gave themselves over to a war without mercy. There were those on both sides who saw such excesses as counterproductive, if not actually inhumane. Francis Marion, an especially successful and popular (with patriots) South Carolina partisan who kept the Low Country outside of Charleston in turmoil, was a prominent example. (Marion was later remembered as the famous "Swamp Fox" – much of the Low Country was wetlands – although he was not called that during the Revolution.) But there was method to Marion's humanity (not that he wasn't sincerely concerned to limit unnecessary bloodshed). He knew excessive brutality on his part could well drive Carolinians to the enemy standard. Indeed, he recognized British and loyalist cruelty as an incentive to join the patriot cause. "Had the enemy wit enough to play a generous game," he told one of his officers, "we should be ruined; but with *them* humanity is out of the question. They will treat the people with severity, rouse opposition in every quarter, and send recruits to our standard, till they accomplish their own destruction."[49]

There were others who took *jus in bello* seriously, usually, like Marion, combining a principled desire to restrain unnecessary violence and a practical hope that minimizing martial excesses might produce favorable political results. Again, however, we look to the highest reaches of command in this regard. Nathanael Greene, having come south to replace Gates in late 1780, blanched at the unrestrained violence in the South. He had no love for the tories, but he blamed both sides for the mayhem and was revolted at what he saw as murder and destruction as neighbors turned against neighbors in a cataclysm of ferocity. From South Carolina he wrote Samuel Huntington, president of the Continental Congress, that the "whole country is in danger of being laid waste by the [whigs] and [loyalists], who pursue each other with as much relentless fury as beasts of prey. People ... are frequently murdered as they ride along the road."[50] "My nature recoils at the horrid scenes which this Country affords," he wrote to his wife, Caty. "Here, turn which way you will, you hear nothing but the mournful widow, and the plaints of the fatherless Child, and behold nothing but houses desolated, and plantations laid waste. Ruin is in every form, and misery in every shape."[51] Greene fully accepted that war was brutal, even necessarily so, but his longing to moderate its excesses was equally genuine – and political. He asked the militia general Andrew Pickens to restrain the vengeful predations of whig partisan bands. "The Idea of exterminating the Tories is not less barbarous than impolitic; and if persisted in, will keep this Country in the greatest confusion and distress, The eyes of the people are much upon you, the disaffected cry of Mercy, and I hope you will exert your self to bring over Tories to our interest."[52]

Greene's chief antagonist shared many of the American commander's qualms. This, of course, was Charles, Second Earl Cornwallis, with whom Greene fenced and parried over late 1780 and into 1781. Cornwallis had every intention of observing the "rules of civilized war." Realizing the necessity of winning hearts and minds, in the Carolinas and Virginia the earl reminded his army of its duty to protect loyalist civilians and to win the populace to the royal cause.[53] And that meant a scrupulous effort to avoid plundering and all unnecessary violence. It was hardly a successful appeal. British commissary operations were stretched thin; hungry soldiers, on very short rations, foraged persistently just to feed themselves. But as Gregory Urwin has made clear, Cornwallis made a good-faith effort to limit military excesses, issuing a succession of orders to deal with illegal foraging and violence against civilians. He even called on paroled rebels "to seize, & Bring to head Quarters all stragglers from the British Army, particularly those whom they may detect in committing depredations & Robberies in the Country, that they may be punished."[54] Thus *jus in bello*, if not observed or interpreted universally, was not a dead letter among all officers.

Still, the conduct of Cornwallis, Marion, Greene, and anyone of like mind were exceptions that proved the rule. On occasion even Marion had to stop his own men from summarily executing captives.[55] And not all senior commanders were above atrocities. Operating outside of Savannah in June 1782, Anthony

Wayne winced at the brutality of whig militia, shocked at their ill-discipline, plunder, and killing of fellow Georgians.[56] But a war-weary Wayne also issued an order as grim as any coming from a vengeful partisan on either side. Late on June 24, Wayne's command had missed a large party of Creeks with a packtrain of furs trekking toward a rendezvous with a tory detachment under Burntfoot Brown. Brown was to escort them to Savannah. Wayne's first knowledge of the Creeks came only when the Indians attacked his camp just after midnight. They almost killed Wayne (they did kill his favorite horse) and inflicted a number of casualties before the general rallied a counterattack that managed to beat off the assault. In the dark Wayne thought Brown or the Savannah garrison had attacked him, and only at daylight did he find the assailants were Creeks. He was enraged, and when he found that his chief subordinate, Lieutenant Colonel Thomas Posey, had taken 30 (or 12, accounts differ) Creek prisoners, Wayne curtly demanded to know why. Posey, Henry Lee recorded, "observed that he thought it wrong to put them to death after they became prisoners." But Wayne ordered them shot.[57] It was murder by any other name.

At the local level, where partisan leaders, desperate groups, and even individuals operated beyond the control of established political authorities or senior military figures, the war proceeded with its prevalent savagery. No one, patriot or loyalist, was really safe in the interior. In North Carolina rebel militia lived in fear for the safety of their homes and families, and they especially dreaded the fates of women left defenseless in the face of marauding loyalist bands. Whether widespread belief in the "ravishment" of patriot women at tory hands was true — and we have no real numbers — the stories aroused fear and outrage. Historian Hershel Parker, based on an extensive examination of southern military pension files, found that sexual assaults against patriot women left in unguarded areas was one of the chief concerns of revolutionary soldiers serving away from home. The evidence was strong enough for Parker to conclude that at least some of the loyalist irregulars were indeed "sexual predators."[58]

In the confused milieu of the times, even supposed friends could be dangerous. George Dowell, a North Carolina Continental at home on furlough, found it impossible to travel north to rejoin Washington's army. He explained that "it is well-known" that in the sections of the country through which he would have had to pass in his way from North Carolina to Virginia, the "sleepless [ceaseless] violence of Whigs and Tories parties" made travel "extremely perilous, if not impracticable." Worse, "Whigs were fierce in that portion of the Country, and ... they were in the practice of killing those who happened to be suspected or strangers without a written pass." Dowell didn't have a pass, and in the face of threats he gave up trying to go north and enlisted with the North Carolina Continentals. "It would perhaps be proper," he later stated in his pension application, "to say he was pressed" – that is, impressed involuntarily into service.[59] In effect he was, and his experience illustrates just how conditions in localities could affect the safety and conduct of individuals as they negotiated their place in the revolutionary struggle.

Prisoners with known backgrounds of political partisanship or brutality could expect little mercy from either side. Examples were legion. Following the Battle of Kettle Creek, rebel irregulars hunted down some of the loyalist survivors and promptly hanged seven of them.[60] South Carolina governor John Rutledge insisted on making examples of those caught in arms against the Revolution, especially men accused of trying to join the British. Trials held at his behest resulted in any number of hangings, including those of slaves caught attempting to decamp to enemy lines.[61] According to a furious loyalist account, an escaped redcoat prisoner fell into the clutches of three Georgia whigs, who promptly hanged him – "audaciously declaring ... they should treat every British soldier they should meet with in the same manner."[62] The unlucky redcoat was hardly alone in Georgia; with the surrender of Augusta to patriot forces in late 1781, three loyalists quickly met the same fate.[63] And so on...

One of the most infamous cases of surrendered troops paying a stiff price for their political loyalties occurred after the Battle of Kings Mountain, South Carolina. The British commander, Major Patrick Ferguson, had led a mixed contingent of tory militia and provincial regulars (including veteran New Jersey loyalists) into western South Carolina; Ferguson's men were the left wing of Cornwallis' army. As he moved west, the major foolishly proclaimed his intention to "lay waste to their country with fire and sword" unless the rebels returned to royal allegiance.[64] Ferguson paid for his bombast. On October 7, 1780, a collection of Trans-Appalachian "Overmountain Men" – from settlements west of the Blue Ridge Mountains, the first of the Appalachian Mountains – and Carolina and Virginia militia cut him off at Kings Mountain. They killed Ferguson and 290 of his men, some as they tried to surrender, and they were in no mood to show compassion to the survivors. They court-martialed tories they considered especially obnoxious, and sentenced over 30 prisoners to death. The rebels hanged nine, some in front of their distraught families, before senior rebel officers halted the executions.[65]

The Kings Mountain executions were notorious, but they were repeated any number of times on a smaller scale. Consider the experience of Nancy Hart. Hart lived in the Broad River Valley of northern Georgia, a frontier region bitterly disputed between patriots and tories. "Aunt Nancy," as locals called her, was typical of the area's whigs; she hated Indians and tories and was a virulent proponent of all-out war. The wife of a respected militia officer, at different times she gathered intelligence for the rebels, and in 1779 she probably fought at Kettle Creek. Hart was best known, however, for an exploit in her own cabin. With her husband away on militia duty, six loyalists suddenly appeared in her yard, killed her favorite turkey, and then burst into her cabin and demanded that she cook it for them. She did, but while they ate she and one of her daughters got hold of their weapons. She killed two men outright and held the other four at gunpoint. When her husband returned (her daughter had run to summon him), he wanted to shoot the remaining four prisoners. But a furious Nancy insisted shooting was too good for them;

she wanted them hanged. A true story? Admittedly the incident has a folkloric air to it — but in 1912 an astonished railroad work crew inadvertently unearthed the six bodies.[66]

As Hart's story illustrates, irregular warfare blurred the lines between combatants and noncombatants, and violence could strike at anyone. In early 1779, patriot raiders struck at the estate of Georgia royal governor James Wright, killing the manager of the property, "first shooting him," reported the *Royal Georgia Gazette*, "and afterwards scalping him and breaking his limbs, to the disgrace of human nature." The same band then murdered and scalped a "Mrs. Hearn," killed her year-old child, and wounded her presumably loyalist husband and brother.[67] From backcountry Augusta a letter in the same issue of the *Gazette* informed readers of the malevolent conduct of patriot militia "under the celebrated horse thief, Capt. [William] Few." Few was actually a prominent whig partisan, and his men did more than steal horses. According to the enraged loyalist writer, they "left the Georgians a lasting impression of rebellious authority, by ravaging the country ... without regard for age or sex, the widow or the orphans cries. Not satisfied with rapine, they have dragged forth the peaceable inhabitants like slaves to war, and, worse than the heathen savages of the wilderness, murdered, in cool blood, a Mr. ---------, who refused to join them in their infamy." "Revenge was the word," as regional loyalists rallied to chase Few out of Georgia into South Carolina. They captured one of Few's officers, and one can only imagine his fate.[68]

Again tories vowed to repay patriot violence in kind. Just wait, they warned the three patriots who had hanged the defenseless redcoat: "What may not those barbarous Rebels expect from the just resentment of his fellow soldiers?" And that incident was only one case crying out for "just resentment." "Alas! So many Loyalists have been hanged by order of Rebel Governors, after suffering the grossest contumely," and after enduring "mock trials" before disgraceful judges. "Hanging has now become familiar to those *virtuous Sons of Liberty*" — the loyalist author certainly knew sarcasm — "and the putting to death of a Tory is highly meritorious among them, but a day of reckoning," he warned, "is hastening on." Soon "all these Murderers, and the Tar and Feathering Gentry, must answer for their crimes."[69] In early 1781 Georgia loyalists shared a British tract that fully articulated their sentiments. "Compassion" was wasted on the rebels, the indignant author fumed, as they only saw it as weakness. He wanted that "quondam President of their infernal Congress" dragged "to Tyburn" to "die the death of a traitor; hang him, draw, and quarter him." "Revenge is now become a virtue," he declared.[70]

There were plenty of loyalists long since convinced of such a course. And no one was better at revenge, or more brutal, than William – "Bloody Bill" – Cunningham. A former Continental, his motives for taking up arms for the King remain obscure; but once he committed to the imperial cause he fought with a fervor bordering on bloodlust. Operating with the approval of British authorities, Cunningham led loyalist bands in the Carolinas, where he proved a terror to patriots. He burned and killed in lightning strikes, usually hitting sparsely defended targets by surprise. His most famous (or infamous) exploit was the so-called "bloody scout" of November 1781. Cunningham led some 250 to 300 men on a raid into the South Carolina backcountry, burning out whig farms, killing any number of known rebels, and perpetrating a genuine atrocity – the Cloud's Creek or Turner House Massacre. On November 17, in modern Saluda County, his loyalists trapped some 28 or 30 militia in a private home. Hopelessly surrounded, the rebels surrendered on a promise of quarter – upon which Cunningham butchered 23 disarmed men in cold blood. There were only two survivors. Cunningham's command then rode to a local blacksmith shop, had their mounts reshod, and killed the blacksmith, his son, and a young slave before burning the smithy. If Cunningham's men gave little quarter, when captured they received just as little – some of them meeting "speedy justice ... under a stooping hickory." Cunningham himself survived the war and went into exile when the British evacuated the South.[71] He had fought without mercy, a true exemplar of existential warfare with a reputation as an ogre that survived for generations in the post-revolutionary South.

There was yet another "Bloody Bill," who earned his grim sobriquet at Gowen's Fort, South Carolina. The fort was located near the South Pacolet River northwest of modern Spartanburg, a region hotly contested by patriot and tory militias. William Bates, a former Indian trader married to a Cherokee woman, had been an active loyalist since 1776 when he had fled for protection among Dragging Canoe's Chickamauga Cherokees. On November 3, 1781, Bates attacked the small fort with a mixed force of loyalists and Indians, probably including Dragging Canoe. After a brief siege, the outnumbered patriots surrendered after Bates had promised quarter. "Bloody Bill" then ordered the slaughter of most of the captives, including women and children, while others were marched away, some to be tortured and killed later. Several escaped to spread the news of the disaster. After the war the cycle of retribution continued. Captured as "a noted horse thief" and imprisoned in Greenville – not far from the infamous site of Gowen's Fort – Bates met his end at the hands of a Gowen's Fort survivor. This was an angry young man named Motley, whose family had died in the massacre. Motley broke Bates out of the jail in broad daylight, then gunned him down in cold blood. There is little doubt Motley's act of vengeance enjoyed popular approval. He was never prosecuted.[72]

The violence associated with Hart, Cunningham, and Bates – and typical of so many others – clearly contravened the humane ideals of *jus in bello*. At least some southerners knew as much. In the summer of 1779 one tory Georgian, correctly citing Vattel, observed that "the laws of war and nations" supposedly afforded all combatants fighting under organized governments – even rebel governments if they assumed the organization and functions of independent states – the protections recognized under the conventions of *jus in bello*. But he accused whigs of having none of this and treating loyalists as traitors, murdering them "merely for their adherence to their King." Such conduct, he insisted, would recoil on the perpetrators.[73] In the fall he returned to his subject, reproving rebels for waging "an unnatural ruinous war" (that "unnatural" adjective again), and threatening dire consequences. "Those who abuse, and even hang, the loyal subjects ... merely for their allegiance, fidelity, and attachment" to their sovereign "act contrary to the practice and law of nations." And in so doing, he warned, they could not themselves justly claim protection under the canons of *jus in bello*. The writer signed himself "VATTEL."[74] Here, of course, was another example of using accusations of brutality, violations of the "laws of war," to shame an enemy and seize the high moral ground and, significantly, to justify retribution.

War Without Mercy

Finger-pointing and counter-accusations of atrocities and violations of the rules of war meant little in any empirical sense. Any provable "truth" meant virtually nothing. The significant fact was that the rival combatants, and their civilian adherents, so readily believed the worst of one another. All concerned accepted that their opponents had perpetrated deliberate atrocities, and any efforts to refute such accusations gained little or no traction in the rival camps. Enemy outrages demanded retribution in kind, and neither side saw any reason to waste any remorse on the other.

The South had descended into a relentless existential war. The whigs had started it, and once they embarked on their campaigns of intimidation, there was no going back. Given the large numbers of hostile (or at least potentially hostile) Indians, slaves, and tories, patriots instinctively understood that the odds against them were considerable in the event of a counter-revolution. Under the circumstances, violence, or credible threats of violence, seemed the only way to control the situation. And as the reader knows, with few exceptions the rebels were able to keep the lid on until the return of the British in 1778, after which all-out civil war consumed the region. With lives, families, homes, and hopes for any kind of reasonable future at stake, everyone fought to win. There seemed no alternative but defeat at the hands of a merciless enemy. Martial restraint made little sense, and the scope of the savagery knew few bounds. One had to pick a side or be seen as an enemy. Those who sought to stay neutral found their position almost impossible to maintain. Both sides mistrusted anyone not overtly with them and acted accordingly. No one knew this better than Light Horse Harry Lee. "In a civil war," he recorded in his memoirs, "no citizen should expect or desire neutrality. Whoever attempts to place himself in that condition misunderstands human nature, and becomes entangled in toils [coils] always dangerous – often fatal."[75]

The southern conflict was yet another reminder of the consequences of war slipping beyond the control of regular armies. It was also, of course, an illustration of how brutal war could be even when regulars and their senior commanders were present – even when waged within the generally recognized bounds of *jus in bello*. But the fact remains that without a Cornwallis or a Greene (or, to give the partisans their due, a Francis Marion) on the scene, the war descended to the level of barbarity that had so shocked the Enlightenment writers. They would easily have identified parallels between the horrors of the Thirty Years War and the tragedy of the American revolutionary South.

The last word goes to a distinguished South Carolinian. As a young man Alexander Garden served as a cornet – a junior dragoon officer – in Henry Lee's Legion. Garden's political loyalty came at a personal cost. He was the son of the South's most prominent naturalist, also Alexander Garden – the "gardenia" is named for him – who saw no reason to forsake the Crown. While the senior Garden took no role in the war, he did congratulate Lord Cornwallis after Camden, and his loyalist sympathies were well known. Carolina whigs finally drove him into exile (he settled in London) and confiscated his estates. He never forgave his son for joining the patriots.[76] The junior Alexander saw some tough service under Lee, and after the war he compiled two volumes of military reminiscences and anecdotes. Having seen the agony and devastation of war firsthand, and from a whig perspective, Garden unsurprisingly threw most of the blame for the South's tribulations on the loyalists. But as for the conflict as a whole? His assessment was as blunt as it was tragic: "It may truly be said to have been a war of extermination."[77] That is, it was an existential war – and so often utterly without mercy.

Epilogue: A Word from Thucydides

The War for Independence represented a violent era. Any notion that the American Revolution was somehow less tragic and costly in human suffering than other Western revolutions is simply wrong; the evidence points conclusively in the opposite direction. Americans are only now coming to grips with the violent realities of the War for Independence; and while we are better informed as to *what* happened, *why* it happened has been the focus of this book. And why was the war so violent? Here we return to the original definition of "existential warfare" – war in which combatants (or at least most of them) believed they had no choice but to fight without restraint or mercy – and the choices of "Liberty or Death." The alternative was defeat, with consequences too terrible to contemplate.

In explaining all of this we have emphasized the local nature of the War for Independence: As we have seen in Peckham, Munn, and Parker, most of the fighting occurred at the local or regional levels. The farther incidents occurred from the main armies, the more likely were local forces to wage war on their own terms – and they were terms under which the ideals encompassed in *jus in bello* crumbled in the face of existential realities. All of our chapters have emphasized the various motives for taking up arms and how they coalesced to produce a war of tragic savagery. In 1775 probably only the most bloodthirsty of individuals could have anticipated the course of events, and by 1783 an affair on the scale of the Boston Massacre would have rated notice only as an insignificant skirmish.

Consider the motives for unrestrained violence: ideology, racism, imperial rivalries, naked fear, threats to traditional homelands and ways of life, cycles of revenge and retribution, land hunger, and in some instances even religious schism. All of these elements were present – not necessarily all at once and not everywhere. But the toxic mix was prevalent enough to assure that the war would develop on an existential basis. There was little mercy.

Certainly over the eight long years of war there were instances of compassion and restraint among all combatants. Recall that Washington and Howe exchanged letters over what was or wasn't fair play in combat. Then there were the musings of Henry Knox on waging an honorable war and the very real efforts of Lord Cornwallis to maintain discipline and restraint among British ranks during his southern campaigns. There were times when Joseph Brant withheld the tomahawk; and for all of his venomous hatred of tories, William Livingston preferred to pursue his enemies under the cover of law. And there were, as the reader knows from these pages, other examples in this regard. But such instances could not obviate the brutal realities of what became an existential struggle for victory, and they were generally exceptions that stood out from the brutal norms. Once again we can stress that the farther the war got from centers of effective political and military authorities, the worse the violence became.

Moreover, even the regular armies and senior leadership on both sides could wink at much of the carnage, especially as the war dragged on. Early on, Washington had frowned on the brutality of "Devil David" Forman; but later in the conflict, knowing full well that Forman was the driving force behind the Monmouth County Retaliators, the commanding general was happy enough with Forman's intelligence operations. Governor William Livingston similarly disapproved of Forman's extra-legal proceedings, but his objections were practical, fearful of Forman driving Jerseymen into the loyalist fold. Yet recall that the governor's own anti-tory rhetoric was absolutely ferocious, and he was more than willing to use all legal means to stamp out loyalism, including the ultimate "Extinction of Life."[1]

And not all patriots were as concerned with legalities. Rebel leadership never took to task George Rogers Clark or Anthony Wayne for the summary and cold-blooded murder of Indian prisoners, acts clearly beyond the bounds of *jus in bello*. Benedict Arnold's New London raid, however, demonstrated just how flexible those bounds could be. The sacking of the town, including civilian property, and the bloody action at Fort Griswold all fell within the limits of the rules of "civilized" warfare. The horrors on the northern, southern, and Trans-Appalachian frontiers rivaled the worst excesses of the Thirty Years War. The hangings after Kings Mountain, the ghastly slaughter of innocent Lenapes at Gnadenhütten, Sullivan's despoiling of Iroquoia, the subsequent Anglo-Indian "Burning of the Valleys," and the heinous massacre of surrendered settlers at Gowen's Fort at the hands of "Bloody Bill" Bates, all indicated a war in which desperation and hatreds overwhelmed any ideals of restraint.

What was the final toll in lives lost and maimed? In homes and livelihoods shattered and blighted? In futures blasted? We can answer only in very general terms. No one really knows how many combatants and noncombatants died fighting, fell victims to terror and murder, succumbed to disease, or simply went missing. Howard Peckham's tally of some 25,324 rebel military deaths is certainly conservative.[2] But what of civilians of all political persuasions and ethnicities and of combatant Indians and loyalists? We don't know; all we can really say is that the numbers were not small. Aside from some of the larger engagements, there are no reliable casualty counts from the hundreds of small-scale clashes in the southern backcountries and on the northern and western frontiers. But the aggregate toll easily must have doubled or tripled Peckham's estimate. And no matter what the total may have been, there is no question of its having derived from a context of bitter and often merciless struggle.

For thousands, the war's legacy was one of dispossession and despair. Among the various British-allied Indian tribes, the

American victory was a catastrophe. The Iroquois Confederacy, torn by its own civil war, never recovered its internal unity or political or military influence. Neither state nor national authorities felt any compunction about prizing lands from the defeated tribes. Those Iroquois who stayed in the new republic progressively lost most of their homelands and found themselves confined to reservations composed of lands least desirable to white settlers. Many followed Brant and other tribal leaders to Canada. Theirs was a lost cause. Warfare continued in the Trans-Appalachian West, and the toll of death, destruction, and dispossession continued unabated. The western tribes would lose out as well – but their death would be drawn out through the 1790s – and even later in the old Southwest. During these years they would inflict considerable pain on the post-revolutionary westward tide of white settlers and the military forces of the fledgling republic. In an existential war, one did not give up short of total defeat or complete victory.

Is it possible to fix some overall blame for all of this? After all, we have seen that combatants on all sides contributed to the mayhem. Still, we need to look hard at the whigs. Certain facts stand out. In deciding on rebellion, and then on revolution, patriots took the initiative and quickly resorted to tactics of intimidation – which then morphed into violence. They truly felt they had little choice. Like revolutionaries in all ages, they could hardly afford to allow counter-revolutionaries to regain their balance and mount an effective opposition. And once going down that road, how could the rebels go back? To have done anything other than keeping the pressure on their antagonists – be they white tories, Indian, black, or anyone else – would have invited retribution from those they had persecuted and driven to frenzied calls for revenge. It was revenge, of course, loyalists inflicted whenever they could.

It was equally noteworthy that in many respects patriot tactics were, by any other name, terrorism. How else can we define the tarring and feathering of a customs official in Boston or a tory in New Jersey? Or the dragging of an elderly parson from his desk and tossing him in a South Carolina river? Or the savage torture of Thomas Brown in Georgia? These were acts to discourage anyone from opposing the rebellion or espousing loyalty to the empire – that is, terror to further political ends. If much of this activity was not officially state-sponsored (and some of it clearly was), it was at least state-condoned. The actions of patriot authorities certainly fit the bill. Forced exiles, property confiscations, the suppression of civil liberties, and prosecutions – and executions – for treason all were part of the context. So were summary executions that were no more than murder. One thinks here of South Carolina's killing of black people taken in arms – acts specifically ordered by patriot authorities – or the murder of Indian prisoners on the orders of Anthony Wayne and George Rogers Clark. And if Governor William Livingston officially deplored the activities of "Devil David" Forman and his Retaliators, he never actually stopped them. Brutal as all of this was, it was part and parcel of the consolidation of patriot authority and efforts to establish effective new governments.

Moreover, as rebel authorities sponsored or condoned terrorist tactics, in many cases they were, in effect, playing catch-up. As we have found, in virtually all theaters of the war efforts to intimidate and suppress the enemies of the Revolution began at the local level. That is, as often as not, local actors launched the rebellion, which in large measure explains the early success against loyalism. Local patriots knew whom to target, assuring that tories would be thrown immediately on the defensive, often with potential tory leadership neutralized. Senior patriot leaders, in condoning and building on such local initiatives, saw no reason to change tactics later.

Faced with such early and then unrelenting brutality, loyalists, when they could, fought back with bitterness and desperation. But they lost, and at a terrible cost. Maya Jasanoff, a meticulous historian, has calculated that some 75,000 surviving loyalists (including 15,000 former slaves) chose to abandon America after Independence, wanting nothing to do with an America governed by victorious rebels. This 75,000 was no small migration; it was "about one in forty members of the American population," and proportionately it represented five times the number of French driven into exile during the French Revolution.[3] Some exiles were voluntary, but it is difficult to imagine so significant an exodus taking place in an atmosphere of restraint among the victors. Most loyalists, having endured as much as they did during the war, were justifiably not convinced they faced a secure or peaceable future in the new republic. Their memories were of violence, terror, disillusion, and death – they knew what and why they were fleeing.

The War for Independence bred such existential fears as to override the moderation and restraint characterizing the ideals of *jus in bello*. Indeed, any notions of *jus in bello* had only marginal influence during the Revolution. Except among certain members of contemporary elites, the ideals of Grotius, Vattel, and other Enlightenment writers meant little in theory and just as little in reality. Indeed, our review of the fighting across the colonies suggests the Revolution represented exactly the "contagion of violence" Enlightenment theorists had hoped to discourage. *Jus in bello* was in part a reaction to a previous age of ideological war, the unrestrained mayhem of Catholic versus Protestant convulsions that had devastated much of Europe during the Thirty Years War. To a significant extent, the War for Independence was a revival of ideological war, with self-perpetuating cycles of revenge and reprisal. Some Americans and British, as well as a number of Indian combatants, certainly did embrace moderation during the conflict. Yet their restraint had limits. It could not contain the brutality born of frontier warfare, the predisposition to violence inherent in patriot republicanism, and loyalist rage at an "unnatural rebellion."[4]

In this respect, we need to see the revolutionary struggle in the context of other wars – wars that have prompted some incisive and troubling observations on how violence can take on a blistering momentum. Abraham Lincoln knew as much as he remarked on the Civil War in Missouri. "Actual war coming, blood grows hot, and blood is spilled. Thought is forced from old channels into confusion. Deception breeds and thrives," he lamented. "Confidence dies, and universal suspicion reigns. Each man feels an impulse to kill his neighbor, lest he be first killed by him. Revenge and retaliation follow... Murders for old grudges, and murders for pelf, proceed under any cloak that will best cover for the occasion."[5] Little more than a decade later, Helmuth von Moltke (Moltke the Elder), Chief of the Great (German) General Staff, reacted similarly to the popular French uprising during the Franco-Prussian War of 1870–71. War was supposed to be the business of regular armies, he noted, and that was grim enough. But once the general populace took up arms, it was horrid: "It is all wrong to lead whole peoples against each other. That is not progress, but a return to barbarism."[6] Yes it was, and James Lovell (remember him?) would have perfectly understood Lincoln and Moltke.

In the 5th century BC Thucydides wrote of the civil conflict in Corcyra during the Peloponnesian War; and his understanding of that bitter struggle, in which mercy gave way to carnage, was every bit as applicable to what happened in America during the War for Independence: "In their struggle for ascendancy nothing was barred; terrible indeed were the actions to which they committed themselves, and in taking revenge they went further still. Here they were deterred neither by claims of justice nor by the interests of the state."[7] As with the ancient Greeks, patriots, loyalists, Americans Indians, and many British combatants saw little middle ground in their war, and they fought accordingly. Thus we end where we began – with Liberty or Death – and the desperate and inhumane consequences of an existential struggle for victory.

Notes

PROLOGUE

1 A number of useful studies have told the Massacre story. Representative are Hilller B. Zobel, *The Boston Massacre* (New York: W. W. Norton, 1970); Eric Hinderaker, *Boston's Massacre* (Cambridge, MA: Harvard University Press, 2017); and Serena Zabin, *The Boston Massacre: A Family History* (Boston: Houghton, Mifflin, Harcourt, 2020).

2 https://www.dictionary.com/browse/massacre. An 18th-century British dictionary defined a massacre as "a Butchery and Slaughter made on People, not in a Condition to defend themselves"; as a verb, it was "to butcher after a barbarous Manner." N. Bailey, *An Universal Etymological English Dictionary* (London: Printed for R. Ware et al., 1775), n.p., under "MASSACRE."

3 *The Bloody Massacre perpetrated in King-Street BOSTON on March 5th 1770 by a party of the 29th REGT … Engrav'd & printed by Paul Revere* (Boston, 1770), Metropolitan Museum of Art, https://en.wikipedia.org/wiki/Boston_Massacre#/media/File:The_Boston_Massacre_MET_DT2086.jpg.

4 James Lovell, *An Oration Delivered April 2d, 1771 at the Request of the Inhabitants of the Town of Boston to Commemorate the Bloody Tragedy of the Fifth of March, 1770* (Boston: Printed by Edes and Gill, 1771), 11, 12, 15–16, 17–18.

5 Abigail Adams to Catharine Sawbridge Macaulay [Oct, 1774], *Adams Family Correspondence*, ed. by L. H. Butterfield et al., 10 vols. (Cambridge, MA: Harvard University Press, 1963–), 1:177.

6 "Speech of His Excellency Archibald Bulloch … to the [Georgia] Provincial Congress … June 5, 1776," in Peter Force, ed., *American Archives*, Ser. 4 (Washington, DC: M. St. Clair and Peter Force, 1846), VI:718.

7 John Adams to Abigail Adams, 17 Feb. 1777. *The Adams Papers: Adams Family Correspondence*, ed. by L. H. Butterfield (Cambridge, MA: Harvard University Press, 1963), 2:162.

INTRODUCTION: TOWARD WAR WITHOUT MERCY

1 E.g., Carlo Botta, *History of the War of the Independence of the United States of America*, trans. by George Alexander Otis, 2 vols., 9th ed. (Cooperstown, NY: H. & E. Phinney, 1847 [orig. in Italian, 1809]), 2:26–28, 460–63; Mercy [Otis] Warren, *History of the Rise, Progress and Termination of the American Revolution. Interspersed with Biographical, Political and Moral Observations*, 3 vols. (Boston: Manning and Loring, 1805), 3:428–31; David Ramsay, *The History of the American Revolution* (Philadelphia: Printed by R. Aitken & Son, 1789).
2 John Ellis, *Armies in Revolution* (New York: Oxford University Press, 1974), 59–63, 71–72. See also Crane Brinton, *The Anatomy of Revolution* (New York: Vintage, 1938), 22, 24; Brinton saw the American Revolution as an effort "to set the English North American colonies up as an independent nation-state" rather than to uproot established socio-economic relationships. In this limited goal it was a distinctly less violent event than other revolutions. Seymour Martin Lipset's *The First New Nation: The United States in Historical and Comparative Perspective* (New York: Basic Books, 1963), 90–98, sees the Revolution and the quick emergence of a relatively stable republic in its aftermath as a product of popularly shared democratic values (albeit with an assist from a charismatic and unifying George Washington). In works such as Brinton's and Lipset's, the war itself is almost incidental to the political, social, cultural, intellectual, and economic aspects of the Revolution. The darker side of the War for Independence has escaped significant emphasis in many very fine general histories of the Revolution: Typical are Walter Millis, *Arms and Men* (New York: New American Library, 1956); Christopher Ward, *The War of the Revolution*, 2 vols. (New York: Macmillan, 1952); Willard Wallace, *Appeal To Arms: A Military History of the American Revolution* (New York: Harper & Brothers, 1951); and John Richard Alden, *A History of the American Revolution* (New York: Da Capo Press, 1989).
3 See, for example, the important study by John Pancake, *This Destructive War: The British Campaign in the Carolinas* (Tuscaloosa, AL: University of Alabama Press, 1985). More recently, see Holger Hoock, *The Scars of*

Independence: America's Violent Birth (New York: Crown Publishers, 2017); W. H. Brands, *Our First Civil War: Patriots and Loyalists in the American Revolution* (New York: Doubleday, 2021); and Allan Paul Crawford, *This Fierce People: The Untold Story of America's Revolutionary War in the South* (New York: Knopf, 2024). Overall, these three descriptive studies do not tackle questions of why there was so much violence.

4 See the findings, for example, of Wayne E. Lee, *Crowds and Soldiers in Revolutionary North Carolina: The Culture of Violence in Riot and War* (Gainesville, FL: University Press of Florida, 2001); Jim Piecuch, *Three Peoples, One King: Loyalists, Indians, and Slaves in the Revolutionary South, 1775–1782* (Columbia, SC: University of South Carolina Press, 2008); and John R. Maass, *"A Complicated Scene of Difficulties": North Carolina and the Revolutionary Settlement, 1776–1789* (Ph.D. Diss., Ohio State University, 2007).

5 The more recent literature on the brutal realities of the War for Independence is actually quite extensive, although much of it has escaped popular notice. For good examples, see: Mark Edward Lender, "The Western Theater: The Theater of Fear," in James Kirby Martin and David L. Preston, eds., *Theaters of the American Revolution: Northern, Middle, Southern, Western, Naval* (Yardley, PA: Westholme, 2017), 139–78; John Buchanan, *The Road to Charleston: Nathanael Greene and the American Revolution* (Charlottesville, VA: University of Virginia Press, 2019); James Kirby Martin, "A Contagion of Violence: The Ideal of *Jus in Bello* Versus the Reality of Fighting on the New York Frontier during the Revolutionary War," *Journal of Military Ethics*, 14 (April 2015), 57–73; James Piecuch, "The Southern Theater: Britain's Last Chance for Victory," in Martin and Preston, eds., *Theaters of the American Revolution*, 89–138; Hoock, *The Scars of Independence*; Mark Edward Lender and James Kirby Martin, "Liberty or Death! *Jus in Bello* and Existential Warfare in the American Revolution," in Glen A. Moots and Philip Hamilton, eds., *Justifying Revolution: Law, Virtue, and Violence in the American War of Independence* (Norman, OK: University of Oklahoma Press, 2018), 147–67.

6 E.g., Michael S. Adelberg, *The American Revolution in Monmouth County: The Theater of Spoil and Destruction* (Charleston, SC: History Press, 2010); Adrian Coulter Leiby, *The Revolutionary War in the Hackensack Valley: The Jersey Dutch and the Neutral Ground, 1775–1783* (New Brunswick, NJ: Rutgers University Press, 1962); Lyman

Copeland Draper, *King's Mountain and Its Heroes: History of the Battle of King's Mountain, October 7th, 1780, and the Events Which Led to It* (Cincinnati, OH: P. G. Thomson, 1881); Edward G. Lengel, *The Battles of Connecticut Farms and Springfield, 1780* (Yardley, PA: Westholme, 2020).

7 Lovell, *An Oration*, 11, 12, 15–16, 17–18.

8 Timothy Campeau, *Dishonored Americans: The Political Death of Loyalists in Revolutionary America* (Charlottesville, VA: University of Virginia Press, 2023), "Introduction: Political Death," and "Chapter 1: Dishonor."

9 Mary Beth Norton, *1774: The Long Year of Revolution* (New York: Vintage Books, 2020), 47, 49, 105–107, 133, 141, 146, 167.

10 T. H. Breen, *American Insurgents, American Patriots: The Revolution of the People* (New York: Hill and Wang, 2010); this is the theme of Breen's entire book, but see esp. pp. 10–19.

11 John Buchanan, *The Road to Guilford Courthouse: The American Revolution in the Carolinas* (New York: John Wiley & Sons, 1997), 95–96; Georgia Council of Safety quoted in ibid., 96; Edward J. Cashin, *The King's Ranger: Thomas Brown and the American Revolution on the Southern Frontier* (New York: Fordham University Press, 1999).

12 Andrew M. Sherman, *Historic Morristown, New Jersey: The Story of Its First Century* (Morristown, NJ: Howard Publishing Co., 1905), 248–49. For the court records, see New Jersey vs. James Hiss to New Jersey vs. John Parks, Morris County Court of Oyer and Terminer, Minutes [1777], Boxed MSS, New Jersey State Library, Trenton; Military Record of Captain Moses Estey (copy of original), New Jersey Department of Defense MSS, 10304B, ibid.

13 "The Reverend Nicholas Collin on the Ravages of War," in Larry R. Gerlach, ed., *New Jersey in the American Revolution, 1763–1783: A Documentary History* (Trenton, NJ: New Jersey Historical Commission, 1975), 303.

14 The term has had scant application to the American Revolution, but see Lender and Martin, "Liberty or Death! *Jus in Bello* and Existential Warfare in the American Revolution," in Moots and Hamilton, eds., *Justifying Revolution*, 147–67.

15 The Mackenzie Institute, "Existential War," 21 Apr. 2008, https://mackenzieinstitute.com/2008/04/existential-war/, accessed 12 Dec. 2019. In our "Liberty or Death!," 148, we used a slightly different definition of our own devising: "warfare in which combatants

believed their very existence is in question, leading to an acceptance of violence against persons and property as preferable to defeat, which is equated with political, cultural, and even physical extinction. This meant war with few restrictions and an expectation of ferocity and brutality, anything to avoid defeat." The import is the same as Mackenzie's.

16 Kaufmann quoted in ibid., and cited from Walter Kaufmann, *Existentialism from Dostoevsky to Sartre*, e-book (Auckland, NZ: Pickle Partners Publishing, 2016 [orig. 1956]), 9–10.

17 For an overview of existentialism, see Steven Crowell, "Existentialism," *Standford Encyclopedia of Philosophy*, https://plato.stanford.edu/entries/existentialism/, accessed 21 June 2021.

18 Mackenzie Institute, "Existential War," https://mackenzieinstitute.com/2008/04/existential-war/, accessed 21 July 2021.

19 Strobe Driver, "A New Age of Violence: Terrorism as an Asymmetrical and 'Existential Threat,'" *E-International Relations*, 27 Sept. 2017, https://www.e-ir.info/2017/09/27/terrorism-as-an-asymmetrical-and-existential-threat/#google_vignette, accessed 27 Jan. 2024.

20 Howard H. Peckham, ed., *The Toll of Independence: Engagements and Battle Casualties of the American Revolution* (Chicago: University of Chicago Press, 1974), viii–x.

21 Peckham, *The Toll of Independence*, 133; David C. Munn, ed., *Battles and Skirmishes of the American Revolution in New Jersey* (Trenton, NJ: Bureau of Geography and Topography, Department of Environmental Protection, 1976), 125–41.

22 Peckham, *The Toll of Independence*, 130, *passim*; Munn, ed., *Battles and Skirmishes*, *passim*.

23 Peckham, *The Toll of Independence*, 133. John W. Gordon, *South Carolina and the American Revolution: A Battlefield History* (Columbia: University of South Carolina Press, 2003), 1–2, claims that South Carolina saw the most fighting, with perhaps a third of all documented engagements (but without citing specific numbers). Whoever the "winner" in this grim contest may have been, the point remains the same: most of the fighting was by local forces.

24 Peckham, *The Toll of Independence*, 23.

25 John C. Parker, *Parker's Guide to the Revolutionary War in South Carolina* (West Conshohocken, PA: Infinity Publishing, 2013). See also Patrick O'Kelley, *Nothing but Blood and Slaughter: Military Operations and Order of Battle of the Revolutionary War in the Carolinas*, 4 vols. (Trenton, GA: Booklocker.com, 2004–2005).

26 As major engagements of the main armies, I have included Long Island, Fort Washington, Kips Bay, Harlem Heights, White Plains, the investment of Fort Ticonderoga, Hubbardston, Fort Stanwix, Oriskany (largely a militia versus Indian action, but a major engagement), Bennington (actually fought just inside New York State), Freeman's Farm, Bemis Heights, Stony Point, Minisink, Newtown, Brodhead's Expedition, Morrisania, Four Corners, New Rochelle, Fort George, Middle Fort (Middleburg), and perhaps (generously) a few others – for a total of about 26.
27 John Grenier, *The First Way of War: American War Making on the Frontier, 1607–1814* (New York: Cambridge University Press, 2005).
28 Patrick Griffin, *American Leviathan: Empire, Nation, and Revolutionary Frontier* (New York: Hill and Wang, 2007), 46–48.
29 Marjoleine Kars, *Breaking Loose Together: The Regulator Rebellion in Pre-revolutionary North Carolina* (Chapel Hill: University of North Carolina Press, 2002); Richard Maxwell Brown, *The South Carolina Regulators* (Cambridge, MA: Belknap Press of Harvard University Press, 1963).
30 E.g., see Richard Maxwell Brown, *Strain of Violence: Historical Studies of American Violence and Vigilantism* (New York: Oxford University Press, 1975).
31 John Adams to John Winthrop, 23 June 1776, *LDC*, 4:299.
32 Elbridge Gerry to Horatio Gates, 25 June 1776, ibid., 4:313. On the same day Gerry wrote similarly to Massachusetts politico James Warren; ibid., 4:317. Caesar Rodney to Thomas Rodney, 10 July 1776, ibid., 4:433.
33 Samuel Peters, *General History of Connecticut: From Its First Settlement under George Fenwick to Its Latest Period of Amity with Great Britain Prior to the Revolution* (New York: D. Appleton and Company, 1877 [orig. 1781]), 274.
34 For an influential discussion of republicanism, see Robert E. Shalhope, "Toward a Republican Synthesis: The Emergence of an Understanding of Republicanism in American Historiography," *William and Mary Quarterly* 29 (1972):49–80. See also Bernard Bailyn, *The Ideological Origins of the American Revolution* (Cambridge, MA: Belknap Press of Harvard University Press, 2017 [orig. 1967]).
35 John A. Lynn II, *Another Kind of War: The Nature and History of Terrorism* (New Haven: Yale University Press, 2019), 4–30.
36 Ruma Chopra, *Unnatural Rebellion: Loyalists in New York City during the Revolution* (Charlottesville, VA: University of Virginia Press, 2011), 4.

CHAPTER 1: "FIGHTING JUSTLY"? *JUS IN BELLO*
AND ITS PROBLEMS

1 John Adams to Samuel Chase, 1 July 1776, *LDC*, 4:347.
2 On the origins and evolution of *jus in bello* particularly and just war ideas generally, see James Turner Johnson, *Ideology, Reason, and the Limitation of War: Religious and Secular Concepts, 1200–1740* (Princeton, NJ: Princeton University Press, 1975); and Andreas Harald Aure, "Just War Theory in the Image of Emer de Vattel," in Moots and Hamilton, eds., *Justifying Revolution*, 21–22.
3 Frederick H. Russell, *The Just War in the Middle Ages* (New York: Cambridge University Press, 1975), 2. For a concise overview of just war theories and their connections to political culture, see Russell's introductory chapter, pp. 1–15.
4 Hugo Grotius, *De Jure Belli ac Pacis Libri Tres* [*On the Law of War and Peace*], trans. and ed. by A. C. Campbell (Kitchener, Ontario: Batoche Books, 2001 [orig. 1625]), http://socserv2.socsci.mcmaster. ca/econ/ugcm/3ll3/grotius/Law2.pdf.
5 Aure, "Just War Theory," 22–23.
6 "What Are Jus ad Bellum and Jus in Bello?" 22 Jan. 2015, International Committee of the Red Cross, https://www.icrc.org/en/document/what-are-jus-ad-bellum-and-jus-bello-0, accessed 8 Jan. 2020.
7 Unless noted otherwise, we have relied on the following for our account of the origins and progress of the war: see "Thirty Years War," *Encyclopedia Britannica*, https://www.britannica.com/event/Thirty-Years-War, accessed 17 Dec. 2019; Geoffrey Parker, *The Thirty Years War* (Boston: Routledge, 1984); Peter H. Wilson, *Europe's Tragedy: A New History of the Thirty Years War* (London: Penguin, 2010).
8 Wilson, *Europe's Tragedy*, 787; Michael Clodfelter, *Warfare and Armed Conflicts: A Statistical Encyclopedia of Casualty and Other Figures, 1492–2015* (Jefferson, NC: McFarland, 2017), 40; Matthew White, "Statistics of Wars, Oppressions and Atrocities of the Nineteenth Century (the 1800s)," http://necrometrics.com/wars19c.htm#Napoleonic, accessed 9 Jan. 2020.
9 Emer de Vattel, *The Law of Nations, Or, Principles of the Law of Nature, Applied to the Conduct and Affairs of Nations and Sovereigns, with Three Early Essays on the Origin and Nature of Natural Law and on Luxury*, ed. by Béla Kapossy and Richard Whatmore (Indianapolis: Liberty Fund, 2008 [orig. 1758]). This biographical sketch of Vattel is drawn from Peter Haggenmacher, "Emer de Vattel," *Dictionnaire Historique de la*

Suisse (7 Feb. 2013), https://hls-dhs-dss.ch/fr/articles/015917/2013-07-02/, accessed 11 Jan. 2020.

10. Vattel, *The Law of Nations*, Book III, Chap. I, Sec. 3:470; http://oll.libertyfund.org/titles/ 2246/212414, accessed 14 Apr. 2017. Unless noted otherwise, subsequent citations to Vattel are to the Kapossy and Whatmore edition. The first English translation of Vattel appeared as *The Law of Nations; Or, Principles of the Law of Nature: Applied to the Conduct and Affairs of Nations and Sovereigns*, 2 vols. (London, 1759–60).

11. For an excellent summary of just war theory, including *jus in bello*, see Alexander Moseley, "Just War Theory," *Internet Encyclopedia of Philosophy*," http://www.iep.utm.edu/justwar/, accessed 12 Aug. 2016. On the history of just war theory and its applications over time, see Michael Walzer, *Just and Unjust Wars: A Moral Argument with Historical Illustrations*, 4th ed. (New York: Basic Books, 1977); and Paul Ramsey, *The Just War* (New York: Charles Scribner's Sons, 1969).

12. Vattel, *The Law of Nations*, xxi.

13. Wayne E. Lee, *Barbarians and Brothers: Anglo-American Warfare, 1500–1865* (New York: Oxford University Press, 2011), 189–90; GW to Robert Cary & Co., 6 Oct. 1773, *The Papers of George Washington Digital Edition* [hereafter *PGWde*], ed. by Theodore J. Crackel, Colonial Ser., 9:344; Reuters, "George Washington's Library Book Returned 221 Years Late," 20 May 2010, http://www.reuters.com/article/2010/05/20/us-library-washington-idUSTRE64J4EG20100520, accessed 14 July 2015.

14. E.g., "Reply of the House to Hutchinson's First Message," 26 Jan. 1773, *The Adams Papers*, ed. by Robert J. Taylor (Cambridge, MA: Harvard University Press, 1977), 1:315–31; "Reply of the House to Hutchinson's Second Message," 2 Mar. 1773, ibid., 1:331–46; James Lovell to John Adams, 1 Jan. 1778, ibid., 13:379–81; "To John Adams from Jean Henri David Uhl, 1 July 1782," *Founders Online*, National Archives, http://founders.archives.gov/documents/Adams/06-13-02-0087-0001; Edmund Randolph to Thomas Jefferson, with a memorandum by Jefferson, 9 Feb. 1781, *PTJ*, 4:571–72. On Franklin, see the "Introduction" by Albert de Lapradelle in Emer [Emmerich] de Vattel, *Le Droit des Gens [The Law of Nations]*, trans. by Charles G. Fenwick (Washington, DC: Carnegie Institution of Washington, 1916 [orig. 1758]), 3. Subsequent citations to Vattel are to this edition.

15. Geoffrey Best, *Humanity in Warfare: The Modern History of the International Law of Armed Conflict* (London: Methuen 1983), 36; Eliga H. Gould, "Zones of Law, Zones of Violence: The Legal Geography of

the British Atlantic, circa 1772," *William and Mary Quarterly*, 3rd Ser., LX, No. 3 (2003):477.
16 John Fabian Witt, *Lincoln's Code: The Laws of War in American History* (New York: Free Press, 2013), Chap. 1.
17 Ibid., 13–20.
18 Stephen Brumwell, *George Washington: Gentleman Warrior* (London: Quercus, 2013), esp. Chapters 6–8; Witt, *Lincoln's Code*, 13–48.
19 Mark Edward Lender and Garry Wheeler Stone, *Fatal Sunday: George Washington, the Monmouth Campaign, and the Politics of Battle* (Norman, OK: University of Oklahoma Press, 2016), 276; Daniel M. Sivilich, *Musket Ball and Small Shot Identification: A Guide* (Norman, OK: University of Oklahoma Press, 2016), 73–89 is Chapter 5: "Musket Balls Altered to Improve Lethality."
20 Phillip Hamilton, "'A Contest of Virtue with vice': Henry Knox's Just and Honorable War for Independence," in *Justifying Revolution*, 127–46.
21 [John Graves] Simcoe, *A Journal of the Operations of the Queen's Rangers: From the End of the Year 1777, to the Conclusion of the Late American War* (Exeter, UK: Printed for the author, 1787), 119; Dansey's letter of 6 July 1776 is quoted in Stephen Conway, "British Army and the War of Independence," 95.
22 "Reminiscences of Read," in R. W. Gibbes, ed., *Documentary History of the American Revolution: Consisting of Letters and Papers Relating to the Contest for Liberty, Chiefly in South Carolina, from the Originals in the Possession of the Editor, and Other Sources*, 3 vols. (New York: D. Appleton, 1853–57), 3:256–57; Michael M. Greenburg, *The Court-Martial of Paul Revere: A Son of Liberty & America's Forgotten Military Disaster* (Lebanon, NH: University Press of New England, 2014), 145–47.
23 Lee, *Barbarians and Brothers*, 169–208.
24 Gregory J. W. Urwin, "'To bring the American Army under strict Discipline': British Army Foraging Policy in the South, 1780–81," *War in History* 26, No. 1 (2019):15; Cornwallis' proclamation of 17 June 1781 quoted in ibid., 19.
25 On the 18th-century aristocratic honor code within the British officer corps, and officers as "gentlemen," see Arthur N. Gilbert, "Law and Honour among Eighteenth-Century British Army Officers," *The Historical Journal* 19, No. 1 (1976):75–87; Armstrong Starkey, "War and Culture, A Case Study: The Enlightenment and the Conduct of the British Army in America, 1755–1781," *War and Society* 8 (1990):1–28; Stephen Conway, "To Subdue America: British Army Officers and

the Conduct of Revolutionary War," *William and Mary Quarterly*, 3rd Ser., 43 (1986):381–407.
26 Vattel, *The Law of Nations*, Book III, Sec. 143:548.
27 Mark Edward Lender, *Cabal! The Plot Against General Washington* (Yardley, PA: Westholme Publishing, 2019), 42.
28 Clinton quoted in Andrew Jackson O'Shaughnessy, *The Men Who Lost America: British Leadership, the American Revolution, and the Fate of the Empire* (New Haven: Yale University Press, 2013), 220.
29 Mark Edward Lender and James Kirby Martin, "A Traitor's Epiphany: Benedict Arnold in Virginia and the Quest for Reconciliation," *Virginia Magazine of History and Biography*, 125 (2017):314–57.
30 James Lovell to John Adams, 1 Jan. 1778, *Adams Papers*, 13:379–81; Edmund Randolph to Thomas Jefferson, with a memorandum by Jefferson, 9 Feb. 1781, *PTJ*, 4:571–72.
31 Vattel appreciated the fact that privateers put their personal resources at risk on behalf of a cause. He saw nothing questionable in the profit motive at work in privateers as long as they carried a letter of marque from a legal government; *The Law of Nations*, Book III, Chap. XV, Sec. 229:400–401 [appears mispaginated, should be 614–15].
32 Ibid., Book III, Chap. XV, Sec. 226:613.
33 David Hackett Fischer, *Paul Revere's Ride* (New York: Oxford University Press, 1994), 215.
34 Vattel, *The Law of Nations*, Book III, Chap. XV, Sec. 226:613.
35 Lender and Stone, *Fatal Sunday*, 145–47; 211–17.
36 Vattel, *The Law of Nations*, Book III, Chap. VIII, Sec. 138:543.
37 Ibid., Book III, Chap. IX, Sec. 164:568; Sec. 166:570.
38 Andrew Jackson O'Shaughnessy, *The Empire Divided: The American Revolution and the British Caribbean* (Philadelphia: University of Pennsylvania Press, 2000), 218.
39 On the "hard-line" view, see Conway, "To Subdue America," 382, 392–99; and Stephen Conway, *The War of American Independence, 1775–1783* (London: Edward Arnold, 1995), 35, 39, 51–52, 166. An overview of Culloden and its painful aftermath is in John Prebble, *The Lion in the North: A Personal View of Scotland's History* (London: Penguin Books, 1973), 300–302.
40 William G. Evelyn to Mrs. Leveson Gower, 19 Aug. 1775, and William G. Evelyn to William Evelyn, 7 July 1775, in C. D. Scull, ed., *Memoir and Letters of Captain Willian G. Evelyn of the 4th Regiment ("King's Own") from North America, 1774–1776* (Oxford: Printed by James Parker and Co., 1879), 65, 71.

41 Vattel, *The Law of Nations*, Book III, Chap. XVIII, Secs. 290–95:642–49.
42 Benjamin Hichborn to John Adams, 10 Dec. 1775, *The Adams Papers*, ed. by Robert J. Taylor, 3:323–224. Some historians have questioned the validity of Hichborn's description or have ignored it. Regardless, British soldiers fought viciously, while taking an unexpected beating themselves at Bunker Hill (Breed's Hill). Warren was well known to them as a preeminent rebel agitator, making him a target for brutal treatment, both during and after the battle. For a fuller discussion of the battle itself and its relation to Warren, see Nathaniel Philbrick, *Bunker Hill: A City, a Siege, a Revolution* (New York: Viking, 2013), 208–30; and James L. Nelson, *With Fire and Sword: The Battle of Bunker Hill and the Beginning of the American Revolution* (New York: St. Martin's Press, 2011), 217–317.
43 John C. Clyde, *Rosbrugh, a Tale of the Revolution, or, Life, Labors and Death of Rev. John Rosbrugh: Pastor of Greenwich, Oxford and Mansfield Woodhouse (Washington) Presbyterian Churches, N.J., from 1764 to 1769, and of Allen Township Church, Pa., from 1769 to 1777: Chaplain in the Continental Army, Clerical Martyr of the Revolution, Killed by Hessians, in the Battle of Assunpink, at Trenton, New Jersey, Jan. 2d, 1777* (Easton, PA: 1880), 59–60; Hoock, *The Scars of Independence*, 159; David Hackett Fischer, *Washington's Crossing* (New York: Oxford University Press, 2004), 300.
44 "Speech of His Excellency Archibald Bulloch … to the [Georgia] Provincial Congress … June 5, 1776," in Force, ed., *American Archives*, Ser. 4, VI:718.
45 27 and 28 Sept. 1781, 1 Oct. 1781, *JCC*, 21:1017–18, 1023, 1029–30.
46 Peckham, ed., *The Toll of Independence*, 130, *passim*; David C. Munn, ed., *Battles and Skirmishes*, *passim*; Parker, *Parker's Guide*, *passim*.
47 Michael S. Adelberg deserves credit for the term. See his "Destitute of Almost Everything to Support Life: The Acquisition and Loss of Wealth in Revolutionary Monmouth County, New Jersey," in James J. Gigantino II, ed., *The American Revolution in New Jersey: Where the Battlefront Meets the Home Front* (New Brunswick: Rutgers University Press, 2015), 110.
48 Military frontiers could shift. During the British occupation of Philadelphia, the surrounding Pennsylvania counties and the Delaware River counties of New Jersey endured foraging sweeps by both armies and the turmoil of clashes between local whigs and tories. With the British departure in 1778, however, relative tranquility returned when whigs reestablished control on both sides of the Delaware.

NOTES

CHAPTER 2: "EXPOSED TO BOTH INTERNAL AND EXTERNAL ENEMIES": WAR TO THE KNIFE IN NEW JERSEY

1 Richard P. McCormick, *New Jersey from Colony to State: 1609–1789*, rev. ed. (Newark, NJ: New Jersey Historical Society, 1981), 81. Population estimates for colonial New Jersey are educated guesses. Various early censuses were incomplete, although New Jersey's size during the revolutionary period relative to other states is clear enough from the first national census of 1790. Peter O. Wacker, *Land & People: A Cultural Geography of Preindustrial New Jersey: Origins and Settlement Patterns* (New Brunswick, NJ: Rutgers University Press, 1975), 121–221; U.S. Bureau of the Census, *Historical Statistics of the United States: Colonial Times to 1957* (Washington, DC: U.S. Government Printing Office, 1960), 13. New Jersey was only larger than New Hampshire, Rhode Island, Delaware, and Georgia.

2 Passed in March 1765, Parliament intended the Stamp Act to raise funds for colonial defense. It required the use of revenue-stamped paper for newspapers, most legal and commercial transactions, and various other documents. Colonial indignation stemmed mostly from the fact that, for the first time, Britain had levied a direct tax on the colonies – violating the traditional understanding that "Englishmen could be taxed only by their own representatives." New Jersey sent representatives to the Stamp Act Congress in New York City to register their protests, and they applauded when, in the face of sustained colonial opposition – including disrupted trade with Britain and threats of violence against anyone willing to distribute the stamps – Parliament repealed the act in March 1766. With this, the excitement tailed off. The province evinced little interest in continued controversy – and there would be no New Jersey James Lovell to keep the pot boiling. McCormick, *New Jersey from Colony to State, 1609–1789*, 109–11.

3 Peckham, ed., *The Toll of Independence*, 133.

4 *New York Journal*, 28 Dec. 1775, cited in Larry R. Gerlach, *Prologue to Independence: New Jersey in the Coming of the American Revolution* (New Brunswick, NJ: Rutgers University Press, 1976), 304.

5 Peter Force, ed., *American Archives: Consisting of a Collection of Authentick Records, State Papers, Debates, and Letters and Other Notices of Publick Affairs, the Whole Forming a Documentary History of the Origin and Progress of the North American Colonies*, 9 vols. (Washington, DC: M. St. Clair Clarke and Peter Force, 1843–53), 4 Ser., 4:235.

6 A fuller discussion of these events is in Gerlach, *Prologue to Independence*, 304.
7 Gerlach, *Prelude to Independence*, 354–55; patriot and loyalist motivations are discussed in depth in Maxine Lurie, *Taking Sides in Revolutionary New Jersey: Caught in the Crossfire* (New Brunswick, NJ: Rutgers University Press, 2022).
8 Chopra, *Unnatural Rebellion*, 4.
9 James Moody, *Narrative of the Exertions and Sufferings of Lieut. James Moody, in Cause of Government since the Year 1776* (New York: Priv. print., 1865 [orig. 1783]), 10.
10 *New-York Gazette and Weekly Mercury*, 21 Oct. 1776.
11 Maxine N. Lurie and Marc Mappen, eds., *Encyclopedia of New Jersey* (New Brunswick, NJ: Rutgers University Press, 2004), 288.
12 "K. L. a Mechanic" to Frances Lagrange, July 1776, Bernardus Lagrange Papers, Special Collections and University Archives, Rutgers University Library, New Brunswick, NJ; "A. Mechanic" to Bernardus Lagrange, as a public "Advertisement," July 1776, ibid.
13 Gerlach, *Prologue to Independence*, 301.
14 Leiby, *The Revolutionary War in the Hackensack Valley*, passim; Adrian C. Leiby, *The Huguenot Settlement of Schraalenburgh: The History of Bergenfield, New Jersey* (Bergenfield, NJ: Free Public Library, 1964), 33.
15 Levi Pawling to George Clinton, 23 Mar. 1777, *Public Papers of George Clinton, First Governor of New York, 1777–1795, 1801–1804*, ed. by Hugh Hastings et al., 10 vols. (Albany, NY: State of New York, 1899–1914), 1:678.
16 David J. Fowler, "Forman, David," in Lurie and Mappen, eds., *Encyclopedia of New Jersey*, 282; Charles Forman, *Three Revolutionary Soldiers: David Forman (1745–1797), Jonathan Forman (1755–1809), Thomas Marsh Forman (1758–1845)* (Cleveland, OH: Forman-Bassett-Hatch, 1902), 7–18.
17 On Monmouth County during 1776 see Adelberg, *The American Revolution in Monmouth County*, 15–18.
18 Wacker, *Land & People*, 190.
19 Gerlach, *Prologue to Independence*, 355.
20 William Livingston to Richard Bache, 22 May 1777, *PWL*, 1:338.
21 Essex County (New Jersey) Committee to GW, 4 July 1776, in Force, ed., *American Archives*, Ser. 4, VI:1262–62.
22 Josiah Bartlett to John Langdon, 19 May 1776, in Force, ed., *American Archives*, Ser. 4, VI:1022.

23 Howe's orders are reprinted in William S. Stryker, *The Battles of Trenton and Princeton* (Trenton, NJ: The Old Barracks Association, 2001 [orig. 1898]), 484.
24 Vattel, *The Law of Nations*, Book III, Chap. XV, Sec. 226:613.
25 Thomas Olden, *A Brief Narrative of the Ravages of the British and Hessians at Princeton, 1776–1777*, ed. by Varnum Lansing Collins (Princeton, NJ: Drumthwacket Foundation, 1999), 20–21, 43–44.
26 Ibid., 6–12, 9–10.
27 Ibid., 14–15.
28 On the tragedy of Abigail Palmer and sexual violence against civilian women, see Holger Hoock, "*Jus in Bello*, Rape and the British Army in the American Revolutionary War," *Journal of Military Ethics*, 14 (April 2015), 74–97.
29 Thomas Nelson to Thomas Jefferson, 2 Jan. 1777, *Founders Online*, National Archives, https://founders.archives.gov/documents/Jefferson/01-02-02-0001, accessed 2 Feb. 2020.
30 Linda Grant DePauw, *Fortunes of War: New Jersey Women and the American Revolution* (Trenton: New Jersey Historical Commission, 1975), 19–20.
31 18 Apr. 1777, *JCC*, 7:276–78.
32 Ibid., 8:565.
33 18 Apr. 1777, *JCC*, 7:278.
34 Ibid., 7:279.
35 Mark Edward Lender, "Small Battles Won: New Jersey and the Patriot Military Revival," *New Jersey Heritage* 1, No. 2 (2002), 30–37; Munn, *Battles and Skirmishes in New Jersey*, 126–27.
36 In mid-July 1777 Washington did send Daniel Morgan with his corps of riflemen to the Hackensack area. Morgan was to gather intelligence and guard against loyalist and British incursions. Washington also warned Morgan against surprise. Only days later, however, the commander-in-chief ordered Morgan back to the main army. Albert Louis Zambone, *Daniel Morgan: A Revolutionary Life* (Yardley, PA: Westholme Press, 2018), 129–30. GW to William Livingston, 29 Apr. 1777, *PGWde*, RWS, 9:302.
37 Petition of Henrietta Blanch, Pension Records, W23632, in Leiby, *Hackensack Valley*, 116.
38 Alexander McDougall to GW, 18 May 1779, *PGWde*, RWS, 20:529.
39 Michael S. Adelberg, "'A Combination to Trample All Law Underfoot': The Association for Retaliation and the American Revolution in Monmouth County" (Unpublished MS, Monmouth

County Historical Association, Freehold, 1997), 2–3. Adelberg based his estimate of 500 Monmouth County New Jersey Volunteers on an examination of unit muster rolls of early 1777 in Special Collections, Rutgers University Library, New Brunswick, NJ. The number of exiles was larger, however, as the muster rolls did not count women and children fleeing with male recruits; nor did they list men, including escaped slaves, not serving in the Volunteers. See also Adelberg, *The American Revolution in Monmouth County*, 18–19.

40 Ibid., 18–19.
41 "West Jersey Volunteers: Memorial of the Inhabitants of West Jersey," [Great Britain] Public Record Office, Audit Office, Class 13, Volume 109, folio 109, in *On-Line Institute for Advanced Loyalist Studies*, http://www.royalprovincial.com/military/rhist/wjv/wjvmem1.htm, accessed 13 July 2020.
42 Ricardo A. Herrera, *Feeding Washington's Army: Surviving the Valley Forge Winter of 1778* (Chapel Hill: University of North Carolina Press, 2022), 78–109.
43 Munn, *Battles and Skirmishes in New Jersey*, 108, 129–32.
44 Nicholas Colin, *The Journal and Biography of Nicholas Collin, 1746–1831: The Journal Translated from the Original Swedish Manuscript*, trans. and ed. by Amandus Johnson (Philadelphia: New Jersey Society of Pennsylvania, 1936), 243–49.
45 Harold E. Selesky, ed., *Encyclopedia of the American Revolution*, 2nd ed. (Detroit: Charles Scribner's Sons, 2006), 2:959; Donald J. Gara, *The Queen's American Rangers* (Yardley, PA: Westholme, 2015), 114–18.
46 Mawhood and Hand quoted in W[illiam] H[enry] Carpenter and T[imothy] S[hay] Arthur, *The History of New Jersey from Its Earliest Settlement to the Present Time* (Philadelphia: Claxton, Remsen & Haffelfinger, 1874), 198–99.
47 Ibid., 99.
48 On June 27 and 28, 1778, in British-occupied Monmouth Court House, New Jersey, rebel homes and other structures went up in flames while tory properties were spared the torch. Lender and Stone, *Fatal Sunday*, 123–48.
49 Ibid., 214–16.
50 "The Reverend Nicholas Collin on the Ravages of War," in Gerlach, ed., *New Jersey in the American Revolution, 1763–1783*, 303. Johnson, ed., *Journal of Nicholas Collin*, 243–49. Collin's account may be trusted. He was a respected cleric on both sides of the Delaware, a friend of

Benjamin Franklin, eventually a correspondent of Jefferson, a member of the American Philosophical Society, and an amateur botanist of some note.

51 Lender and Stone, *Fatal Sunday*, 420.
52 James J. Gigantino II, *William Livingston's Revolution* (Philadelphia: University of Pennsylvania Press, 2018), 41, refers to Livingston as a "Reluctant Patriot." On the governor's early support of loyalty oaths for tories, see ibid., 101. On tory paroles and other lenient treatment, see William Livingston to Stephen Skinner, 8 July 1776, *PWL*, 1:83; William Livingston to Samuel Tucker, 8 July 1776, ibid., 1:84; Pass for Andrew Elliot, 25 Sept. 1776, ibid., 1:151.
53 *The Papers of Alexander Hamilton*, ed. by Harold C. Syrett and Jacob E. Cooke, 27 vols. (New York: Columbia University Press, 1961–87), 1:242–44.
54 William Livingston to John Witherspoon, 7 May 1777, ibid., 1:222–24; Gigantino, *Livingston's Revolution*, 119.
55 William Livingston to GW, 5 Oct. 1777, *PWL*, 2:86.
56 William Livingston to George Clinton, 15 Jan. 1778, *PWL*, 1:198–99.
57 William Livingston to the Assembly, 29 May 1778, *PWL*, 2:348–51.
58 *Royal Gazette* (New York), 24 Oct. 1778.
59 *Royal American Gazette* (New York), 8 June 1778.
60 Ambrose Serle, *The Journal of Ambrose Serle, Secretary to Lord Howe, 1776–1778*, ed. by Edward H. Tatum, Jr. (San Marino, CA: Huntington Library, 1940), 308.
61 Olden, *A Brief Narrative*, 40.
62 Sherman, *Historic Morristown*, 246–47.
63 Philip R. N. Katchur, *Encyclopedia of British, Provincial, and German Army Units, 1775–1783* (Harrisburg, PA: Stackpole Books, 1973), 93; William Livingston to GW, 3 Sept. 1777, *PWL*, 2:60–61; "A History of the 1st Battalion, New Jersey Volunteers," *On-Line Institute of Advanced Loyalist Studies*, http://www.royalprovincial.com/military/rhist/njv/1njvhist.htm, accessed 25 Aug. 2020; "A History of the 5th Battalion, New Jersey Volunteers," ibid., http://www.royalprovincial.com/military/rhist/njv/5njvhist.htm, accessed 25 Aug. 2020.
64 William Livingston to GW, 5 Nov. 1777, *PWL*, 2:102–103; Sherman, *Historic Morristown*, 248–49. For the court records, see New Jersey vs. James Hiss to New Jersey vs. John Parks, Morris County Court of Oyer and Terminer, Minutes [1777], Boxed MSS, New Jersey State Library, Trenton; Military Record of Captain Moses Estey (copy of original), New Jersey Department of Defense MSS, 10304B, ibid.

65 Samuel Adams, Jr., to Sally Adams, 19–20 July 1778, Sol Feinstone Collection, No. 28, David Library of the American Revolution, Washington Crossing, PA.
66 Compiling such a list would entail at least a thorough examination of period New Jersey court records, loyalist muster rolls, British military records, and Continental and militia courts-martial. To date (2024), no such study exists.
67 Christian McBurney, *Abductions in the American Revolution: Attempts to Kidnap George Washington, Benedict Arnold and Other Military and Civilian Leaders* (Jefferson, NC: McFarland & Company, 2016), 74.
68 These actions occurred in those areas roughly from modern Elizabeth north along the Hudson River to the New York border, and inland to include modern Bergen, Union, and Essex Counties. See Munn, *Battles and Skirmishes*, 133–41.
69 Leiby, *Hackensack Valley*, 200–201, 204–205.
70 "Extract of a letter from New-Barbadoes, Bergen County, April 22, 1779," in *Documents Relating to the Revolutionary History of the State of New Jersey* [hereafter *NJA*], ed. by William Nelson (Trenton, NJ: John L. Murphy Publishing Company, 1901), Ser. 2, 3:358–59.
71 *Royal Gazette* (New York), No. 272, 8 May 1779, in *NJA*, Ser. 2, 3:345.
72 Adelberg, *Revolution in Monmouth County*, 19–20; Peckham, *The Toll of Independence*, 51; Munn, *Battles and Skirmishes in New Jersey*, 51, 54.
73 Adelberg, *Revolution in Monmouth County*, 85.
74 *New Jersey Gazette*, 24 Apr. 1782.
75 Mark Edward Lender, *The War for American Independence* (Santa Barbara, CA: ABC-CLIO, 2016), 266–67.
76 Alan Gilbert, *Black Patriots and Loyalists: Fighting for Emancipation in the War for Independence* (Chicago: University of Chicago Press, 2012), 142.
77 Leiby, *Hackensack Valley*, 192.
78 Ibid., 191–99; Harry M. Ward, *Between the Lines: Banditti of the American Revolution* (Santa Barbara, CA: Praeger, 2002).
79 Leiby, *Hackensack Valley*, 193.
80 Hugh Hastings et al., ed., *Public Papers of George Clinton*, 4:588–89; Leiby, *Hackensack Valley*, 195; Carl Van Doren, *Secret History of the American Revolution: An Account of The Conspiracies of Benedict Arnold and Numerous Others, Drawn from the Secret Service Papers of the British Headquarters in North America, Now for the First Time Examined and Made Public* (New York: Viking Press, 1941), 140.
81 Leiby, *Hackensack Valley*, 197.

82 David J. Fowler, *Egregious Villains, Wood Rangers, and London Traders: The Pine Robber Phenomenon in New Jersey During the Revolutionary War* (New Brunswick, NJ: Rutgers University Press, 1987), 235–92.
83 Adelberg, *Monmouth County*, 35–36.
84 William Livingston to Moore Furman, 7 Feb. 1779, *PWL*, 3:30–31. The militia captain who brought down Fagan was a Benjamin Dennis. Through a case of poor timing (and a legal technicality), however, Dennis did not collect the reward, as Fagan met his end just *before* the state had authorized the bounty. But in November 1778 the legislature did agree to reimburse Dennis and his men for expenses incurred in the pursuit of Fagan as a "recompense for their risqué & trouble as may be a suitable encouragement for others to undertake the like Enterprizes." William Livingston to the Assembly, 30 Nov. 1778, ibid., 2:487.
85 Ben Ruset, "The Refugee John Bacon," *JNPineBarrens*, 24 June 2011, https://www.njpinebarrens.com/the-refugee-john-bacon/.
86 "Articles of the Associated Loyalists, under the Honourable Board of Directors," New York, *c.*1781, Printed Ephemera Collection; Portfolio 111, Folder 4, Library of Congress, https://www.loc.gov/resource/rbpe.11100400/, accessed 14 Aug. 2020; Vattel, *The Law of Nations*, Book III, Chap. XV, Sec. 229:614.
87 Henry Clinton, *The American Rebellion: Sir Henry Clinton's Narrative of His Campaigns, 1775–1782, with an Appendix of Original Documents*, William B. Willcox, ed. (New Haven: Yale University Press, 1954), 237–38.
88 T. Cole Jones, *Captives of Liberty: Prisoners of War and the Politics of Vengeance in the American Revolution* (Philadelphia: University of Pennsylvania Press, 2020), 232–33; Holly A. Mayer, *Congress's Own: A Canadian Regiment, the Continental Army, and American Union* (Norman, OK: University of Oklahoma Press, 2022).
89 Adelberg, *Monmouth County*, 124–25, 127.
90 David Forman to GW, 23 June 1780, *PGWde*, RWS, 26:534–35.
91 Anti-Retaliator Petition, quoted in Adelberg, *Monmouth County*, 136.
92 "Existential War," 21 Apr. 2008, The Mackenzie Institute, https://mackenzieinstitute.com/2008/04/existential-war/, accessed 12 Dec. 2019. In our "Liberty or Death!," 148, we used a slightly different definition of our own devising: "warfare in which combatants believed their very existence is in question, leading to an acceptance of violence against persons and property as preferable to defeat, which is equated with political, cultural, and even physical extinction. This meant war

with few restrictions and an expectation of ferocity and brutality, anything to avoid defeat." The import is the same as Mackenzie's.
93 Peckham, ed., *The Toll of Independence*, 130, *passim*; Munn, ed., *Battles and Skirmishes*, *passim*.
94 These numbers derive from the body of Munn's compilation, although he did not total the casualties himself; ibid., *passim*. The estimate of 1,000 is certainly conservative inasmuch as Munn did not have casualty figures for a number of engagements (e.g., Second Trenton and Monmouth) where state militia were involved and in which they suffered losses. In other cases Munn was only able to report that British or loyalist raiders took New Jersey prisoners, but without reporting numbers. These estimates do not include Continental casualties.
95 Adelberg, *Monmouth County*, 37.
96 "Revolutionary War Damage Claims, 1776–1782," *New Jersey State Archives*, https://wwwnet-dos.state.nj.us/DOS_ArchivesDBPortal/RevWarDamages.aspx, accessed 9 Oct. 2020. None of these claims were paid.
97 Edward Alfred Jones, *The Loyalists of New Jersey: Their Memorials, Petitions, Claims, Etc. from English Records*, intro. by George Athan Billias (Boston: Gregg Press, 1972 [orig. 1927]), x; Paul H. Smith, "New Jersey Loyalists and the British 'Provincial' Corps in the War of Independence," *New Jersey History* 87, no. 2 (1969):69–78; Dennis P. Ryan, *New Jersey's Loyalists*, New Jersey's Revolutionary Experience, No. 20 (Trenton, NJ: New Jersey Historical Commission, 1975), 6. For an older but still useful operational account of the Volunteers, see William S. Stryker, *The New Jersey Volunteers (Loyalists) in the Revolutionary War* (Trenton, NJ: Naar, Day & Naar, printers, 1887). The best single source of information on the six loyalist New Jersey Volunteer battalions, including transcriptions of original documents from various archives in Canadian, British, and American sources, is the *On-Line Institute for Advanced Loyalist Studies* [hereafter *OIALS*], the website created and maintained by Todd Braisted, http://www.royalprovincial.com/military/rhist/njv/njvlist.htm.
98 Jones, *New Jersey Loyalists*, 91–92.
99 Ibid., 6, 8.

CHAPTER 3: THEATER OF FEAR: EXISTENTIAL WAR IN THE WEST

1 Selesky, *Encyclopedia*, 2:941–42.
2 Tenuous as Iroquois claims south of the Ohio were, they made the cession partially in hopes of taking American settlement pressure off

of their central homelands in upper and western New York; that is, the Iroquois wanted white settlers moving south, not north. Colin G. Calloway, *The American Revolution in Indian Country: Crisis and Diversity in Native American Communities* (New York: Cambridge University Press, 1995), 161, 189.

3 On Dunmore's War, see Glenn F. Williams, *Dunmore's War: The Last Conflict of America's Colonial Era* (Yardley, PA: Westholme, 2017). On the Mingos, see Michael N. McConnell, *A Country Between: The Upper Ohio Valley and Its Peoples, 1724–1774* (Lincoln, NB: University of Nebraska Press, 1992).

4 Michael Toomey, "Daniel Boone (1734–1829)," *The Tennessee Encyclopedia of History and Culture*, http://tennesseeencyclopedia.net/entry.php?rec=111, accessed 13 Nov. 2016; John Mack Faragher, *Daniel Boone: The Life and Legend of an American Pioneer* (New York: Holt, 1992), 374–76; John E. Kleber, ed., "Harrod, James," *The Kentucky Encyclopedia* (Lexington, KY: University Press of Kentucky, 1992), 413–14.

5 Griffin, *American Leviathan*, 171.

6 Grenier, *The First Way of War*, 10; Peter Silver, *Our Savage Neighbors: How Indian Warfare Transformed Early America* (New York: W. W. Norton, 2007); Griffin, *American Leviathan*, 49, 171; Alan Taylor, *The Divided Ground: Indians, Settlers, and the Northern Borderland of the American Revolution* (New York: Alfred A. Knopf, 2006), 33. Taylor was writing of the Pennsylvania frontier, but we can say as much of frontier settlers generally.

7 Grenier, *The First Way of War*, 10.

8 Griffin, *American Leviathan*, 48.

9 Cameron's transcription of Dragging Canoe's speech is in John P. Brown, *Old Frontiers: The Story of the Cherokee from Earliest Times to the Date of Their Removal to the West* (Kingsport: Southern Publishers, 1938). Cameron was agent to the Cherokees for 15 years until his death in 1781. In August 1779 Britain appointed him superintendent of Indian affairs for the entire Southwest. As such Cameron was influential in Cherokee affairs (he had three children with Cherokee consorts) and worked unceasingly to keep the tribe allied to the British cause. How close his version of Dragging Canoe's speech is to the chief's actual words is unknown, but it certainly captured Dragging Canoe's sentiments. On Cameron, see Tara Mitchell Mielnik, "Alexander Cameron," *The Tennessee Encyclopedia of History and Culture*, 25 Dec. 2009, https://tennesseeencyclopedia.net/entries/alexander-cameron/, accessed 10 Feb. 2016.

10 Henry Stuart to John Stuart, 25 Aug. 1776, *Colonial Records of North Carolina*, ed. by William L. Saunders, 10 vols. (Raleigh, NC: Josephus Daniels, 1886–90), 10:778.
11 Cornstalk quoted in Gary B. Nash, *The Unknown American Revolution: The Unruly Birth of Democracy and the Struggle to Create America* (New York: Penguin, 2006), 260.
12 Ethan Schmidt, *Native Americans in the American Revolution: How the War Divided, Devastated, and Transformed the Early American Indian World* (Praeger: Santa Barbara, 2014), 143.
13 Captain Thomas Cook quoted in Claudio Saunt, *West of the Revolution: An Uncommon History of 1776* (New York: W. W. Norton, 2014), 4.
14 Hamilton was one of Quebec's five lieutenant governors. For a concise biography, see Elizabeth Arthur, "Hamilton, Henry," *Dictionary of Canadian Biography*, IV (1771–1800), http://www.biographi.ca/en/bio/hamilton_henry_4E.html, accessed 29 Feb. 2016.
15 Ibid., 143–45.
16 On the British Indian agents generally, see Colin Calloway, *The American Revolution in Indian Country*, passim. For specific individuals, see Richard A. Colbert, "James Logan Colbert of the Chickasaw, The Man and the Myth," *North Carolina Genealogical Society Journal*, XX, No. 2 (1994):82, http://www.angelfire.com/ok3/greybird7/genealogy.html, accessed 7 Mar. 2016; Consul Willshire Butterfield, *History of the Girtys: Being a Concise Account of the Girty Brothers, Thomas, Simon, James and George...* (Cincinnati, OH: Robert Clarke and Co., 1890); R. Douglas Hurt, *The Ohio Frontier: Crucible of the Old Northwest, 1720–1830* (Bloomington, IN: Indiana University Press, 1996), 73–75; Larry L. Nelson, *A Man of Distinction among Them: Alexander McKee and the Country Frontier, 1754–1799* (Kent, OH: Kent State University Press, 1999); Tara Mitchell Mielnik, "Alexander Cameron," *The Tennessee Encyclopedia of History and Culture*, 25 Dec. 2009, https://tennesseeencyclopedia.net/entries/alexander-cameron/, accessed 10 Feb. 2016; John Walton Caughey, *McGillivray of the Creeks* (Columbia: University of South Carolina Press, 2007).
17 A. B. Brooks, "Story of Fort Henry," *West Virginia History* 1, No. 2 (1940):110–18; Otis Rice, *West Virginia: A History*, 2nd ed. (Lexington, KY: University Press of Kentucky, 1993), 43; "History of Fort Randolph," *First Biennial Report of the* [West Virginia] *Department of Archives and History*, 1906, 236–39, http://www.wvculture.org/HiStory/settlement/fortrandolph04.html, accessed 14 Apr. 2016.

18 Daniel Boone thought a few settlers held out at the Falls of the Ohio around modern Louisville, although there is little evidence of this. Michael A. Lofaro, *Daniel Boone: An American Life* (Lexington, KY: University Press of Kentucky, 2003), 83; John Filson, *The Discovery, Purchase, and Present State of Kentucky: and an Essay towards the Topography and Natural History of That Important Country*... (Wilmington: Printed by James Adams, 1784), 9, 48; An Online Text Edition, Paul Royster, ed. (Lincoln, NB: DigitalCommons@University of Nebraska), http://digitalcommons.unl.edu/cgi/viewcontent.cgi?article=1002&context=etas, accessed 14 Feb. 2016.

19 Brown, *Old Frontiers*, 162–63; William Anderson and James A. Lewis, eds., *A Guide to Cherokee Documents in Foreign Archives* (Metuchen, NJ: Scarecrow Press, 1995), 160. The Creeks never fully committed to the British, but war parties occasionally sallied against the Americans.

20 Greg O'Brien, "Southeastern Indians and the American Revolution," *Encyclopedia of Alabama*, http://www.encyclopediaofalabama.org/article/h-1133, accessed 14 Feb. 2016.

21 On republicanism as an ideology generally, see Bailyn, *Ideological Origins*; for the American belief in conspiracies, see pp. 94–159.

22 On the interplay between fears of Indian conspiracies and republican ideology during the Revolution, see Robert M. Owens, *Red Dreams, White Nightmares: Pan-Indian Alliances in the Anglo-American Mind, 1763–1814* (Norman, OK: University of Oklahoma Press, 2015), 59–70.

23 Saunt, *West of the Revolution*, 27.

24 Department commanders were brigadier generals Edward Hand (1777–78) and Lachlan McIntosh (May 1778–March 1779) and colonels Daniel Brodhead (March 1779–May 1781) and John Gibson (May–September 1781). Thereafter Brigadier General William Irvine commanded for the rest of the war. Robert K. Wright, Jr., *The Continental Army* (Washington, DC: Center of Military History, United States Army, 1989), 151; Fred Anderson Berg, *Encyclopedia of Continental Army Units: Battalions, Regiments, and Independent Corps* (Harrisburg, PA: Stackpole Books, 1972), 97, 129. Because of its assignment to the Western Department, the 9th Virginia (it was originally the 13th Virginia, and occasionally appears as such in accounts of the war in the West) was the only Virginia regiment to escape the surrender of the rest of the Virginia Line at Charleston in 1780; ibid., 129. "Military History of William Irvine," The State Society of the Cincinnati of Pennsylvania, http://www.pasocietyofthecincinnati.org/Names/WilliamIrvine.html, accessed 14 Apr. 2016.

Charles H. Lesser, ed., *The Sinews of Independence: Monthly Strength Reports of the Continental Army* (Chicago: University of Chicago Press, 1976), 104, 141, 145, 154, 164, 169, 192.

25 Daniel Brodhead to John Clark, 4 Apr. 1779, "Instructions to Officers," Brodhead Papers; Brodhead to Clark, 27 July 1779, ibid.

26 Hurt, *The Ohio Frontier*, 68–69.

27 The Indians with Bird were Delawares, Wyandots, and Mingos. Thomas Pieper and James B. Gidney, *Fort Laurens, 1778–1779: The Revolutionary War in Ohio* (Kent, OH: Kent State University Press, 1976).

28 Consul Willshire Butterfield, *History of George Rogers Clark's Conquest of the Illinois and the Wabash Towns, 1778–1779* (Columbus, OH: F. J. Heer, 1903), 88–89.

29 Filson, *Discovery of Kentucky*, 31–37. In summer 1776 Captain George Gibson led 20 men on the Fort Pitt to New Orleans journey under Virginia authority. They conducted no raid, but did sound out the Spanish on their reactions should the Americans attack the British on the Mississippi and in Pensacola – proposals that met only a diplomatic coolness. (Washington knew nothing about any of this.) Gibson, however, did make the return trip with 10,000 pounds of gunpowder for the patriot cause; and he clearly demonstrated the practicality of commercial links with Spanish Louisiana. See David Narrett, *Adventurism and Empire: The Struggle for Mastery in the Louisiana-Florida Borderlands, 1762–1803* (Chapel Hill: University of North Carolina Press, 2015), 70–71.

30 Michael A. McDonnell, *Masters of Empire: Great Lakes Indians and the Making of America* (New York: Hill and Wang, 2015), 289–90.

31 The 8th Foot deployed to North America in 1768. Its ten companies were dispersed as follows: Detroit, three companies; Fort Michilimackinac, two companies; Fort Niagara, four; Fort Oswego, one; J. A. Houlding, *Fit for Service: The Training of the British Army, 1715–1795* (New York: Oxford University Press, 1981), 17. On the composition of the expedition, see "Henry Hamilton's Journal," 7 Oct. 1778, Indiana Historical Bureau, http://www.in.gov/history/3013.htm, accessed 7 Mar. 2016.

32 "Henry Hamilton's Journal," 10 Dec. & 17 Dec. 1778, ibid., http://www.in.gov/history/3011.htm, accessed 7 Mar. 2016.

33 For a full account of Sullivan's expedition, see Glenn F. Williams, *Year of the Hangman: George Washington's Campaign Against the Iroquois* (Yardley, PA: Westholme Publishing, 2005).

34 Daniel Brodhead to Frederick Vernon, 28 Apr. 1779, "Instructions to Officers," Brodhead Papers.
35 A concise account of Brodhead's expedition is in Crytzer, "Allegheny Burning," https://allthingsliberty.com/2015/05/allegheny-burning-george-washington-daniel-brodhead-and-the-battle-of-thompsons-island/#_edn18, accessed 14 Apr. 2016.
36 General Orders, 18 Oct. 1779, John C. Fitzpatrick, ed. *Writings of George Washington* (Washington, DC: United States Government Printing Office, 1936), 16:480–81.
37 David A. Armour, "De Peyster, Arent Schuyler," *Dictionary of Canadian Biography*, IV (1821–35), http://www.biographi.ca/en/bio.php?id_nbr=2831, accessed 16 Feb. 2016.
38 Nelson, *A Man of Distinction*.
39 Willing's expedition receives thorough treatment in Narrett, *Adventurism and Empire*, 79–88.
40 Arent De Peyster to Frederick Haldimand, 8 Mar. 1780, *Collections and Researches Made by the Pioneer Society of the State of Michigan* [various titles, hereafter *MPHC*] X (1908):378–79.
41 Arent De Peyster to Frederick Haldimand, 8 Mar. 1780, *MPHC* X (1908):379.
42 At Detroit, De Peyster did notify Sinclair of his plans to seize the Falls while Sinclair's expedition was moving south, but that was the extent of their coordination. Neither man seems to have been in touch with Campbell in West Florida, who in any case was already on the defensive. Arent De Peyster to Patrick Sinclair, 12 Mar. 1780, *MPHC* IX (1908):580–81.
43 Arent De Peyster to Sinclair, 18 May 1780, *MPHC* IX (1908):582.
44 Alexander McKee to Major [Arent] De Peyster, 8 July 1780, Haldimand Papers, NG21, Add. Mss. 21760 (B-100), National Archives of Canada, http://www.frontierfolk.net/ramsha_research/mckee.html, accessed 5 Feb. 2016; Frederick Haldimand to Arent De Peyster, 12 Feb. 1780, *MPHC* IX (1908):634.
45 J. Winston Coleman, Jr., *The British Invasion of Kentucky* (Lexington, KY: Winburn Press, 1951), http://www.walthertree.com/BritishInvasionofKentucky.html, accessed 5 Feb. 2016. Coleman's account is grotesquely anti-Indian, but it provides an accurate account of Bird's expedition based on primary sources.
46 Clark even tried to halt land sales, insisting Americans should serve in an attack on Detroit before settling. R. E. Banta, *The Ohio* (Lexington, KY: University Press of Kentucky, 1998 [orig. 1949]), 159.

47 John Hancock to GW, 12 Oct. 1777, *PGWde*, RWS, 11:492–93.
48 Bradley J. Birzer, "French Imperial Remnants on the Middle Ground: The Strange Case of August de la Balme and Charles Beaubien," *Journal of the Illinois State Historical Society* 93, No. 2 (2000):135–54; Harvey Lewis Carter, *The Life and Times of Little Turtle: First Sagamore of the Wabash* (Urbana, IL: University of Illinois Press, 1987).
49 Daniel Brodhead to John Clark, 11 Oct. 1779 (Urbana, IL: University of Illinois Press, 1987). "Instructions to Officers," Brodhead Papers; Louise Phelps Kellogg, ed., *Frontier Retreat on the Upper Ohio, 1779–1781* (Madison, WI: Wisconsin Historical Society, 1917), 376–77.
50 Calloway, *American Revolution in Indian Country*, 228–333. Fort Carlos was also known as Post Charles III.
51 Schmidt, *Native Americans in the American Revolution*, 147–48.
52 After the war, South Carolina authorities arrested Bates and sentenced him to hang. Instead, a Gowen's Fort survivor entered the jail and shot him to death; and South Carolinians lauded the vigilante avenger as a hero. Edward McCrady, *The History of South Carolina in the Revolution, 1780–1783* (New York: Macmillan Company, 1902), 477–79.
53 At different times other Indians suspected the Gnadenhütten Lenapes (Delawares) were in sympathy with the Americans. Williamson didn't care. His men had a reputation for wanton barbarity, and learning of the militia commander's target, at Fort Pitt Continental colonel John Gibson actually tried to warn the Delawares of the impending assault, for which his life was threatened. Banta, *The Ohio*, 160–61; Rob Harper, "Looking the Other Way: The Gnadenhutten Massacre and the Contextual Interpretation of Violence," *William and Mary Quarterly*, 3rd Ser., 64, No. 3 (2007):633–42.
54 Peckham, *The Toll of Independence*, 94–96; Ted Franklin Belie, "Crawford's Sandusky Expedition," in *The American Revolution, 1775–1783: An Encyclopedia*, ed. by Richard L. Blanco (New York: Garland, 1993), 1:416–20.
55 George Washington to William Irvine, 6 Aug. 1782, Fitzpatrick, ed., *Writings of George Washington*, 24:474. See also Eric Sterner, *The Battle of Upper Sandusky, 1782* (Yardley, PA: Westholme Publishers, 2023).
56 E. M. Sanchez-Saavedra, *A Guide to Virginia Military Organizations in the American Revolution, 1774–1787* (Westminster, MD: Heritage Books, 1978).
57 Bessie Taul Conkright, "Estill's Defeat or the Battle of Little Mountain March 22, 1782," *Register of Kentucky State Historical Society*, 22, No. 66 (1924):311–22; Michael C. C. Adams, "An Appraisal of the Blue Licks Battle," *Filson Club History Quarterly* 75, No. 2 (2001):181–203.

58 David Curtis Scaggs, ed., *The Old Northwest in the American Revolution: An Anthology* (Madison, WI: The State Historical Society of Wisconsin, 1977), 132.
59 William Irvine to GW, 2 Dec. 1781, Founders Online, National Archives, http://founders.archives.gov/documents/Washington/99-01-02-07473, accessed 3 May 2016.
60 Arent De Peyster to Patrick Sinclair, 8 Mar. 1780, *MPHC* IX (1908):378–79.
61 Indeed, from a few outposts in 1777, by 1782 Kentucky's population had increased to some 8,000 settlers, and then soared to 50,000 by 1787, and 73,677 by 1790. In Tennessee, the beleaguered settlements of the 1780s grew to 35,691 residents in 1790, and to over 105,000 in 1800. Narrett, *Adventurism and Empire*, 129; Richard L. Forstall, comp. and ed., *Population of the States and Counties of the United States: 1790–1990* (Washington, DC: U.S. Department of Commerce, Bureau of the Census, 1996), 4.
62 Some historians, however, persist in crediting Clark for the British conceding the West to the new republic. E.g., Selesky, *Encyclopedia*, 2:1257.
63 Jonathan R. Dull, *A Diplomatic History of the American Revolution* (New Haven: Yale University Press, 1985), 159–64.
64 "Existential War," 21 Apr. 2008, The Mackenzie Institute, https://mackenzieinstitute.com/2008/04/existential-war/, accessed 12 Dec. 2019.

CHAPTER 4: "A CONTAGION OF VIOLENCE":
THE NEW YORK FRONTIER

1 William N. Fenton, *The Great Law and the Longhouse: A Political History of the Iroquois Confederacy* (Norman, OK: University of Oklahoma Press, 1998), 51–119; Joseph T. Glatthaar and James Kirby Martin, *Forgotten Allies: The Oneida Indians and the American Revolution* (New York: Hill & Wang, 2006), 7–46.
2 The Scots-Irish were Protestants who first migrated from Scotland to the Ulster region in the north of Ireland; many of their descendants then migrated to America during the 18th century. See Ronald Chepesiuk, *The Scotch-Irish: From the North of Ireland to the Making of America* (Jefferson, NC: McFarland, 2000).
3 David L. Preston, *The Texture of Contact: European and Indian Settler Communities on the Frontiers of Iroquoia, 1667–1783* (Lincoln, NE:

University of Nebraska Press, 2009); Fintan O'Toole, *White Savage: William Johnson and the Invention of America* (New York: Farrar, Straus and Giroux, 2005).

4   Glatthaar and Martin, *Forgotten Allies*, 66–71; Preston, *Texture of Contact*, 91–115; Colin G. Calloway, *The Scratch of a Pen: 1763 and the Transformation of North America* (New York: Oxford University Press, 2006), 99–100.

5   Glatthaar and Martin, *Forgotten Allies*, 76–99.

6   Ibid., 91–92; Isabel T. Kelsay, *Joseph Brant, 1743–1807: Man of Two Worlds* (Syracuse, NY: Syracuse University Press, 1984), 138–60.

7   Continental Congress quoted in Barbara Graymont, *The Iroquois in the American Revolution* (Syracuse, NY: Syracuse University Press, 1972), 72.

8   Glatthaar and Martin, *Forgotten Allies*, 92–99; Graymont, *Iroquois in the Revolution*, 69–73.

9   Glatthaar and Martin, *Forgotten Allies*, 100–105; Gavin K. Watt, *Rebellion in the Mohawk Valley: The St. Leger Expedition of 1777* (Toronto: Dundurn Press, 2002), 27–33.

10 Kelsay, *Joseph Brant*, 176–90; Glatthaar and Martin, *Forgotten Allies*, 134–48; "The Examination of Moabary Owen Taken by Henry Wisenor, Esqr," in Hugh Hastings et al., ed., *Public Papers of George Clinton*, 5:163.

11 Philip R. N. Katcher, *Encyclopedia of British, Provincial, and German Army Units, 1775–1783* (Harrisburg, PA: Stackpole Books, 1973), 84, 88.

12 Brant's letter of 10 Apr. 1780 was written in Mohawk and translated into English by Rev. Samuel Kirkland; quoted in Graymont, *Iroquois in the American Revolution*, 231.

13 Major James Gray quoted in Kelsay, *Joseph Brant*, 193.

14 John Stark to Ichabod Alden, 15 Aug. 1778, in Caleb Stark, *Memoir and Official Correspondence of Gen. John Stark, with Notices of Several Other Officers of the Revolution. Also, a Biography of Capt. Phinehas Stevens and of Col. Robert Rogers, with an Account of His Services in America during the "Seven Years' War"* (Concord, NH: Parker Lyon, 1860), 185. Caleb Stark's editorial comment is on the same page.

15 The details of the British plans are in Kevin J. Weddle, *The Compleat Victory: Saratoga and the American Revolution* (New York: Oxford University Press, 2021); Richard M. Ketchum, *Saratoga: Turning Point of America's Revolutionary War* (New York: Henry Holt and Company, 1997); John F. Luzader, *Saratoga: A Military History of the Decisive Campaign of the American Revolution* (New York: Savas Beatie, 2008).

16 James Kirby Martin and Mark Edward Lender, *A Respectable Army: The Military Origins of the Republic, 1763–1789*, 3rd ed. (Malden, MA: Wiley Blackwell, 2015), 83–87; Watt, *Rebellion in the Mohawk Valley*, 56–80.

17 Glatthaar and Martin, *Forgotten Allies*, 149–57; Watt, *Rebellion in the Mohawk Valley*, 107–25. Unless noted otherwise, the following narrative of military operations is based on these sources.

18 Anonymous soldier, Extract of a letter from Fort Schuyler, 28 July 1777, *New York Journal*, 4 Aug. 1777.

19 Blacksnake quoted in Thomas S. Abler, ed., *Chainbreaker: The Revolutionary War Memoirs of Governor Blacksnake as Told to Benjamin Williams* (Lincoln, NE: University of Nebraska Press, 1989), 128–30. For estimates of casualties at the Oriskany battle see Glatthaar and Martin, *Forgotten Allies*, 168–69, and Watt, *Rebellion in the Mohawk Valley*, 317–18.

20 Allan D. Foote, *Liberty March: The Battle of Oriskany* (Utica, NY: North Country Books, 1998), 175–76; Graymont, *Iroquois in the Revolution*, 138–39.

21 Martin and Lender, *A Respectable Army*, 115–27.

22 Daniel Claus to William Knox, 6 Nov. 1777, in *Documents Relative to the Colonial History of the State of New York*, ed. by Edmund B. O'Callaghan et al., 15 vols. (Albany, NY: Weed, Parsons and Company, printers, 1853–87), 8:725. Like Glatthaar and Martin, Graymont, *Iroquois in the Revolution*, 142–43, views the Battle of Oriskany and the sacking of Oriska as the starting points of the damaging civil war among the Six Nations.

23 Quoted in Graymont, *Iroquois in the Revolution*, 165–66.

24 John Stark to Meshech Weare, 28 June 1778, in Stark, *Memoir and Official Correspondence of Gen. John Stark*, 172–73.

25 "Springfield, New York," in Selesky, *Encyclopedia*, 2:1102; Peckham, *The Toll of Independence*, 51, 52; Jeptha R. Simms, *The Frontiersmen of New York: Showing Customs of the Indians, Vicissitudes of the Pioneers White Settlers, and Border Strife in Two Wars. With a Great Variety of Romantic and Thrilling Stories Never before Published*, 2 vols. (Albany, NY: Geo. C. Riggs, 1882–83), 2:170–71; Daniel Barr, *Unconquered: The Iroquois League at War in Colonial America* (Westport, CT: Praeger, 2006), 152.

26 Johann Ewald, *Diary of the American War: A Hessian Journal*, trans. and ed. by Joseph P. Tustin (New Haven: Yale University Press, 1979), 166–67.

27 Ernest Alexander Cruikshank, "The Story of Butler's Rangers and the Settlement of Niagara," in Ernest Alexander Cruikshank, Henry U. Swinnerton, and Isaac A. Chapman, eds. *Butler's Rangers: Three Accounts of the American War of Independence* (Driffield, UK: Leonaur,

2011 [orig. 1893]), 39–55; Williams, *Year of the Hangman*, 114–33; Graymont, *Iroquois in the Revolution*, 168–74.
28 Williams, *Year of the Hangman*, 130; Richard Berleth, *Bloody Mohawk: The French and Indian War & American Revolution* (Hensonville, NY: Black Dome Press, 2009), 259–60.
29 Graymont, *Iroquois in the Revolution*, 171; Mark G. Dziak, *The Battle of Wyoming: For Liberty and Life* (self published, 2008–18).
30 Abler, *Chainbreaker*, 101–103; Graymont, *Iroquois in the Revolution*, 184.
31 "William Butler Journal," 9 Oct. [1778], Hugh Hastings et al., ed., *Public Papers of George Clinton*, 4:225–27. For more information on this important Indian village and base of operations for Brant, see Calloway, *The American Revolution in Indian Country*, 108–28; Glatthaar and Martin, *Forgotten Allies*, 49–53.
32 Graymont, *Iroquois in the Revolution*, 184–85; Henry U. Swinnerton, "The Story of Cherry Valley," in Cruikshank, *Butler's Rangers*, 117–30.
33 Graymont, *Iroquois in the Revolution*, 185–86; Glatthaar and Martin, *Forgotten Allies*, 230–32.
34 Graymont, *Iroquois in the Revolution*, 184–91; Swinnerton, "The Story of Cherry Valley," 131–35.
35 Quoted in Graymont, *Iroquois in the Revolution*, 190. See also quotes in Glatthaar and Martin, *Forgotten Allies*, 231–32.
36 Haldimand quoted in Cruikshank, "The Story of Butler's Rangers," 62–63.
37 John Hathorn to [Gov. George Clinton], [Col. John Hathorn's Official Report], 27 July 1779, Draper Manuscript Collection, Wisconsin Historical Society, http://www.albertwisnerlibrary.org/Factsandhistory/History/Minisink.htm; Selesky, *Encyclopedia*, 2:726–27; Mark Hendrickson, Jon Inners, and Peter Osborne, *So Many Brave Men: A History of the Battle at Minisink Ford* (Easton, PA: Pienpack Publishing, 2010), 19, 55–64.
38 Sullivan quoted in Glatthaar and Martin, *Forgotten Allies*, 256. For differing interpretations of the controversial Sullivan Expedition, see Joseph R. Fischer, *A Well-Executed Failure: The Sullivan Campaign against the Iroquois, July–September 1779* (Columbia, SC: University of South Carolina Press, 1997), 34–197; Barbara A. Mann, *George Washington's War on Native America* (Westport, CT: Praeger, 2005), 51–110; and Williams, *Year of the Hangman*, 240–89.
39 Glatthaar and Martin, *Forgotten Allies*, 252–54; Graymont, *Iroquois in the Revolution*, 216–17.

NOTES

40 Martin and Lender, *A Respectable Army*, 142–44; Fischer, *A Well-Executed Failure*, 235, n71.
41 Williams, *Year of the Hangman*, 225, 245; Frederick Cook, ed., *Journals of the Military Expedition of Major General John Sullivan against the Six Nations of Indians in 1779 with Records of the Centennial Celebration* (Auburn, NY: Knapp, Peck & Thomson, printers, 1887), 439–40.
42 Gavin K. Watt, *The Burning of the Valleys: Daring Raids from Canada against the New York Frontier in the Fall of 1780* (Toronto: Dundurn Press, 1997), 259–69; Cruikshank, "The Story of Butler's Rangers," 87–88.
43 Charles Gehring, *Agriculture and the Revolution in the Mohawk Valley* (St. Johnsville, NY: Fort Klock Historic Restoration, n.d. [1980?]), 5–6.
44 Claim 266 (McKay), 276 (Fenny), in Alexander Fraser, *Second Report of the Bureau of Archives for the Province of Ontario*, 2 vols. (Toronto: L. K. Cameron, Printer to the King's Most Excellent Majesty, 1905), 1:358, 364.
45 A current historiographical debate focusing on Native Americans in American history has pitted models of "ethnic cleansing" versus "genocide" in reaching conclusions about the fate of American Indians over time. See Gary C. Anderson, *Ethnic Cleansing and the Indian: The Crime that Should Haunt Humanity* (Norman, OK: University of Oklahoma Press, 2004), 36–109; and Benedict Kiernan, *Blood and Soil: A World History of Genocide and Extermination from Sparta to Darfur* (New Haven, CT: Yale University Press, 2007), 213–48, 310–63. Neither of these potentially explanatory models fits well with the realities of the Revolutionary War, since such warfare often pitted British partisans and Indians fighting together against rebel partisans and their supporting Indian allies. That was the situation on the New York frontier. Furthermore, each of these competing models tends to turn Native Americans into little more than victims of white aggression. Much scope remains in the secondary literature to reinstate their historical agency.

CHAPTER 5: TARGET NEW LONDON: BENEDICT ARNOLD FROM *JUS IN BELLO* TO "HARD LINE"

1 *Freeman's Journal: Or, the North-American Intelligencer* (Philadelphia), 14 Nov. 1781; 1 Oct. 1781, *JCC*, 21:1029–30.
2 Jared Sparks, *The Life and Treason of Benedict Arnold* (New York: Harper & Brothers, 1835), 325.

3 Some accounts of Arnold have been even-handed, trying to explain – although not excuse – Arnold's treason and subsequent conduct in a British uniform, but to a greater or lesser extent most have mirrored Sparks' animosity. George Canning Hill certainly did. His 1858 narrative of the New London raid easily matched Sparks' portrayal of Arnold as a ruthless barbarian. Dave R. Palmer, who has much good to say about Arnold before his treason, offers a grim view of the New London operation and terms the Fort Griswold action a "gruesome atrocity." Claire Brandt's psychological biography sees little restraint in Arnold's attack on his native region; Willard Stern Randall views the raid simply as an example of Arnold's willingness to wage "ruthless, total, modern warfare." See George Canning Hill, *Benedict Arnold: A Biography* (Boston: A. O. Libby & Company, 1858), 289–91; Dave R. Palmer, *George Washington and Benedict Arnold: A Tale of Two Patriots* (Washington, DC: Regnery Publishing, 2006), 382; Clare Brandt, *The Man in the Mirror: A Life of Benedict Arnold* (New York: Random House, 1994), 249–52; Willard Sterne Randall, *Benedict Arnold: Patriot and Traitor* (New York: Quill/William Morrow, 1990), 585–86. For similar accounts, see Brian Richard Boylan, *Benedict Arnold: The Dark Eagle* (New York: W. W. Norton, 1973); and Willard Mosher Wallace, *Traitorous Hero: The Life and Fortunes of Benedict Arnold* (New York: Harper and Brothers, 1954), 278–83. A more sympathetic treatment of Arnold, which still sees New London as a "blot" on his reputation, is in Audrey Wallace, *Benedict Arnold: Misunderstood Hero* (Shippensburg, PA: Burd Street Publishers, 2003), 81–83. Eric D. Lehman, *Homegrown Terror: Benedict Arnold and the Burning of New London* (Middletown, CT: Wesleyan University Press, 2016).

4 Ernest E. Rogers, *Connecticut's Naval Office at New London during the War of the American Revolution; Including the Mercantile Letter Book of Nathaniel Shaw, Jr.* (New London, CT: New London County Historical Society, 1933), 6; Lehman, *Homegrown Terror*, 16.

5 Rogers, *Connecticut's Naval Office*, 54–55, 72. Built in 1778, *General Putnam* was lost in the disastrous Massachusetts expedition against Penobscot (modern Maine) in 1779. On the Shaw mansion, see National Register of Historic Places, "Nomination for Shaw Mansion," 1970, National Park Service, https://npgallery.nps.gov/pdfhost/docs/NRHP/Text/70000713.pdf, accessed 13 Oct. 2017.

6 David Syrett, *Shipping and the American War, 1775–83: A Study of British Transport Organization* (London: Athlone Press, 1970), 77; Walter Powell, *Murder or Mayhem? Benedict Arnold's New England Connecticut Raid,*

1781 (Gettysburg, PA: Thomas Publications, 2000), 7–9; Edgar Stanton Maclay, *A History of American Privateers* (New York: D. Appleton and Company, 1899), ix, 216–17.
7 *Annual Register* (London), 1778, p. 36.
8 Clinton quoted in Franklin W. Kemp, *A Nest of Rebel Pirates: The Account of an Attack by the British Forces on the Privateer Stronghold at Little Egg Harbor*, 2nd ed. (Batsto, NJ: Batsto Citizens Committee, 1993).
9 Willian Scudder Stryker, *The Affair at Egg Harbor, New Jersey, October 15, 1778* (Trenton, NJ: Naar, Day & Naar, 1894), 8–9, 17–20.
10 Charles Townshend, *The British Invasion of New Haven, Connecticut, Together with Some Account of Their Landing and Burning the Towns of Fairfield and Norwalk, July 1779* (New Haven, CT: Tuttle, Morehouse and Taylor Printers, 1879), 33–49.
11 George E. Buker, *The Penobscot Expedition: Commodore Saltonstall and the Massachusetts Conspiracy of 1779* (Annapolis, MD: Naval Institute Press, 2002), 4–5; Michael M. Greenburg, *The Court-Martial of Paul Revere: A Son of Liberty and America's Forgotten Military Disaster* (Lebanon, NH: University Press of New England, 2014).
12 Frances H. Kennedy, ed., *The American Revolution: A Historical Guidebook* (New York: Oxford University Press, 2014), 190; Richard Buel, Jr., *Dear Liberty: Connecticut's Mobilization for the Revolutionary War* (Middletown, CT: Wesleyan University Press, 1980), 157; *The Continental Journal and Weekly Advertiser* (Boston), 22 Oct. 1778 [p. 2], in the Annotated Newspapers of Harbottle Dorr, Jr., Massachusetts Historical Society.
13 Powell, *Murder or Mayhem?*, 7–9.
14 Maclay, *American Privateers*, viii.
15 Ibid., 157, 192–93, 230.
16 Ibid.
17 Henry B. Carrington, *Battles of the American Revolution, 1775–1781* (New York: A. S. Barnes & Company, 1876), 626, 631. Powell, *Murder or Mayhem?*, 10–23, has the best description of New London's defenses (and the sorry state thereof).
18 Frances Manwaring Caulkins, *History of New London, Connecticut: from the First Survey of the Coast in 1612, to 1860* (New London, CT: H. D. Utley, 1895), 541–45.
19 Frederick Mackenzie, *Diary of Frederick Mackenzie: Giving a Daily Narrative of His Military Service as an Officer of the Regiment of the Royal Welsh Fusiliers during the Years 1775–1781 in Massachusetts, Rhode Island*

      and New York, 2 vols. (Cambridge, MA: Harvard University Press, 1930), 2:611.
20 Maclay, *American Privateers*, 157.
21 Clinton, *American Rebellion*, 331. While Clinton did use the word "diversion" in reference to the New London raid, we should not read too much into it. In fact, there is little contemporary evidence to link New London with a diversion in favor of Cornwallis. In later controversies over his conduct in America, and specifically in justifying his conduct relative to Cornwallis' predicament in Virginia, Clinton *never* mentioned the New London raid (at least not in any known documents), although he did discuss sending Arnold and Major General William Phillips to Virginia in early 1781. See *The Narrative of Lieutenant General Henry Clinton, K.B. Relative to His Conduct during Part of His Command of the King's Troops in North America; Particularly to That Which Reflects the Unfortunate Issue of the Campaign of 1781: with an Appendix, Containing Copies and Extracts of Those Parts of His Correspondence with Lord George Germain, Earl Cornwallis, Rear Admiral Graves, &c. Which Are Referred to Therein* (London: J. Debrett, 1783), 49–50, 37–38.
22 On Arnold suggesting the New London operation, see Robert K. Wright, Jr., "New London Raid, Connecticut," in Selesky, *Encyclopedia*, 2:814.
23 Powell, *Murder or Mayhem?*, 28.
24 George Washington to Benedict Arnold, 14 Dec. 1776, *PGWde*, RWS, 7:331.
25 Mark Edward Lender and James Kirby Martin, "A Traitor's Epiphany: Benedict Arnold in Virginia and His Quest for Reconciliation," *Virginia Magazine of History and Biography* 125, no. 4 (2017), 315–57. For earlier and less benign views of Arnold's conduct in Virginia, see Bruce Lancaster, *The American Revolution* (Boston: Houghton Mifflin Co., 2001 [orig. 1971]), 317. Lancaster's account, typical of other histories, claims Clinton dispatched Arnold to Virginia because he knew Arnold "would not be hampered by any nicety of feeling in dealing with arrant Rebels and their property." The turncoat general supposedly was an agent of "havoc and destruction wherever he went." Michael Kranish, *Flight from Monticello: Thomas Jefferson at War* (New York: Oxford University Press, 2010), 164–99, also found Arnold's conduct deplorable but offers a much more nuanced interpretation.
26 Lender and Martin, "A Traitor's Epiphany," *Virginia Magazine of History and Biography*, 315–57.

27 Ibid.
28 Powell, *Murder or Mayhem?*, 29–30.
29 Ibid., 29.
30 Dave R. Palmer is surely correct in concluding "the raid ... had absolutely no impact on General Washington's march to Yorktown." Palmer, *Washington and Arnold*, 382.
31 Vattel, *The Law of Nations*, Book III, Chap. VIII, Sec. 143:548. "Rufus Avery's Narrative, from His Original Manuscript," in William W. Harris, *The Battle of Groton Heights: A Collection of Narratives, Official Reports, Records, Etc., of the Storming of Fort Griswold, the Massacre of Its Garrison, and the Burning of New London by British Troops Under the Command of Brig.-Gen. Benedict Arnold, on the Sixth of September, 1781*, revised by Charles Allyn (New London, CT: Charles Allyn, 1882), 32.
32 "Narrative of Stephen Hempstead," in ibid., 49–50; "Narrative of Thomas Hertell," in ibid., 71.
33 "Narrative of Stephen Hempstead," 50.
34 George Middleton, "A Narrative of the Capture of Fort Griswold," in Harris, *Battle of Groton Heights*, 92.
35 Powell, *Murder or Mayhem?*, 43–52.
36 Ibid., 55; Robert K. Wright, Jr., "New London Raid, Connecticut," in Selesky, *Encyclopedia*, 2:814.
37 Caulkins, *New London*, 569–70; Benedict Arnold to Henry Clinton, 8 Sept. 1781, reprinted in Harris, *Battle of Groton Heights*, 103.
38 Quoted in Rogers, *Connecticut's Naval Office*, 73. The wording of the article ("this town") implies publication in New London, and the *Connecticut Gazette* was the local newspaper, which must have resumed publication relatively soon after the raid. On the rise of Norwich, see Caulkins, *New London*, 574.
39 "Norwich," *New-Jersey Gazette* (Trenton), 26 Sept. 1781.
40 *Independent Chronicle* (Boston), 6 Dec. 1781.
41 *The Freeman's Journal: Or, the North-American Intelligencer* (Philadelphia), 10 Oct. 1781.
42 Jonathan Trumbull to George Washington, 13 Sept. 1781, *Founders Online*, National Archives, http://founders.archives.gov/documents/Washington/99-01-02-06956; 20 Sept. 1781, *JCC*, 21:977–98.
43 27 Sept. and 28 Sept. 1781, ibid., 21:1017–18, 1023; 1 Oct. 1781, ibid., 21:1029–30.
44 Benedict Arnold to Henry Clinton, 8 Sept. 1781, reprinted in Harris, *Battle of Groton Heights*, 105; Henry Clinton, General Orders (per Frederick Mackenzie), reprinted in ibid., 112.

45 James Robertson to Lord Amherst, 25 Sept. 1781, in Milton M. Klein and Ronald W. Howard, eds., *The Twilight of British Rule in Revolutionary America: The New York Letters Book of General James Robertson, 1780–1783* (Cooperstown, NY: New York State Historical Association, 1983), 215–16.
46 Joshua Upham to William Franklin, 13 Sept. 1781, in Harris, *Battle of Groton Heights*, 110.
47 Daniel Mark Epstein, *The Loyal Son: The War in Ben Franklin's House* (New York: Ballantine Books, 2017), 325–30.
48 Rivington's *Royal Gazette*, Sept. 1781; reprinted in Harris, *Battle of Groton Heights*, 97. Rivington's account was republished in the *Connecticut Gazette* (New London), 21 Sept. 1781, "with a view of convincing our Readers what infamous Falsehoods our Enemies are capable of publishing to the world"; ibid., 94.
49 Vattel, *The Law of Nations*, Book III, Chap. VIII, Sec. 137:542.
50 Ibid.
51 Ibid., Book III, Chap. VIII, Sec. 138:543.
52 Ibid., Book III, Chap. IX, Sec. 164:568; Sec. 166:570.
53 Ibid., Book III, Chap. IX, Sec. 167:570.
54 Randall accepts the account of a British officer murdering Ledyard with his own sword, attributing the crime to a New Jersey loyalist officer, Lieutenant Colonel Abraham Van Buskirk, who actually was nowhere near Ledyard when Fort Griswold fell. Randall, *Benedict Arnold*, 588–89; Brandt, *Man in the Mirror*, 249–52, makes the same mistake. The loyalists, delayed by difficult terrain, took no part in storming the fort. Powell, *Murder or Mayhem?*, 60–62, 64–69; "A History of the 4th Battalion, New Jersey Volunteers – Part 2 of 2," *OIALS*, http://www.royalprovincial.com/military/rhist/njv/4njvhist2.htm, accessed 26 Feb. 2017.
55 Carl P. Borick, "Waxhaws, South Carolina," in Selesky, *Encyclopedia*, 2:1245–46. Hoock, *The Scars of Independence*, 311–12, takes a similar view, but in not directly considering the issue of command and control he still considers the actions of Tarleton's men excessive.
56 "Norwich," *New-Jersey Gazette* (Trenton), 26 Sept. 1781. The *Gazette* credited the British for restoring "humanity" and, after the fighting stopped, treating survivors properly "as courage, policy, nay, and every principle required." This reference was brief and part of a longer article savaging Arnold and the British for their conduct; even so, it was perhaps the only contemporary patriot account to treat British actions at New London or Groton with anything less than indignation.

NOTES

57 William Heath, *Memoirs of Major-General Heath: Containing Anecdotes, Details of Skirmishes, Battles, and Other Military Events, during the American War* (Boston: I. Thomas and E. T. Andrews, 1798), 307–308.
58 Vattel, *The Law of Nations*, Book III, Chap. VIII, Sec. 143:548.

CHAPTER 6: THE SOUTH: TERROR FROM THE START

1 The military potential of these three groups – white loyalists, black slaves, and American Indians – is fully explored in Jim Piecuch, *Three Peoples, One King: Loyalists, Indians, and Slaves in the Revolutionary South, 1775–1782* (Columbia: University of South Carolina Press, 2008).
2 Breen, *American Insurgents*, 291.
3 Piecuch, *Three Peoples, One King*, 45–46, 54–55.
4 Rod Andrew, Jr., *The Life and Times of General Andrew Pickens: Revolutionary War Hero, American Founder* (Chapel Hill: University of North Carolina Press, 2017), 28–42; Breen, *American Insurgents*, 291; Robert M. Weir, *Colonial South Carolina: A History* (Millwood, NY: KTO Press, 1983), 324.
5 H. G. Jones, *North Carolina Illustrated, 1524–1984* (Chapel Hill: University of North Carolina Press, 1983), 113; Hugh T. Lefler and William S. Powell, *Colonial North Carolina: A History* (New York: Charles Scribner's Sons, 1973), 264, 266–67.
6 Buchanan, *The Road to Guilford Courthouse*, 95–96; Georgia Council of Safety quoted in ibid., 96.
7 Robert K. Wright, Jr., "Great Bridge, Virginia," *Encyclopedia.com*, https://www.encyclopedia.com/history/encyclopedias-almanacs-transcripts-and-maps/great-bridge-virginia, accessed 25 Apr. 2021; Lawrence E. Babits, "Moores Creek Bridge," in Selesky, *Encyclopedia*, 2:745–47.
8 Breen, *American Insurgents*, 9–19.
9 Jim Piecuch, "The Southern Theater: Britain's Last Chance for Victory," in Martin and Preston, eds., *Theaters of the American Revolution*, 90–91; Wright quoted on p. 90.
10 Benjamin Arthur Quarles, *The Negro in the American Revolution* (Chapel Hill: University of North Carolina Press, 1996 [orig. 1961]), 19–32.
11 "The Capital: Municipal Common Hall to Governor Dunmore, An Humble Address," in Robert L. Scribner and William J. Van Schreeven, eds., *Revolutionary Virginia: The Road to Independence* (Charlottesville: University of Virginia Press, 1973), 3:54–55; "Norfolk County

Committee: Remissness and Most Unfriendly Disposition," in ibid., 3:452–53. Alan Taylor, *The Internal Enemy: Slavery and War in Virginia, 1771–1832* (New York: W. W. Norton & Company, 2013), 22–23.
12 Charles Lee, "Minutes of Council of War," 8 May 1776, in Force, ed., *American Archives*, Ser. 4, VI:407.
13 Breen, *American Insurgents*, 293; Lefler and Powell, *Colonial North Carolina*, 277.
14 "A Declaration of the Delegates of Maryland," 6 July 1776, in Force, ed., *American Archives*, Ser. 4, VI:1506.
15 Piecuch, *Southern Theater*, 92–93.
16 Weir, *Colonial South Carolina*, 202–203; Taylor, *The Internal Enemy*, 20–26.
17 Minutes of the Virginia Convention, 18 May 1776, in Force, ed., *American Archives*, Ser. 4, VI:1526–27, and 7 June 1776, ibid., 1552–53; Taylor, *The Internal Enemy*, 25.
18 Lefler and Powell, *Colonial North Carolina*, 277.
19 Gilbert, *Black Patriots and Loyalists*, 119; Howe quoted in Emma Nogrady Kaplan and Sidney Kaplan, *The Black Presence in the Era of the American Revolution* (Amherst, MA: University of Massachusetts Press, 1989), 79.
20 Piecuch, "Southern Theater," 91–92.
21 Weir, *Colonial South Carolina*, 322.
22 R. Rea to Archibald Bulloch, 3 July 1776, in Force, ed., *American Archives*, Ser. 4, VI:2228.
23 Andrew, *Andrew Pickens*, 44.
24 James Creswell to William Henry Drayton, 27 July 1776, in Gibbes, *Documentary History*, 2:30–33; Henry Laurens to John Laurens, 14 Aug. 1776, *The Papers of Henry Laurens*, ed. by David R. Chesnutt and C. James Taylor, 16 vols. (Columbia, SC: University of South Carolina Press, 1968–2002), 11:227.
25 "Instructions to Archibald Bullock, John Houston, Lyman Hall, Button Gwinnett, and George Walton, *Esquires*," 5 Apr. 1776, in Force, ed., *American Archives*, Ser. 4, VI:1674.
26 "Speech of His Excellency Archibald Bullock ... to the [Georgia] Provincial Congress ... June 5, 1776," in Force, ed., *American Archives*, Ser. 4, VI:718.
27 Timothy quoted in Piecuch, *Three Peoples, One King*, 47.
28 "Helvetius," *Royal Georgia Gazette* (Savannah), 27 July 1780.
29 William Hooper to James Duane, 22 Nov. 1774, *LDC*, 1:263. On the Chandler controversy, see the editorial notes in ibid., 263. On Hooper, see Mary Claire Engstrom, "Hooper, William," *NCPedia*,

University of North Carolina Press, https://www.ncpedia.org/biography/hooper-william, accessed 26 Mar. 2023.
30 William Hooper to Samuel Johnston, 2 Dec. 1775, ibid., 2:425; William Hooper to Samuel Johnston, 6 Feb. 1776, ibid., 3:210–11; William Hooper to Joseph Trumbull, 13 Mar. 1776, ibid., 3:372–73.
31 North Carolina Delegates to the North Carolina Council of Safety, 7 Aug. 1776, ibid., 4:640–41.
32 Cashin, *The King's Ranger*, 33–52.
33 Edward J. Cashin, "Revolutionary War in Georgia," *New Georgia Encyclopedia*, https://www.georgiaencyclopedia.org/articles/history-archaeology/revolutionary-war-georgia, accessed 11 Mar. 2021.
34 "Strictures on the Measures used in order to reduce the American Rebels," *Royal Georgia Gazette* (Savannah), 12 Aug. 1779.
35 Katcher, *Encyclopedia*, 86, 95, 100–101, has listed the "regular" loyalist units and provided strength estimates based on available records: Georgia Loyalists (raised in 1779, 175 of all ranks, disbanded 1782 in New York); North Carolina Highlanders (also called the North Carolina Volunteers, raised 1780, 611 all ranks, disbanded Canada 1783); Royal North Carolina Regiment (raised 1780, 600 men, disbanded St. Augustine, Florida, 1783); South Carolina Dragoons (raised 1781, 38 men, merged with the South Carolina Royalists); South Carolina Rangers (raised 1780, 81 men, disbanded 1783, St. Augustine); South Carolina Royalists (raised 1778 in East Florida, served in Georgia and South Carolina, 660 men, disbanded in New York, 1783).
36 Kenneth Coleman, *Colonial Georgia: A History* (New York: Charles Scribner's Sons, 1976), 295–96, 299.
37 Rutledge, unable to find any real security in South Carolina, actually spent considerable time in Philadelphia as a delegate to the Continental Congress. J. D. Lewis, "The American Revolution in South Carolina: The Provincial & State Government in SC during the American Revolution," https://www.carolana.com/SC/Revolution/sc_revolution_provincial_government.html, accessed 23 Apr. 2021; David Ramsay, *The History of South-Carolina: From Its First Settlement in 1670 to the Year 1808* (Newberry, SC: W. J. Duffie, 1858 [orig. 1809]), 198–99; Edward McCrady, *The History of South Carolina in the Revolution, 1775–1780* (New York: The Macmillan Company, 1901), 463–66, 533, 539, 623, 764–65.
38 Lee, *Crowds and Soldiers*, 176–211.
39 Andrew, *Andrew Pickens*, 119–21; Henry Lee, *Memoirs of the War in the Southern Department of the United States* (New York: University Publishing Company, 1869 [orig. 1812]), 154–57.

40 O'Kelley, *Nothing but Blood and Slaughter*, 3:99.
41 Ibid., 120; Lee, *Memoirs of the War in the Southern Department of the United States*, 111–12, 242–54, 250.
42 David Fanning, *The Narrative of Colonel David Fanning, (a Tory in the Revolutionary War with Great Britain;) Giving an Account of His Adventures in North Carolina, from 1775 to 1783, as Written by Himself* (Richmond, VA: Privately published, 1861), 34–35; Lindley S. Butler, "David Fanning," in William S. Powell, ed., *Dictionary of North Carolina Biography* (Chapel Hill: University of North Carolina Press, 1986), 2:179–80.
43 E.g., Pancake, *This Destructive War*; Hooke, *The Scars of Independence*; O'Kelley, *Nothing but Blood and Slaughter*.
44 Piecuch, *Three Peoples, One King*, 5–6.
45 Michael Bellesiles, "Sumter, Thomas," in Selesky, *Encyclopedia*, 2:1128–30.
46 Ian Saberton, "The Campaigns of 1780 and 1781 in the Southern Theatre of the American Revolutionary War" (Ph.D. essay, History Department, University of Warwick, 2015), 36–37, http://wrap.warwick.ac.uk/80231/1/WRAP_THESIS_Saberton_2015.pdf, accessed 31 Mar. 2021.
47 Ibid., 37.
48 Quoted in Weir, *Colonial South Carolina*, 335–36.
49 Remarks attributed to Marion by militia officer Colonel Peter Horry, in Alexander Garden, *Anecdotes of the Revolutionary War in America: With Sketches of Character of Persons Most Distinguished, in the Southern States, for Civil and Military Services* (Charleston, SC: Printed by A. E. Miller, 1822), 250. Garden himself was a veteran of the Southern Theater.
50 Greene quoted in Terry Golway, *Washington's General: Nathanael Greene and the Triumph of the American Revolution* (New York, Henry Holt and Company, 2005), 240.
51 Greene quoted in ibid., 278.
52 Greene quoted in ibid., 273.
53 Urwin, "'To bring the American Army under strict Discipline,'" 15; Saberton, "The Campaigns of 1780 and 1781," 23. Indeed, Ian Saberton has suggested that the earl, a "humane, cultivated man" as well as an aggressive but traditional officer, simply lacked the stomach for the mayhem born of the civil war in the Carolinas.
54 Cornwallis proclamation of 17 June 1781 quoted in Urwin, "British Army Foraging Policy," 19.
55 Weir, *Colonial South Carolina*, 336.
56 Mary Stockwell, *Unlikely General: "Mad" Anthony Wayne and the Battle for America* (New Haven, CT: Yale University Press, 2018), 207–208.

57 Lee, *Memoirs of the War in the Southern Department of the United States*, 409–10.
58 Hershel Parker, "A 'Heavenly Harvest' of Vulnerable Women in North Carolina: Tory Troops as Sexual Predators," *Journal of the American Revolution*, 27, Feb. 2017, https://allthingsliberty.com/02/heavenly-harvest-vulnerable-women-north-carolina-tory-troops-sexual-predators/, accessed 2 Feb. 2020.
59 Pension application of George Dowell, S32222, fn71 NC/SC, statement of 28 Feb. 1838, "Southern Campaign American Revolution Pension Statements & Rosters," https://revwarapps.org/s32222.pdf, accessed 14 Feb. 2020.
60 Louise Frederick Hays, *Hero of Hornet's Nest: A Biography of Elijah Clark, 1733 to 1799* (New York: Stratford House, 1946), 59.
61 Piecuch, *Three Peoples, One King*, 143, 166.
62 "Savannah," *Royal Georgia Gazette* (Savannah), 13 Jan. 1780.
63 "Savannah," ibid., 20 Sept. 1781.
64 Ferguson quoted in Buchanan, *The Road to Guilford Court House*, 208.
65 Ibid., 225–41; Draper, *King's Mountain and Its Heroes*, 332–43.
66 Clay Ouzts, "Nancy Hart (ca. 1735–1830)," *The New Georgia Encyclopedia*, https://www.georgiaencyclopedia.org/articles/history-archaeology/nancy-hart-ca-1735-1830, accessed 25 Feb. 2021; E. Merton Coulter, "Nancy Hart, Georgia Heroine of the Revolution: The Story of the Growth of a Tradition," *Georgia Historical Quarterly* 39 (1955):118–51.
67 "[Notice by] Arch. McArthur, Commandant," *Royal Georgia Gazette* (Savannah), 11 Feb. 1779.
68 "Extract of a letter from Augusta, February 6, 1779," ibid., 11 Feb. 1779; Coleman, *Colonial Georgia*, 299.
69 "Savannah," ibid., 13 Jan. 1780.
70 "To the Printer of the *Morning Chronicle*," ibid., 22 Feb. 1781.
71 J. B. O. Landrum, *Colonial and Revolutionary History of Upper South Carolina* (Greenville, SC: Shannon & Co., Printers and Binders, 1897), 342–58; Peckham, *The Toll of Independence*, 93; "Cloud's Creek," *The American Revolution in South Carolina*, https://www.carolana.com/SC/Revolution/revolution_clouds_creek_2.html
72 Archie Vernon Huff, Jr., *Greenville: The History of the City and County in the Southern Piedmont* (Columbia: University of South Carolina Press, 1995), 27–28; Landrum, *Upper South Carolina*, 359–64.
73 "An Address to any People, that have been attacked, and may be attacked, that they may consider," *Royal Georgia Gazette*, 19 Aug. 1779.
74 "VATTEL," *Royal Georgia Gazette*, 25 Nov. 1779.

75 Lee, *Memoirs of the War in the Southern Department of the United States*, 450.
76 David Taylor, ed., *South Carolina Naturalists: An Anthology, 1700–1860* (Columbia, SC: University of South Carolina Press, 1998), 31.
77 Garden, *Anecdotes of the American Revolution*, 172.

EPILOGUE: A WORD FROM THUCYDIDES

1 William Livingston to GW, 5 Oct. 1777, *PWL*, 2:86.
2 Peckham, *The Toll of Independence*, 132.
3 Maya Jasanoff, *Liberty's Exiles: American Loyalists in the Revolutionary World* (New York: Alfred A. Knopf, 2011), 6, 343–50, 351–58.
4 The role of religion in existential warfare is beyond the immediate ken of this book, but the relationship invites further investigation. There are two initial questions in this regard. First, to what extent did patriots consider their cause a "Holy War"? John D. Carlson, citing some impressive scholarship, thinks that most rebels did not. However, some patriots certainly *did*, and how widespread this belief may have been begs clarification. Second, if some patriots believed they were engaged in a crusade – that God was on their side – how might this conviction have justified the measures they employed in waging their crusade? Finally, if, as Carlson further suggests, religious fervor blended with republican ideology in sustaining faith in the Revolution, to what extent did this conflation of religion and ideology fuel belief that almost any military measures were acceptable to secure victory? Carlson does not raise questions of existential warfare, but we believe his article implicitly suggests a religious dimension to the matter. See John D. Carlson, "A Just or Holy War of Independence? The Revolution's Legacy for Religion, Violence, and American Exceptionalism," in John D. Carlson and Jonathan H. Ebel, eds., *From Jeremiad to Jihad: Religion, Violence, & America* (Berkeley: University of California Press, 2012), 208.
5 Abraham Lincoln to Charles Drake and others, 5 Oct. 1863, *Collected Works of Abraham Lincoln*, ed. by Roy P. Basler, 9 vols. (New Brunswick, NJ: Rutgers University Press, 1953), 6:500.
6 Moltke quoted in Walter Goerlitz, *The German General Staff, 1657–1945*, trans. by Brian Battershaw (New York: Frederick A. Praeger, 1964), 93.
7 Thucydides, *History of the Peloponnesian War*, trans. by Rex Warner (New York: Penguin, 1972), 243–44.

Bibliography

Manuscript Sources

Anthony Wayne Papers, Historical Society of Pennsylvania, Philadelphia.
Bernardus Lagrange Papers, Special Collections and University Archives, Rutgers University Library, New Brunswick, NJ.
Daniel Brodhead Papers, Archives and Special Collections, University of Pittsburgh Library.
Gilder Lehrman Collection, Gilder Lehrman Institute, New York.
Morris County Court of Oyer and Terminer, Minutes [1777], Boxed MSS, New Jersey State Library, Trenton.
Horatio Gates Papers, New-York Historical Society, New York.
Horatio Gates Papers, Manuscripts and Archives Division, New York Public Library.
Philip Schuyler Papers, Letters Received, Manuscripts and Archives Division, New York Public Library Digital Collections.
Society Collection, Historical Society of Pennsylvania, Philadelphia.
Sol Feinstone Collection, American Philosophical Society, Philadelphia.
Transcripts of Letters from Maj. Gen. Horatio Gates, Papers of the Continental Congress, Library of Congress.
Transcripts of Letters from Philip Schuyler, Papers of the Continental Congress, Library of Congress.
William A. Oldridge Collection of George Washington's Headquarters Staff Writings, Library of Congress.

Memoirs, Published Papers, and Related

Abler, Thomas S., ed. *Chainbreaker: The Revolutionary War Memoirs of Governor Blacksnake as Told to Benjamin Williams.* Lincoln, NE: University of Nebraska Press, 1989.

Adams, John. *Diary and Autobiography of John Adams*, 4 Vols. Edited by L. H. Butterfield et al. New York: Atheneum, 1964.

----------. *Papers of John Adams*. 17 Vols. Edited by Robert J. Taylor et al. Cambridge, MA: Harvard University Press, 1977–2014.

Adams, Samuel. *The Writings of Samuel Adams*, 4 Vols. Edited by Harry Alonzo Cushing. New York: G. P. Putnam's Sons, 1907.

Beebe, Lewis. "Journal of a Physician on the Expedition Against Canada, 1776." Edited by Frederick R. Kirkland. *Pennsylvania Magazine of History and Biography* 59 (1935):321–61.

Bloomfield, Joseph. *Citizen Soldier: The Revolutionary War Journal of Joseph Bloomfield.* 2nd ed. Edited by Mark Edward Lender and James Kirby Martin. Yardley, PA: Westholme Press, 2018.

Boudinot, Elias. *Journal of Historical Recollections of American Events during the Revolutionary War.* Philadelphia: F. Bourquin, 1894.

Brymner, Douglas, ed. *Report on Canadian Archives, 1885*. Ottawa: Printed by Maclean, Roger & Co., 1886.

----------. *Report on Canadian Archives, 1886*. Ottawa: Printed by Maclean, Roger & Co., 1887.

----------. *Report on Canadian Archives, 1888*. Ottawa: Printed for the Queen's Printer and Controller of Stationery, 1889.

Clinton, George. *Public Papers of George Clinton, First Governor of New York: 1777–1795, 1801–1804.* Edited by Hugh Hastings, vols. 1–8, and J. A. Holden, vols. 9–10. 10 Vols. Albany: James B. Lyon, State Printer, 1899–1914.

Clinton, Henry. *The Narrative of Lieutenant General Henry Clinton, K.B. Relative to His Conduct during Part of His Command of the King's Troops in North America; Particularly to That Which Reflects the Unfortunate Issue of the Campaign of 1781: with an Appendix, Containing Copies and Extracts of Those Parts of His Correspondence with Lord George Germain, Earl Cornwallis, Rear Admiral Graves, &c. Which Are Referred to Therein.* London: J. Debrett, 1783.

----------. *The American Rebellion: Sir Henry Clinton's Narrative of His Campaigns, 1775–1782, with an Appendix of Original Documents.* Edited by William B. Willcox. New Haven: Yale University Press, 1954.

Colin, Nicholas. *The Journal and Biography of Nicholas Collin, 1746–1831: The Journal Translated from the Original Swedish Manuscript.* Trans. and ed. by Amandus Johnson. Philadelphia: New Jersey Society of Pennsylvania, 1936.

Collections and Researches Made by the Pioneer Society of the State of Michigan: Michigan Pioneer Collections X (1908).

Continental Congress. *Journals of the Continental Congress, 1774–1789.* 34 Vols. Edited by Worthington C. Ford et al. Washington, DC: U.S. Government Printing Office, 1904–37.

Cook, Frederick, ed. *Journals of the Military Expedition of Major General John Sullivan against the Six Nations of Indians in 1779 with Records of the Centennial Celebration.* Auburn, NY: Knapp, Peck & Thomson, printers, 1887.

Crary, Catherine S. ed. *The Price of Loyalty: Tory Writings from the Revolutionary Era.* New York: McGraw Hill Book Company, 1973.

Cruikshank, Ernest Alexander, Henry U. Swinnerton, and Isaac A. Chapman, eds. *Butler's Rangers: Three Accounts of the American War of Independence.* Driffield, UK: Leonaur, 2011 [orig. 1893].

Dann, John C., ed. *The Revolution Remembered: Eyewitness Accounts of the War for Independence.* Chicago: University of Chicago Press, 1980.

Davies, Kenneth Gordon, ed. *Documents of the American Revolution, 1770–1783.* 21 Vols. Dublin: Irish University Press, 1972–81.

Denny, Ebenezer. *Military Journal of Major Ebenezer Denny, an Officer in the Revolutionary and Indian Wars, with an Introductory Memoir.* Philadelphia: J. B. Lippincott, 1859.

Digby, William. *The British Invasion from the North: The Campaigns of Generals Carleton and Burgoyne, from Canada, 1776–1777, with the Journal of Lieut. William Digby, of the 53d, Or Shropshire Regiment of Foot.* Edited by James Finney Baxter. Albany, NY: Joel Munsell's Sons, 1887.

Egle, William Henry, ed. *Journals and Diaries of the Revolution, with Lists of Officers and Soldiers, 1775–1783.* Harrisburg, PA: E. K. Myers, 1893.

Enys, John. *The American Journals of Lt. John Enys.* Edited by Elizabeth Cometti. Syracuse, NY: Syracuse University Press, 1976.

Ewald, Johann. *Diary of the American War: A Hessian Journal.* Trans. and ed. by Joseph P. Tustin. New Haven: Yale University Press, 1979.

"Extracts from a Letter from General Haldimand, Governor and Commander in Chief of His Majesty's Forces in the Province of Quebec to Lord George Germain, One of His Majesty's Secretaries of State," *Bulletin of the Fort Ticonderoga Museum* 7, No. 4 (1946):29–31.

Fanning, David. *The Narrative of Colonel David Fanning, (a Tory in the Revolutionary War with Great Britain;) Giving an Account of His Adventures in North Carolina, from 1775 to 1783, as Written by Himself.* Richmond, VA: Privately published, 1861.

Force, Peter and M. St. Clair, eds., *American Archives: Consisting of a Collection of Authentick Records, State Papers, Debates, and Letters and Other Notices of Publick Affairs, the Whole Forming a Documentary History of the Origin and Progress of the North American Colonies.* 9 Vols. Washington, DC: M. St. Clair Clarke and Peter Force, 1837–53.

Fraser, Alexander, ed. *Second Report of the Bureau of Archives for the Province of Ontario.* 2 Vols. Toronto: L. K. Cameron, Printer to the King's Most Excellent Majesty, 1905.

Gerlach, Larry R., ed., *New Jersey in the American Revolution, 1763–1783: A Documentary History.* Trenton, NJ: New Jersey Historical Commission, 1975.

Gibbes, R. W., ed. *Documentary History of the American Revolution: Consisting of Letters and Papers Relating to the Contest for Liberty, Chiefly in South Carolina, from the Originals in the Possession of the Editor, and Other Sources.* 3 Vols. New York: D. Appleton, 1853–57.

Haldimand, Frederick. "The Haldimand Papers, with Contemporaneous History." *Collections of the Vermont Historical Society.* 2 Vols. Montpelier, VT: J. & M. Polard, printer, 1870–71, 2:59–366.

Hamilton, Alexander. *The Papers of Alexander Hamilton.* Edited by Harold C. Syrett and Jacob E. Cooke. 27 Vols. New York: Columbia University Press, 1961–87.

Harris, William W. *The Battle of Groton Heights: A Collection of Narratives, Official Reports, Records, Etc., of the Storming of Fort Griswold, the Massacre of Its Garrison, and the Burning of New London by British Troops Under the Command of Brig.-Gen. Benedict Arnold, on the Sixth of September, 1781;* revised by Charles Allyn. New London, CT: Charles Allyn, 1882.

Heath, William. *The Heath Papers. Collections of the Massachusetts Historical Society,* 5th Ser., Vol. 4 (1878); 7th Ser., Vols. 4 and 5 (1904–1905). Boston: Massachusetts Historical Society, 1878–1905.

Heath, William. *Memoirs of Major-General Heath: Containing Anecdotes, Details of Skirmishes, Battles, and Other Military Events, during the American War.* Boston: I. Thomas and E. T. Andrews, 1798.

Klein, Milton M. and Ronald W. Howard, eds. *The Twilight of British Rule in Revolutionary America: The New York Letters Book of General James Robertson, 1780–1783.* Cooperstown, NY: New York State Historical Association, 1983.

Laurens, Henry. *The Papers of Henry Laurens*. Edited by David R. Chesnutt and C. James Taylor. 16 Vols. Columbia, SC: University of South Carolina Press, 1968–2002.

Lee, Henry. *Memoirs of the War in the Southern Department of the United States*. New York: University Publishing Company, 1869 [orig. 1812].

Lesser, Charles H., ed. *The Sinews of Independence: Monthly Strength Reports of the Continental Army*. Chicago: University of Chicago Press, 1976.

Lincoln, Abraham. *Collected Works of Abraham Lincoln*. Edited by Roy P. Basler. 9 Vols. New Brunswick, NJ: Rutgers University Press, 1953.

Livingston, William. *The Papers of William Livingston*. Edited by Carl E. Prince and Dennis P. Ryan. 5 Vols. Trenton, NJ: New Jersey Historical Commission, 1979–88.

Mackenzie, Frederick. *Diary of Frederick Mackenzie: Giving a Daily Narrative of His Military Service as an Officer of the Regiment of the Royal Welsh Fusiliers during the Years 1775–1781 in Massachusetts, Rhode Island and New York*. 2 Vols. Cambridge, MA: Harvard University Press, 1930.

Mather, Frederic G., ed., *New York in the Revolution as a Colony and State: A Collection of Documents and Records from the Office of the State Comptroller*. 2nd ed. 2 Vols. Albany, NY: J. B. Lyon Company, printers, 1904.

McMichael, James. "Diary of Lieutenant James McMichael, of the Pennsylvania Line, 1776–1778." *Pennsylvania Magazine of History and Biography* 16, No. 2 (1892):129–59.

Moody, James. *Narrative of the Exertions and Sufferings of Lieut. James Moody, in Cause of Government since the Year 1776*. New York: Privately print., 1865 [orig. 1783].

Moore, Frank, ed. *Diary of the American Revolution: From Newspapers and Original Documents*. 2 Vols. New York: Charles Scribner, 1860.

Nelson, William, ed. *Documents Relating to the Revolutionary History of the State of New Jersey*. Ser. 2. Trenton, NJ: John L. Murphy Publishing Company, 1901.

O'Callaghan, Edmund B. et al., eds. *Documents Relative to the Colonial History of the State of New York*. 15 Vols. Albany, NY: Weed, Parsons and Company, printers, 1853–87.

Putnam, Rufus. *The Memoirs of Rufus Putnam and Certain Official Papers and Correspondence*. Edited by Rowena Buell. Boston: Houghton, Mifflin and Company, 1905.

Saunders, William L., ed. *Colonial Records of North Carolina*. 10 Vols. Raleigh, NC: Josephus Daniels, 1886–90.

Scribner, Robert L. and William J. Van Schreeven, eds. *Revolutionary Virginia: The Road to Independence*. Charlottesville: University of Virginia Press, 1973.

Scull, C. D., ed. *Memoir and Letters of Captain Willian G. Evelyn of the 4th Regiment ("King's Own") from North America, 1774–1776.* Oxford: Printed by James Parker and Co., 1879.

Simcoe, [John Graves]. *A Journal of the Operations of the Queen's Rangers: From the End of the Year 1777, to the Conclusion of the Late American War.* Exeter, UK: Printed for the author, 1787.

Smith, Paul H. and Ronald M. Gephart, eds. *Letters of Delegates to Congress, 1774–1789.* 26 Vols. Washington, DC: Library of Congress, 1976–2000.

Specht, Johann Friedrich. *The Specht Journal: A Military Journal of the Burgoyne Campaign.* Trans. by Helga Doblin. Edited by Mary C. Lynn. Westport, CT: Greenwood Press, 1995.

Stark, Caleb. *Memoir and Official Correspondence of Gen. John Stark, with Notices of Several Other Officers of the Revolution. Also, a Biography of Capt. Phinehas Stevens and of Col. Robert Rogers, with an Account of His Services in America during the "Seven Years' War."* Concord, NH: Parker Lyon, 1860.

Stedman, Charles. *The History of the Origin, Progress, and Termination of the American War.* London: Printed for the author, 1794.

Stillé, Charles J. *Major-General Anthony Wayne and the Pennsylvania Line in the Continental Army.* Philadelphia: J. B. Lippincott Company, 1893.

Thacher, James. *Military Journal of the American Revolution.* Boston: Richardson and Lord, 1823.

Trumbull, John. *Autobiography, Reminiscences and Letters of John Trumbull, from 1756 to 1841.* New York: Wiley and Putnam, 1841.

Trumbull, Jonathan. "Letter from His Late Excellency Jonathan Trumbull, Esq. to Baron J. D. Vander Capellan." *Collections of the Massachusetts Historical Society,* Ser. 1, 6 (1799):154–86.

Washington, George. *The Papers of George Washington.* Edited by W. W. Abbot et al. Charlottesville: University of Virginia, 1987–.

----------. *The Papers of George Washington Digital Edition.* Edited by Theodore J. Crackel et al. Charlottesville: University of Virginia Press, Rotunda, 2007.

----------. *The Writings of George Washington from the Original Manuscript Sources, 1745–1799.* 39 Vols. Edited by John. C. Fitzpatrick. Washington, DC: U.S. Government Printing Office, 1931–44.

----------. *The Writings of George Washington: Being the Correspondence, Addresses, Messages, and Other Papers, Official and Private, Selected and Published from the Original Manuscripts.* 12 Vols. Edited by Jared Sparks. Boston: Russell, Odiorne, and Metcalf, and Hilliard, Gray, and Co., 1833–39.

Wayne, Anthony. "Original Letters from Gen. Wayne," *Historical Magazine* V (Feb. 1861):58.
Wilkinson, James. *Memoirs of My Own Times*. 3 Vols. Philadelphia: Printed by Abraham Small, 1816.

Secondary Sources

Adams, Michael C. C. "An Appraisal of the Blue Licks Battle." *Filson Club History Quarterly* 75, No. 2 (2001):181–203.
Adelberg, Michael S. *The American Revolution in Monmouth County: The Theater of Spoil and Destruction*. Charleston SC: History Press, 2010.
----------. "'A Combination to Trample All Law Underfoot': The Association for Retaliation and the American Revolution in Monmouth County." Unpublished MS, Monmouth County Historical Association, Freehold, 1997.
Allen, Paul. *A History of the American Revolution: Comprehending All the Principal Events both in the Field and in the Cabinet*. 2 Vols. Baltimore: Printed for Franklin Betts, 1822.
Anderson, Fred. *Crucible of War: The Seven Years' War and the Fate of Empire in British North America, 1754–1766*. New York: Vintage, 2000.
Anderson, Gary C. *Ethnic Cleansing and the Indian: The Crime that Should Haunt Humanity*. Norman, OK: University of Oklahoma Press, 2004.
Andrew, Rod, Jr. *The Life and Times of General Andrew Pickens: Revolutionary War Hero, American Founder*. Chapel Hill: University of North Carolina Press, 2017.
Bailyn, Bernard. *The Ideological Origins of the American Revolution*. Cambridge, MA: Belknap Press of Harvard University Press, 2017 [orig. 1967].
Banta, R. E. *The Ohio*. Lexington, KY: University Press of Kentucky, 1998 [orig. 1949].
Barr, Daniel. *Unconquered: The Iroquois League at War in Colonial America*. Westport, CT: Praeger, 2006.
Berleth, Richard. *Bloody Mohawk: The French and Indian War & American Revolution*. Hensonville, NY: Black Dome Press, 2009.
Best, Geoffrey. *Humanity in Warfare: The Modern History of the International Law of Armed Conflict*. London: Methuen 1983.
Birzer, Bradley J. "French Imperial Remnants on the Middle Ground: The Strange Case of August de la Balme and Charles Beaubien." *Journal of the Illinois State Historical Society* 93, No. 2 (2000):135–54.

Botta, Carlo. *History of the War of the Independence of the United States of America.* Trans. by George Alexander Otis. 2 Vols. 9th ed. Cooperstown, NY: H. & E. Phinney, 1847 [orig. in Italian, 1809].

Brands, W. H. *Our First Civil War: Patriots and Loyalists in the American Revolution.* New York: Doubleday, 2021.

Breen, T. H. *American Insurgents, American Patriots: The Revolution of the People.* New York: Hill and Wang, 2010.

Brooks, A. B. "Story of Fort Henry." *West Virginia History* 1, No. 2 (1940):110–18.

Brown, John P. *Old Frontiers: The Story of the Cherokee from Earliest Times to the Date of Their Removal to the West.* Kingsport: Southern Publishers, 1938.

Brown, Richard Maxwell. *Strain of Violence: Historical Studies of American Violence and Vigilantism.* New York: Oxford University Press, 1975.

Brumwell, Stephen. *George Washington: Gentleman Warrior.* London: Quercus, 2013.

Buchanan, John. *The Road to Guilford Courthouse: The American Revolution in the Carolinas.* New York: John Wiley & Sons, 1997.

Buchanan, John. *The Road to Charleston: Nathanael Greene and the American Revolution.* Charlottesville, VA: University of Virginia Press, 2019.

Buel, Richard, Jr. *Dear Liberty: Connecticut's Mobilization for the Revolutionary War.* Middletown, CT: Wesleyan University Press, 1980.

Buker, George E. *The Penobscot Expedition: Commodore Saltonstall and the Massachusetts Conspiracy of 1779.* Annapolis, MD: Naval Institute Press, 2002.

Bush, Martin R. *Revolutionary Enigma: A Reappraisal of General Philip Schuyler of New York.* Empire State Historical Publications Series, No. 80. Port Washington, NY: Ira J. Friedman, 1969.

Butterfield, Consul Willshire. *History of the Girtys: Being a Concise Account of the Girty Brothers, Thomas, Simon, James and George.* Cincinnati, OH: Robert Clarke and Co., 1890.

Calloway, Colin G. *The American Revolution in Indian Country: Crisis and Diversity in Native American Communities.* New York: Cambridge University Press, 1995.

----------. *The Scratch of a Pen: 1763 and the Transformation of North America.* New York: Oxford University Press, 2006.

----------. *The Indian World of George Washington: The First President, the First Americans, and the Birth of the Nation.* New York: Oxford University Press, 2018.

Campeau, Timothy. *Dishonored Americans: The Political Death of Loyalists in Revolutionary America.* Charlottesville: University of Virginia Press, 2023.

BIBLIOGRAPHY

Carlson, John D. and Jonathan H. Ebel, eds. *From Jeremiad to Jihad: Religion, Violence, & America*. Berkeley: University of California Press, 2012.

Carpenter, W[illiam] H[enry] and T[imothy] S[hay] Arthur. *The History of New Jersey from Its Earliest Settlement to the Present Time*. Philadelphia: Claxton, Remsen & Haffelfinger, 1874.

Carter, Harvey Lewis. *The Life and Times of Little Turtle: First Sagamore of the Wabash*. Urbana, IL: University of Illinois Press, 1987.

Cashin, Edward J. *The King's Ranger: Thomas Brown and the American Revolution on the Southern Frontier*. New York: Fordham University Press, 1999.

Caughey, John Walton. *McGillivray of the Creeks*. Columbia: University of South Carolina Press, 2007.

Caulkins, Frances Manwaring. *History of New London, Connecticut: from the First Survey of the Coast in 1612, to 1860*. New London, CT: H. D. Utley, 1895.

Chopra, Ruma. *Unnatural Rebellion: Loyalists in New York City during the Revolution*. Charlottesville, VA: University of Virginia Press, 2011.

Clodfelter, Michael. *Warfare and Armed Conflicts: A Statistical Encyclopedia of Casualty and Other Figures, 1492–2015*. Jefferson, NC: McFarland, 2017.

Clyde, John C. *Rosbrugh, a Tale of the Revolution, or, Life, Labors and Death of Rev. John Rosbrugh: Pastor of Greenwich, Oxford and Mansfield Woodhouse (Washington) Presbyterian Churches, N.J., from 1764 to 1769, and of Allen Township Church, Pa., from 1769 to 1777: Chaplain in the Continental Army, Clerical Martyr of the Revolution, Killed by Hessians, in the Battle of Assunpink, at Trenton, New Jersey, Jan. 2d, 1777*. Easton, PA: 1880.

Cohen, Eliot A. *Conquered into Liberty: Two Centuries of Battles Along the Great Warpath that Made the American Way of War*. New York: Free Press, 2012.

Coleman, J. Winston, Jr. *The British Invasion of Kentucky*. Lexington, KY: Winburn Press, 1951.

Conkright, Bessie Taul. "Estill's Defeat or the Battle of Little Mountain March 22, 1782." *Register of Kentucky State Historical Society* 22, No. 66 (1924):311–22.

Conway, Stephen. "To Subdue America: British Army Officers and the Conduct of Revolutionary War," *William and Mary Quarterly*. 3rd Ser., 43 (1986):381–407.

----------. *The War of American Independence, 1775–1783*. London: Edward Arnold, 1995.

Corbett, Theodore. *No Turning Point: The Saratoga Campaign in Perspective*. Norman, OK: University of Oklahoma Press, 2014.

Coulter, E. Merton. "Nancy Hart, Georgia Heroine of the Revolution: The Story of the Growth of a Tradition." *Georgia Historical Quarterly* 39 (1955):118–51.

Crawford, Allan Pell. *This Fierce People: The Untold Story of America's Revolutionary War in the South.* New York: Knopf, 2024.

DePauw, Linda Grant. *Fortunes of War: New Jersey Women and the American Revolution.* Trenton: New Jersey Historical Commission, 1975.

Draper, Lyman Copeland. *King's Mountain and Its Heroes: History of the Battle of King's Mountain, October 7th, 1780, and the Events Which Led to It.* Cincinnati: P. G. Thomson, 1881.

Epstein, Daniel Mark. *The Loyal Son: The War in Ben Franklin's House.* New York: Ballantine Books, 2017.

Fenton, William N. *The Great Law and the Longhouse: A Political History of the Iroquois Confederacy.* Norman, OK: University of Oklahoma Press, 1998.

Filson, John. *The Discovery, Purchase, and Present State of Kentucky: and an Essay towards the Topography and Natural History of That Important Country.* Wilmington: Printed by James Adams, 1784.

Fischer, David Hackett. *Paul Revere's Ride.* New York: Oxford University Press, 1994.

----------. *Washington's Crossing.* New York: Oxford University Press, 2004.

Fischer, Joseph R. *A Well-Executed Failure: The Sullivan Campaign against the Iroquois, July–September 1779.* Columbia, SC: University of South Carolina Press, 1997.

Forman, Charles. *Three Revolutionary Soldiers: David Forman (1745–1797), Jonathan Forman (1755–1809), Thomas Marsh Forman (1758–1845).* Cleveland, OH: Forman-Bassett-Hatch, 1902.

Fowler, David J. *Egregious Villains, Wood Rangers, and London Traders: The Pine Robber Phenomenon in New Jersey During the Revolutionary War.* New Brunswick, NJ: Rutgers University Press, 1987.

Garden, Alexander. *Anecdotes of the Revolutionary War in America: With Sketches of Character of Persons Most Distinguished, in the Southern States, for Civil and Military Services.* Charleston, SC: Printed by A. E. Miller, 1822.

Gehring, Charles. *Agriculture and the Revolution in the Mohawk Valley.* St. Johnsville, NY: Fort Klock Historic Restoration, n.d. [1980?].

Gerlach, Don R. *Proud Patriot: Philip Schuyler and the War of Independence, 1775–1783.* Syracuse, NY: Syracuse University Press, 1964.

Gerlach, Larry R. *Prologue to Independence: New Jersey in the Coming of the American Revolution.* New Brunswick, NJ: Rutgers University Press, 1976.

Gigantino, James J., II, ed. *William Livingston's Revolution*. Philadelphia: University of Pennsylvania Press, 2018.

----------. *The American Revolution in New Jersey: Where the Battlefront Meets the Home Front*. New Brunswick: Rutgers University Press, 2015.

Gilbert, Alan. *Black Patriots and Loyalists: Fighting for Emancipation in the War for Independence*. Chicago: University of Chicago Press, 2012.

Gilbert, Arthur N. "Law and Honour among Eighteenth-Century British Army Officers," *The Historical Journal* 19, No. 1 (1976):75–87.

Glatthaar, Joseph T. and James Kirby Martin, *Forgotten Allies: The Oneida Indians and the American Revolution*. New York: Hill & Wang, 2006.

Gordon, John W. *South Carolina and the American Revolution: A Battlefield History*. Columbia: University of South Carolina Press, 2003.

Gordon, William. *The History of the Rise, Progress, and Establishment of the Independence of the United States of America; Including an Account of the late War; and of the Thirteen Colonies, from their Origin to that Period*. 4 Vols. London: Printed for the author, 1788.

Gould, Eliga H. "Zones of Law, Zones of Violence: The Legal Geography of the British Atlantic, circa 1772," *William and Mary Quarterly*. 3rd Ser., LX, No. 3 (2003):477.

Graymont, Barbara. *The Iroquois in the American Revolution*. Syracuse, NY: Syracuse University Press, 1972.

Greenburg, Michael M. *The Court-Martial of Paul Revere: A Son of Liberty & America's Forgotten Military Disaster*. Lebanon, NH: University Press of New England, 2014.

Grenier, John. *The First Way of War: American War Making on the Frontier, 1607–1814*. New York: Cambridge University Press, 2005.

Griffin, Patrick. *American Leviathan: Empire, Nation, and Revolutionary Frontier*. New York: Hill and Wang, 2007.

Grotius, Hugo. *De Jure Belli ac Pacis Libri Tres [On the Law of War and Peace]*. Trans. and ed. by A. C. Campbell. Kitchener, Ontario: Batoche Books, 2001 [orig. 1625].

Harper, Rob. "Looking the Other Way: The Gnadenhutten Massacre and the Contextual Interpretation of Violence." *William and Mary Quarterly*. 3rd Ser., 64, No. 3 (2007):633–42.

Hays, Louise Frederick. *Hero of Hornet's Nest: A Biography of Elijah Clark, 1733 to 1799*. New York: Stratford House, 1946.

Heitman, Francis B. *Historical Register of Officers of the Continental Army during the War of the Revolution, April 1775, to December, 1783*. Washington, DC: Rare Book Shop Publishing Company, 1914.

Herrera, Ricardo A. *Feeding Washington's Army: Surviving the Valley Forge Winter of 1778.* Chapel Hill: University of North Carolina Press, 2022.

Hoock, Holger. "*Jus in Bello,* Rape and the British Army in the American Revolutionary War," *Journal of Military Ethics,* 14 (April 2015):74–97.

----------. *The Scars of Independence: America's Violent Birth.* New York: Broadway Books, 2017.

Houlding, J. A. *Fit for Service: The Training of the British Army, 1715–1795.* New York: Oxford University Press, 1981.

Huff, Archie Vernon, Jr. *Greenville: The History of the City and County in the Southern Piedmont.* Columbia: University of South Carolina Press, 1995.

Hurt, R. Douglas. *The Ohio Frontier: Crucible of the Old Northwest, 1720–1830.* Bloomington, IN: Indiana University Press, 1996.

Jasanoff, Maya. *Liberty's Exiles: American Loyalists in the Revolutionary World.* New York: Alfred A. Knopf, 2011.

Johnson, James Turner. *Ideology, Reason, and the Limitation of War: Religious and Secular Concepts, 1200–1740.* Princeton, NJ: Princeton University Press, 1975.

Jones, Edward Alfred. *The Loyalists of New Jersey: Their Memorials, Petitions, Claims, Etc. from English Records.* Intro. by George Athan Billias. Boston: Gregg Press, 1972 [orig. 1927].

Jones, T. Cole. *Captives of Liberty: Prisoners of War and the Politics of Vengeance in the American Revolution.* Philadelphia: University of Pennsylvania Press, 2020.

Kaplan, Emma Nogrady and Sidney Kaplan, *The Black Presence in the Era of the American Revolution.* Amherst, MA: University of Massachusetts Press, 1989.

Kars, Marjoleine. *Breaking Loose Together: The Regulator Rebellion in Pre-revolutionary North Carolina.* Chapel Hill: University of North Carolina Press, 2002.

Katcher, Philip R. N. *Encyclopedia of British, Provincial, and German Army Units, 1775–1783.* Harrisburg, PA: Stackpole Books, 1973.

Kaufmann, Walter. *Existentialism From Dostoevsky To Sartre.* e-book. Auckland, NZ: Pickle Partners Publishing, 2016 [orig. 1956].

Kellogg, Louise Phelps, ed. *Frontier Retreat on the Upper Ohio, 1779–1781.* Madison, WI: Wisconsin Historical Society, 1917.

Kelsay, Isabel T. *Joseph Brant, 1743–1807: Man of Two Worlds.* Syracuse, NY: Syracuse University Press, 1984.

Kemp, Franklin W. *A Nest of Rebel Pirates: The Account of an Attack by the British Forces on the Privateer Stronghold at Little Egg Harbor.* 2nd ed. Batsto, NJ: Batsto Citizens Committee, 1993.

Landrum, J. B. O. *Colonial and Revolutionary History of Upper South Carolina*. Greeneville, SC: Shannon & Co., Printers and Binders, 1897.

Lasseray, André. *Les Français sous les Treize Étoiles, 1775–1783*. Paris: Macon, 1935.

Lee, Wayne E. *Crowds and Soldiers in Revolutionary North Carolina: The Culture of Violence in Riot and War*. Gainesville, FL: University Press of Florida, 2001.

----------. *Barbarians and Brothers: Anglo-American Warfare, 1500–1865*. New York: Oxford University Press, 2011.

Lehman, Eric D. *Homegrown Terror: Benedict Arnold and the Burning of New London*. Middletown, CT: Wesleyan University Press, 2016.

Leiby, Adrian Coulter. *The Revolutionary War in the Hackensack Valley: The Jersey Dutch and the Neutral Ground, 1775–1783*. New Brunswick, NJ: Rutgers University Press, 1962.

----------. *The Huguenot Settlement of Schraalenburgh: The History of Bergenfield, New Jersey*. Bergenfield, NJ: Free Public Library, 1964.

Lender, Mark Edward. "Small Battles Won: New Jersey and the Patriot Military Revival." *New Jersey Heritage* 1, No. 2 (2002):30–37.

----------. *The War for American Independence*. Santa Barbara, CA: ABC-CLIO, 2016.

Lender, Mark Edward and James Kirby Martin. "Target New London: Benedict Arnold's Raid, Just War, and 'Homegrown Terror' Reconsidered." *Journal of Military History* 82, No. 4 (2018):67–97.

Lender, Mark Edward and Garry Wheeler Stone. *Fatal Sunday: George Washington, the Monmouth Campaign, and the Politics of Battle*. Norman, OK: University of Oklahoma Press, 2016.

Lender, Mark Edward and James Kirby Martin, "A Traitor's Epiphany: Benedict Arnold in Virginia and His Quest for Reconciliation," *Virginia Magazine of History and Biography* 125, No. 4 (2017):315–57.

Lengel, Edward G. *The Battles of Connecticut Farms and Springfield, 1780*. Yardley, PA: Westholme, 2020.

Lesser, Charles H. *The Sinews of Independence: Monthly Strength Reports of the Continental Army*. Chicago: University of Chicago Press, 1976.

Lofaro, Michael A. *Daniel Boone: An American Life*. Lexington, KY: University Press of Kentucky, 2003.

Lossing, Benson John, ed. *The American Historical Record, and Repository of Notes and Queries*. Philadelphia: John E. Potter and Company, 1874.

----------. *The Pictorial Field-Book of the American Revolution: Or, Illustrations, by Pen and Pencil, of the History, Biography, Scenery, Relics, and Traditions of the War for Independence*. 2 Vols. New York: Harper & Brothers, 1852.

Lovell, James. *An Oration Delivered April 2d, 1771 at the Request of the Inhabitants of the Town of Boston to Commemorate the Bloody Tragedy of the Fifth of March, 1770*. Boston: Printed by Edes and Gill, 1771.

Lugusz, Michael O. *With Musket and Tomahawk: The Saratoga Campaign and the Wilderness War of 1777*. Philadelphia: Casemate, 2010.

Lurie, Maxine. *Taking Sides in Revolutionary New Jersey: Caught in the Crossfire*. New Brunswick, NJ: Rutgers University Press, 2022.

Lynn, John A., II. *Another Kind of War: The Nature and History of Terrorism*. New Haven: Yale University Press, 2019.

Maass, John R. *"A Complicated Scene of Difficulties": North Carolina and the Revolutionary Settlement, 1776–1789*. Ph.D. Diss. Ohio State University, 2007.

Maclay, Edgar Stanton. *A History of American Privateers*. New York: D. Appleton and Company, 1899.

Mann, Barbara A. *George Washington's War on Native America*. Westport, CT: Praeger, 2005.

Martin, James Kirby. *Benedict Arnold, Revolutionary Hero: An American Warrior Reconsidered*. New York: New York University Press, 1997.

----------. "A Contagion of Violence: The Ideal of *Jus in Bello* Versus the Reality of Fighting on the New York Frontier during the Revolutionary War." *Journal of Military Ethics*, 14 (April 2015): 57–73.

Martin, James Kirby and Mark Edward Lender, *A Respectable Army: The Military Origins of the Republic, 1763–1789*. 3rd ed. Malden, MA: Wiley Blackwell, 2015.

Martin, James Kirby and David L. Preston, eds., *Theaters of the American Revolution: Northern, Middle, Southern, Western, Naval*. Yardley, PA: Westholme, 2017.

Mayer, Holly A. *Congress's Own: A Canadian Regiment, the Continental Army, and American Union*. Norman, OK: University of Oklahoma Press, 2022.

McBurney, Christian. *Abductions in the American Revolution: Attempts to Kidnap George Washington, Benedict Arnold and Other Military and Civilian Leaders*. Jefferson, NC: McFarland & Company, 2016.

McCormick, Richard P. *New Jersey from Colony to State: 1609–1789*, rev. ed. Newark, NJ: New Jersey Historical Society, 1981.

McDonnell, Michael A. *Masters of Empire: Great Lakes Indians and the Making of America*. New York: Hill and Wang, 2015.

McIlwraith, Jean N. *Sir Frederick Haldimand*. London, ONT: T. C. & E. C. Jack, 1905.

BIBLIOGRAPHY

Moots, Glen A. and Philip Hamilton, eds. *Justifying Revolution: Law, Virtue, and Violence in the American War of Independence*. Norman, OK: University of Oklahoma Press, 2018.

Munn, David C., ed. *Battles and Skirmishes of the American Revolution in New Jersey*. Trenton, NJ: Bureau of Geography and Topography, Department of Environmental Protection, 1976.

Narrett, David. *Adventurism and Empire: The Struggle for Mastery in the Louisiana–Florida Borderlands, 1762–1803*. Chapel Hill: University of North Carolina Press, 2015.

Nash, Gary B. *The Unknown American Revolution: The Unruly Birth of Democracy and the Struggle to Create America*. New York: Penguin, 2006.

Nelson, James L. *With Fire and Sword: The Battle of Bunker Hill and the Beginning of the American Revolution*. New York: St. Martin's Press, 2011.

Nelson, Larry L. *A Man of Distinction among Them: Alexander McKee and the Country Frontier, 1754–1799*. Kent, OH: Kent State University Press, 1999.

Norton, Mary Beth. *1774: The Long Year of Revolution*. New York: Vintage Books, 2020.

O'Driscoll, Cian. "Heartfelt Truths: Towards an Existentialist Ethics of War." *Review of International Studies* 49, No. 5 (2023):872–84.

O'Kelley, Patrick. *Nothing but Blood and Slaughter: Military Operations and Order of Battle of the Revolutionary War in the Carolinas*. 4 Vols. Trenton, GA: Booklocker.com, 2004–2005.

Olden, Thomas. *A Brief Narrative of the Ravages of the British and Hessians at Princeton, 1776–1777*. Ed by Varnum Lansing Collins. Princeton, NJ: Drumthwacket Foundation, 1999.

O'Shaughnessy, Andrew Jackson. *The Empire Divided: The American Revolution and the British Caribbean*. Philadelphia, University of Pennsylvania Press, 2000.

O'Toole, Fintan. *White Savage: William Johnson and the Invention of America*. New York: Farrar, Straus and Giroux, 2005.

Owens, Robert M. *Red Dreams, White Nightmares: Pan-Indian Alliances in the Anglo-American Mind, 1763–1814*. Norman, OK: University of Oklahoma Press, 2015.

Pancake, John S. *1777: The Year of the Hangman*. Tuscaloosa: University of Alabama Press, 1977.

----------. *This Destructive War: The British Campaign in the Carolinas*. Tuscaloosa, AL: University of Alabama Press, 1985.

Parker, John C. *Parker's Guide to the Revolutionary War in South Carolina*. West Conshohocken, PA: Infinity Publishing, 2013.

Peckham, Howard K., ed. *The Toll of Independence: Engagements and Battle Casualties of the American Revolution.* Chicago: University of Chicago Press, 1974.

Peters, Samuel. *General History of Connecticut: From Its First Settlement under George Fenwick to Its Latest Period of Amity with Great Britain Prior to the Revolution.* New York: D. Appleton and Company, 1877 [orig. 1781].

Piecuch, James. *Three Peoples, One King: Loyalists, Indians, and Slaves in the Revolutionary South, 1775–1782.* Columbia, SC: University of South Carolina Press, 2008.

Pieper, Thomas and James B. Gidney. *Fort Laurens, 1778–1779: The Revolutionary War in Ohio.* Kent, OH: Kent State University Press, 1976.

Powell, Walter. *Murder or Mayhem? Benedict Arnold's New England Connecticut Raid, 1781.* Gettysburg, PA: Thomas Publications, 2000.

Preston, David L. *The Texture of Contact: European and Indian Settler Communities on the Frontiers of Iroquoia, 1667–1783.* Lincoln, NE: University of Nebraska Press, 2009.

Puls, Mark. *Henry Knox: Visionary General of the American Revolution.* New York: Palgrave Macmillan, 2008.

Quarles, Benjamin Arthur. *The Negro in the American Revolution.* Chapel Hill: University of North Carolina Press, 1996 [orig. 1961].

Ramsay, David. *The History of the American Revolution.* Philadelphia: Printed by R. Aitken & Son, 1789.

----------. *The History of South-Carolina: From Its First Settlement in 1670 to the Year 1808.* Newberry, SC: W. J. Duffie, 1858 [orig. 1809].

Rogers, Ernest E. *Connecticut's Naval Office at New London during the War of the American Revolution; Including the Mercantile Letter Book of Nathaniel Shaw, Jr.* New London, CT: New London County Historical Society, 1933.

Russell, Frederick H. *The Just War in the Middle Ages.* New York: Cambridge University Press, 1975.

Ryan, Dennis P. *New Jersey's Loyalists*, New Jersey's Revolutionary Experience, No. 20. Trenton, NJ: New Jersey Historical Commission, 1975.

Saffell, W. T. R. *Records of the Revolutionary War: Containing the Military and Financial Correspondence of Distinguished Officers.* New York: Pudney & Russell, 1858.

Sanchez-Saavedra, E. M. *A Guide to Virginia Military Organizations in the American Revolution, 1774–1787.* Westminster, MD: Heritage Books, 1978.

Saunt, Claudio. *West of the Revolution: An Uncommon History of 1776.* New York: W. W. Norton, 2014.

Scaggs, David Curtis, ed. *The Old Northwest in the American Revolution: An Anthology*. Madison, WI: The State Historical Society of Wisconsin, 1977.

Schmidt, Ethan. *Native Americans in the American Revolution: How the War Divided, Devastated, and Transformed the Early American Indian World*. Praeger: Santa Barbara, 2014.

Shalhope, Robert E. "Toward a Republican Synthesis: The Emergence of an Understanding of Republicanism in American Historiography," *William and Mary Quarterly* 29 (1972):49–80.

Sherman, Andrew M. *Historic Morristown, New Jersey: The Story of Its First Century*. Morristown, NJ: Howard Publishing Co., 1905.

Silver, Peter. *Our Savage Neighbors: How Indian Warfare Transformed Early America*. New York: W. W. Norton, 2007.

Simms, Jeptha R. *The Frontiersmen of New York: Showing Customs of the Indians, Vicissitudes of the Pioneers White Settlers, and Border Strife in Two Wars. With a Great Variety of Romantic and Thrilling Stories Never before Published*. 2 Vols. Albany, NY: Geo. C. Riggs, 1882–83.

Smith, Paul H. "New Jersey Loyalists and the British 'Provincial' Corps in the War of Independence," *New Jersey History* 87, No. 2 (1969):69–78.

Sparks, Jared. *The Life and Treason of Benedict Arnold*. New York: Harper & Brothers, 1835.

Starkey, Armstrong. "War and Culture, A Case Study: The Enlightenment and the Conduct of the British Army in America, 1755–1781," *War and Society* 8 (1990):1–28.

Stockwell, Mary. *Unlikely General: "Mad" Anthony Wayne and the Battle for America*. New Haven: Yale University Press, 2018.

Stryker, Willian Scudder. *The New Jersey Volunteers (Loyalists) in the Revolutionary War*. Trenton, NJ: Naar, Day & Naar, 1887.

—————. *The Affair at Egg Harbor, New Jersey, October 15, 1778*. Trenton, NJ: Naar, Day & Naar, 1894.

—————. *The Battles of Trenton and Princeton*. Trenton, NJ: The Old Barracks Association, 2001 [orig. 1898].

Swiggett, Howard. *War out of Niagara: Walter Butler and the Tory Rangers*. New York: Columbia University Press, 1933.

Syrett, David. *Shipping and the American War, 1775–83: A Study of British Transport Organization*. London: Athlone Press, 1970.

Taylor, Alan. *The Divided Ground: Indians, Settlers, and the Northern Borderland of the American Revolution*. New York: Vintage Books, 2007.

—————. *The Internal Enemy: Slavery and War in Virginia, 1771–1832*. New York: W. W. Norton & Company, 2013.

Thucydides. *History of the Peloponnesian War.* Trans. by Rex Warner. New York: Penguin, 1972.

Townshend, Charles. *The British Invasion of New Haven, Connecticut, Together with Some Account of Their Landing and Burning the Towns of Fairfield and Norwalk, July 1779.* New Haven, CT: Tuttle, Morehouse and Taylor Printers, 1879.

Urwin, Gregory J. W. "'To bring the American Army under strict Discipline': British Army Foraging Policy in the South, 1780–81." *War in History* 26, No. 1 (2019):15.

Van Doren, Carl. *Secret History of the American Revolution: An Account of The Conspiracies of Benedict Arnold and Numerous Others, Drawn from the Secret Service Papers of the British Headquarters in North America, Now for the First Time Examined and Made Public.* New York: Viking Press, 1941.

Vattel, Emer de. *The Law of Nations, Or, Principles of the Law of Nature, Applied to the Conduct and Affairs of Nations and Sovereigns, with Three Early Essays on the Origin and Nature of Natural Law and on Luxury.* Edited by Béla Kapossy and Richard Whatmore. Indianapolis: Liberty Fund, 2008 [orig. 1758].

------- *The Law of Nations; Or, Principles of the Law of Nature: Applied to the Conduct and Affairs of Nations and Sovereigns.* 2 Vols. London, 1759–60.

Wacker, Peter O. *Land & People: A Cultural Geography of Preindustrial New Jersey: Origins and Settlement Patterns.* New Brunswick, NJ: Rutgers University Press, 1975.

Ward, Harry M. *Between the Lines: Banditti of the American Revolution.* Santa Barbara, CA: Praeger, 2002.

Warren, Mercy [Otis]. *History of the Rise, Progress and Termination of the American Revolution. Interspersed with Biographical, Political and Moral Observations.* 3 Vols. Boston: Manning and Loring, 1805.

Watt, Gavin K. *The Burning of the Valleys: Daring Raids from Canada against the New York Frontier in the Fall of 1780.* Toronto: Dundurn Press, 1997.

------------. *Rebellion in the Mohawk Valley: The St. Leger Expedition of 1777.* Toronto: Dundurn Press, 2002.

------------. *Fire & Desolation: The Revolutionary War's 1778 Campaign as Waged from Quebec and Niagara Against the American Frontiers.* Toronto: Dundurn Press, 2017.

Weddle, Kevin J. *The Compleat Victory: Saratoga and the American Revolution.* New York: Oxford University Press, 2021.

Whittemore, Charles. *A General of the Revolution: John Sullivan of New Hampshire.* New York, Columbia University Press, 1961.

Williams, Glenn F. *Year of the Hangman: George Washington's Campaign Against the Iroquois.* Yardley, PA: Westholme, 2005.
———. *Dunmore's War: The Last Conflict of America's Colonial Era.* Yardley, PA: Westholme, 2017.
Wilson, Peter H. *Europe's Tragedy: A New History of the Thirty Years War.* London: Penguin, 2010.
Witt, John Fabian. *Lincoln's Code: The Laws of War in American History.* New York: Free Press, 2013.
Wright, Robert K., Jr. *The Continental Army.* Washington, DC: Center of Military History, U.S. Army, 1983.

Newspapers

Annual Register (London)
Boston Gazette
Connecticut Gazette (New London)
Continental Journal and Weekly Advertiser (Boston)
Dunlap's Pennsylvania Packet, or, the General Advertiser (Philadelphia)
Gentleman's Magazine and Historical Chronicle (London)
Freeman's Journal: Or, the North-American Intelligencer (Philadelphia)
Independent Chronicle (Boston)
London Gazette
Maryland Gazette (Annapolis)
New Jersey Gazette (Trenton)
New-York Gazette and Weekly Mercury
New York Journal
Pennsylvania Evening Post (Philadelphia)
Register of Pennsylvania (Philadelphia, Samuel Hazard)
Rivington's Royal Gazette (New York)
Royal Georgia Gazette (Savannah)

Internet Sources

American Revolution.org. http://www.americanrevolution.org
Biographical Directory of the United States Congress. http://bioguide.congress.gov/scripts/biodisplay.pl?index=L000463.

"Cloud's Creek." *The American Revolution in South Carolina.* https://www.carolana.com/SC/Revolution/revolution_clouds_creek_2.html

Colbert, Richard A. "James Logan Colbert of the Chickasaw, The Man and the Myth." *North Carolina Genealogical Society Journal* XX, No. 2 (1994). http://www.angelfire.com/ok3/greybird7/genealogy.html.

Dictionary of Canadian Biography. http://www.biographi.ca/en/.

Driver, Strobe. "A New Age of Violence: Terrorism as an Asymmetrical and 'Existential Threat.'" *E-International Relations*, 27 Sept. 2017. https://www.e-ir.info/2017/09/27/terrorism-as-an-asymmetrical-and-existential-threat/#google_vignette.

Engstrom, Mary Claire. "Hooper, William," *NCPedia*, University of North Carolina Press. https://www.ncpedia.org/biography/hooper-william.

Founders Online. https://founders.archives.gov/.

Haggenmacher. Peter. "Emer de Vattel." *Dictionnaire Historique de la Suisse* (7 Feb. 2013). https://hls-dhs-dss.ch/fr/articles/015917/2013-07-02/, accessed 11 Jan. 2020.

Haldimand Papers. *Heritage Canadiana.* http://heritage.canadiana.ca.

"History of Fort Randolph." *First Biennial Report of the* [West Virginia] *Department of Archives and History, 1906,* 236–39. http://www.wvculture.org/HiStory/settlement/fortrandolph04.html.

Library of Congress. Printed Ephemera Collection. Portfolio 111, Folder 4. https://www.loc.gov/resource/rbpe.11100400/.

Mackenzie Institute. "Existential War." https://mackenzieinstitute.com/2008/04/existential-war/.

Moseley, Alexander. "Just War Theory." *Internet Encyclopedia of Philosophy.* http://www.iep.utm.edu/justwar/.

New Jersey State Archives. "Revolutionary War Damage Claims, 1776–1782." https://wwwnet-dos.state.nj.us/DOS_ArchivesDBPortal/RevWarDamages.aspx.

O'Brien, Greg. "Southeastern Indians and the American Revolution." *Encyclopedia of Alabama.* http://www.encyclopediaofalabama.org/article/h-1133.

On-Line Institute for Advanced Loyalist Studies. http://www.royalprovincial.com/military/rhist/wjv/wjvmem1.htm.

Parker, Hershel. "A 'Heavenly Harvest' of Vulnerable Women in North Carolina: Tory Troops as Sexual Predators." *Journal of the American Revolution,* 27 Feb. 2017. https://allthingsliberty.com /02/heavenly-harvest-vulnerable-women-north-carolina-tory-troops-sexual-predators/.

Ruset, Ben. "The Refugee John Bacon." *JNPineBarrens,* 24 June 2011. https://www.njpinebarrens.com/the-refugee-john-bacon/.

BIBLIOGRAPHY

Saberton, Ian. "The Campaigns of 1780 and 1781 in the Southern Theatre of the American Revolutionary War." Ph.D. essay. History Department, University of Warwick, 2015. http://wrap.warwick.ac.uk/80231/1/WRAP_THESIS_Saberton_2015.pdf.

"Southern Campaign American Revolution Pension Statements & Rosters." https://revwarapps.org/s32222.pdf.

Tennessee Encyclopedia of History and Culture. http://tennesseeencyclopedia.net/.

The New Georgia Encyclopedia. https://www.georgiaencyclopedia.org/articles/history-archaeology/.

"What Are Jus ad Bellum and Jus in Bello?" 22 Jan. 2015, International Committee of the Red Cross. https://www.icrc.org/en/document/what-are-jus-ad-bellum-and-jus-bello-0.

Index

Note: page numbers in **bold** refer to illustrations.

Adams, Abigail   19–20, 39
Adams, John   18, 19–20, 21, 32, 41, 46, 53, 189–191
Adams, Samuel, Jr.   88
Adelberg, Michael   99
Albany   137, 147–148
Alden, Ichabod   151–152
American Civil War   217
American Legion   171
American whigs
  political ideology   33–34
Anglo-Dutch War   57
anti-British sentiments, surge in   35
Arnold, Benedict   38, 52, 146, 160–161, 163, 167–168, 170–173, 175, 177, 178–180, 184, 213
Asgill, Charles   96
"Asgill affair"   95–96
Association for Retaliation   30–31, 96–98
atrocities   21, 213
  New York frontier   155
  southern theater   201–208, 207
  Trans-Appalachian West   129–130

Bacon, John   93
banditti   91–93

Barton, Joseph   87
Bates, William "Bloody Bill"   129, 207, 213
Bird, Henry   117, 125–126
black population   35
  loyalists   90–91
  slaves and slavery   35, 72–73, 77, 185, 187, 189–191, 195–196
  threat   72–73, 189–191
blame   22–23, 198–208, 210
Blue Licks, Battle of   130
Board of Associated Loyalists   94–98
Boone, Daniel   106
Boston   67, 176
Boston Massacre   17–19, 211
bounties   112–113
Boyd, Thomas   154–155
Brant, Joseph   127, 139, 140–143, 143, 143–145, 145, 147–148, 150–154, 212, 214
Brant's Volunteers   140–143, 143–144, 147–148, 150–154, 156, 192
Breen, T. H.   23, 187
British Army   154
  disdain for rebels   32
  hard line   73–78, 81–82

INDEX

hard-line men   57–59
and *jus in bello*   48, 50–52, 62
punishment   50, 77
withdrawal from
   Philadelphia   84
Brodhead, Daniel   117, 121–122, 127
Brown, Thomas ("Burntfoot")   24,
   38, 59, 188, 194, 202, 215
Buford, Abraham   181–182
Bulloch, Archibald   20, 59, 189–191,
   191, 192
Bunker Hill, Battle of   58–59
Burgoyne, John   53, 143–146, 181
Burke, Thomas   198
Butler, John   143, 144, 145, 149–
   150, 151, 154, 155, 157
Butler, William   151
Butler's Rangers   144, 149–150,
   151–152, 154, 155

Camden, Battle of   195
Cameron, Alexander   109–110, 113
Campbell, John   124–125
Campbell, Lord William   188–189,
   194
Carleton, Guy   96
Carolinas, the   111, 128, 185, 187,
   187–188, 188–189, 189–191,
   191, 191–192, 193–194, 194,
   196, 196–198, 197, 200, 201,
   203, 204, 206–207
   casualties   29
   South Carolina   29, 30
casualties, undercount   28–30, 213
character assassination   23
Charleston   49, 51, 192, 193, 194,
   200
Cherokee War of 1776:   111–112
Cherokees   29, 105, 108, 109–110,
   111–112, 116, 128–129, 188,
   191–193, 194, 197–198
Cherry Valley massacre   151–153, 154

Chickasaws   114, 127–128
civilians   74–75, 83, 152, 204–205
   and *jus in bello*   45, 52, 54
   targeting   55, 159–160, 161–162,
      163, 178–179
Clark, George Rogers   117–120, 121,
   122, 125, 127, 128, 131, 213, 215
Clark, John   92
Clinton, Sir Henry   49, 52, 55, 83,
   84, 94, 95, 96, 97, 165, 166,
   167–168, 170, 177, 180
Clouds, Battle of the   130
Colbert, James   113, 128
Cole, William   92
Collier, George   166
Collin, Nicholas   24, 83–84
combatants   60–63
command and control   181–182
conspiracy theories   33–34, 35,
   115–116, 191–192
Continental Army
   hard line   80
   hard-line men   59–60
   and *jus in bello*   47–50, 52, 62
   in New Jersey   71–72
   New York frontier   144,
      151–152, 154–156
   Northern Department   139
   in Trans-Appalachian West
      116–117, 121–122, 127
Continental Congress, First   19–20,
   67, 69
Cornelius, Titus (Colonel Tye)   90,
   91
Cornstalk   110, 112–113
Cornwallis, Charles, Second
   Earl   50–51, 98, 168, 176–177,
   181, 201, 212
Crawford, William   130
Creeks   108, 113, 202
Creswell, James   192
Crockett, David   114

281

Crouse, Robert   146
Culloden, Battle of   57, 77
Cunningham, William "Bloody
    Bill"   206–207

De Peyster, Arent   122, 123–124,
    125, 131–132
Declaration of Independence
    32–33, 47, 60, 69–70
Delaware Valley   153–154
Dennison, Nathan   149–150, 150
Detroit   117, 120, 123, 126, 127, 131,
    131–132
Dowell, George   203
Dragging Canoe   109–110, 111,
    111–112, 113, 114, 116, 128–129,
    132–133
Dunmore, John Murray, Lord   73,
    189, 190
Dutch Reformed Church   71

Edwards, Stephan   80
engagements
    New Jersey   99
    scale   28, 30, 61
    southern theater   192
Evelyn, William Glanville   58, 60
Ewald, Johann   149–150
executions   60, 87–88, 92, 95,
    203–204, 205–206, 213
existential warfare   25–27, 62–63,
    98–99, 211–212
    New Jersey   67, 91–98
    New York frontier   158
    southern theater   199, 208–210
    Trans-Appalachian West   133
existentialism   25–26
"extirpative" warfare   107–108, 133
Eyre, Edmund   172–173, 181

Fagan, Jacob   93
Fanning, David   198

Fenny, Peter   157
Ferguson, Patrick   165, 204
Florida   123, 126
Forman, "Devil David"   71–72,
    77–78, 80, 89, 97, 98, 212, 215
Fort Griswold   60, 172–174, 178,
    180–184
France   168
Franco-Prussian War   217
Franklin, Benjamin   46, 76
Franklin, William   65, 69–70, 77, 91,
    94, 95, 96, 97, 177–178
free speech   24
Freehold, sack of   82
French and Indian War   103, 138

Garden, Alexander   209–210
Gates, Horatio   195
George III, King   105, 111
Georgia   185, 187, 188, 189,
    189–191, 194–197, 201–202,
    205
Georgia Council of Safety   24
Georgia Provincial Congress   20
Gerry, Elbridge   32–33
Girty brothers   113
Gowen's Fort   129, 207
Great Lakes region   120–121
Greene, Nathanael   200–201
Grenier, John   31, 107, 157–158
Grotius, Hugo   42–43, 44, 45–46,
    46, 53, 216
Groton Heights   **169**, 174

Haldimand, Sir Frederick   122,
    152–153
Hamilton, Alexander   85, 116,
    119–121
Hamilton, Henry   112–113
Hancock's Bridge   81–82
Hand, Edward   116
Harrod, James   106

INDEX

Hart, Nancy 204–205
Haten, Nathaniel 68
Haw River, Battle of 197–198
Heath, William 183
Henry, Patrick 20, 33, 39, 113, 117–118
Herkimer, Nicholas 138, 145
Hessian forces 59, 75
Hooper, William 193–194, 197
Hopper, Jonathan 89
Howe, Robert 190–191
Howe, William 48, 52, 72, 73–75, 78, 81, 212
Huddy, Joshua 95–96
Hudson River 137, 143
Huntington, Samuel 200–201
Hutchinson, Thomas 46

Illinois 117–119, 126–127
Indian wars 31, 105–110; see also Native Americans
intelligence 54
Iroquois 38, 105–106, 121–122, 140–143, 144–145, 153, 154–156, 157–158
Iroquois Confederacy 135, 137, 139, 214

Jacobite rising of 1745–46: 32, 57, 75, 77
Jasanoff, Maya 215–216
Jefferson, Thomas 46, 53, 76, 116
Johnson, Guy 138–139, 157
Johnson, Sir John 139–140, 143, 144, 145, 157
Johnson, Sir William 138
Jumonville, Joseph Coulon de 48
jus in bello 26, 28, 37, 38, 39, 41–63, 196, 207–208, 216
American context 46–52
British Army hard line 57–59, 73–78, 81–82

and civilians 45
and combatants 60–62
Continental Army hard line 80
hard-line men 57–60
historical development 41–46
limits 52–57
proportionality 45, 179–180
raid on New London assessment 178–184
and realities of the war 30

Kaufmann, Walter 25–26
Kentucky 106–107, 109, 110, 115–116, 117, 126, 127
Kettle Creek, Battle of 203
Kings Mountain, Battle of 204
executions 203–204, 213
King's Royal Regiment of New York (Royal Greens) 140, 141, 144, 156, 157
Kirkland, Samuel 138
Klock, George 138
Knox, Henry 48–49, 212

La Balme, Augustin de 126–127
Lagrange, Bernardus 70
land hunger 105
Laurens, Henry 192
Ledyard, William 173–174, 176, 180–184
Lee, Henry 197–198, 209
Lee, Wayne E. 49, 197
"Liberty or Death" 20, 22, 39, 211, 217
Lincoln, Abraham 217
Lincoln, Benjamin 181
Little Turtle 127, 132, 133
Livingston, William 84–86, 87–88, 94, 97–98, 98, 212, 212–213, 215
local context 28, 30–31
Long Beach Island Massacre 93
looting 91

Lord Dunmore's War   191
Louisiana   123, 124–125
Louisville   118–119
Lovell, James   19, 20, 21, 23, 33, 36, 39, 53
loyalists   68–70
   American Legion   171
   black   90–91
   counter-insurgency movement   71
   crack down on   32
   intimidation   68
   irregular activity   91–98
   migration   215–216
   New Jersey   68–70, 74, 79–80, 81, 84, 85–90, 91–98, 100
   New York frontier   157
   psychological disconnect   35–36
   Queen's American Rangers   49, 81–82
   and raid on New London   171
   southern theater   185, 187, 188, 193, 194–197, 197
   terrorism   34

McDougall, Alexander   79
McGillivray, Alexander   113
McIntosh, Lachlan   116–117
McKee, Alexander   113, 125
Mackenzie, Frederick   167
Mackenzie Institute   25, 26, 99, 133
McLean, Francis   49–50
Madison, James   189–191
Marion, Francis   200, 201
Martin, Josiah   188, 189–191
Mathews, John   176–177
Matthews, David   91
Mawhood, Charles   81–83
military frontiers   61–62
military narrative   22
militia warfare   54
Minisink, Battle of   153–154

Mississippi River   105, 114, 119, 123, 126, 128
Mohawk Valley   38, 135, 137–140, 143–146, 150–154
Mohawks   139, 146
momentum   36
Monckton, Henry   49
Monmouth, Battle of   49, 88
Monmouth Courthouse   55, 79–80
Montgomery, William   174
Moody, James   69, 89
Morristown   24
motivations   27–36, 212
Munn, David   29, 61–62, 99, 101, 211

Native Americans   29, 31, 34–35, 37–38, 61, 92, 216
   alliances with the British   111
   British agents   113, 116, 128
   and coming of the Revolution   108–109
   fear of   107, 115–116
   Great Lakes region   120–121
   impact on   213–214
   Indian-Anglo offensive   123–130
   loyalties   111
   neutrality   110–111, 112, 139
   New York frontier   135, 137–158
   resentments   106, 107
   southern theater   185, 187, 188, 191–193, 194, 197, 198, 202
   Trans-Appalachian West wars   105–133
   treaties with   105–106
naval threat   163–166
Nelson, Thomas   76
New England   108
New Jersey   27, 28–29, 31, 37, 55, 65–101, **66**
   Association for Retaliation   30–31, 96–98

INDEX

Bergen County 70–71, 92, 98
black loyalists 90–91
black threat 72–73
Board of Associated
    Loyalists 94–98
casualties 99–101
Council of Safety 86, 87
Dutch population 71
engagements 61–62, 99
Essex County 73
existential warfare 67, 91–98
fissures 67–73
Hackensack Valley 71, 78–79
insurrection 78–84
intimidation of loyalists 68
invasion of 70–71, 73–78, 78
irregular activity 91–98
loyalist collapse 84
loyalist counter-insurgency
    movement 71
loyalists 68–70, 74, 79–80, 81,
    84, 85–90, 91–98, 100
militia mobilization 67–68
Monmouth County 71–72,
    72, 79–80, 91, 92–93, 95–96,
    98, 99
Penn's Neck 83–84
Pine Robbers 92–93, 98
psychological dimension 101
Refugee Town 89–90
reign of terror 86–89
slaves 72–73, 77, 190
Somerset County 72
theater of operations **66**
uncontrolled warfare 84–91
New London, raid on 38, 159–168,
    169, 170–184, 213
    aftermath 174–178
    assault on Fort Griswold 160,
        172–174, 178, 180–184
    assessment 178–184
    British forces 171

civilian and military activities
    intertwined 161–163
civilian casualties 178–179
defenses 166–167
landing 172
loyalist reactions 177–178
massacre charge 180–184
military context 163–167, 168
moral question 160–163
propaganda 174, 176
property damage 179
proportionality 179–180
the raid 167–168, 170–174
sack of New London 175
shock of 175–176
New Orleans 124
New York City 29, 29–30, 31, 37,
    65
New York frontier 38, 135, **136**,
    137–158
    aftermath 156–158
    atrocities 155
    Battle of Minisink 153–154
    Battle of Oriskany 145–146
    Brant's raids 147–148
    Brant's Volunteers 140–143,
        142–143, 147–148, 150–154, 156
    Burgoyne's defeat 143–146
    "Burning of the Valleys" 156
    Cherry Valley massacre 151–153,
        154
    Cobleskill raid 147
    Continental Army 144,
        151–152, 154–156
    existential warfare 158
    expansion into 137–138
    Fort Stanwix 144–145
    Forty Fort 150
    loyalists 157
    Mohawk Valley 135, 137–140,
        150–154
    Native Americans 135, 137–158

retribution 147–150, 151–153
Sullivan Expedition 121–122, 154–156, 158
Wyoming Valley 148–150
North Carolina
  blame 202–203
  engagements 192
  lack of oversight 30
  loyalists 30, 188
  loyalist defeat 188
  Native Americans 111–112
  patriot unraveling 196, 197, 198
  preemptive tyranny 188, 190–191, 192, 193–194
  Regulator crisis 31–32
  slave threat 190–191
Northwest Indian War 133

Ohio Valley 105, 112–113
Olden, Thomas 75–76, 87
Oneidas 138, 146
Orangeburg 199
Oriskany, Battle of 145–146
oversight, lack of 30–31

Palmer, Abigail 76
Paris, Treaty of 132
Parker, John 29, 61, 211
Paxton Boys 31, 108
Peckham, Howard H. 28, 30, 61–62, 211, 213
Pennsylvania 31
Penobscot 49, 165
Peters, Samuel 33
Philadelphia 29, 37, 61–62, 65, 73, 80–81, 84, 176
Phillips, William 170
Pickens, Andrew 128
Piecuch, Jim 198–199
Pine Robbers 92–93, 98
plundering 75–77, 97, 99
political ideology 33–34

Pontiac's "rebellion" 108
Portsmouth, raid on 170–171
preemptive tyranny 187–194
Preston, Thomas 17, 18
prisoners of war 48, 49, 53, 59, 120, 126, 203–204
privateers and the privateer war 162–166, 167, 168, 179
propaganda 174, 176
proportionality 45, 179–180
psychological disconnect 35–36
Pyle, John 197

Quakers 68, 100
Queen Esther Montour 149–150
Queen's American Rangers 49, 81–82
Quinton Bridge 81–82

racial tensions 34–35
Randolph, Edmund 53
Randolph, Thomas 68
rape 75–77
Read, William 49
Revere, Paul 18
Rhode Island 168
Robertson, James 177
Rodney, George 56–57
Rosbrugh, John 59
Royal Navy 163–166, 168, 172
Rutledge, John 203

St. Augustine 192
St. Leger, Barrimore (Barry) 143–145, 146
St. Louis 124
Saratoga, Battle of 51, 53, 181
Schuyler, Philip 139
Second World War 159, 161
Senecas 121–122, 146, 149–150, 152
Serle, Ambrose 86
Sevier, John 128

INDEX

sexual violence 75–77, 202
Shaw, Nathaniel, Jr. 162–163
Shawnees 106, 108, 110, 112, 116, 123, 127, 129, 133, 191
Sherman, William Tecumseh 156
Shreve, William 55
Simcoe, John Graves 48–49, 81–82
Sinclair, Patrick 124
situational loyalty 70
slaves and slavery 35, 72–73, 77, 185, 187, 189–191, 195–196
Smith, Claudius 92
Smith Hatfield, John 100
South Carolina 23, 199
   Battle of Kettle Creek 195, 203
   casualties 29
   Charleston 49, 51, 181, 200
   engagements 61
   existential warfare 200
   Kings Mountain executions 204
   lack of oversight 30
   loyalists 189, 203
   Native Americans 112, 114, 128, 129, 191–192
   patriot unraveling 194, 195–197
   preemptive tyranny 187–188
   terrorism 215
   slave threat 190
   Turner House Massacre 206
   Waxhaws 182
southern theater 38–39, 185, **186**, 187–210
   atrocities 202–208, 207
   Battle of Camden 195
   Battle of Haw River 197–198
   Battle of Kettle Creek 203
   Battle of Kings Mountain 204
   blame 198–208, 210
   British invasion of Georgia 194–197
   British troops return to 187
   conspiracy theories 191–192
   engagements 192
   existential warfare 199, 208–210
   Kings Mountain executions 203–204, 213
   loyalists 185, 187, 188, 189, 193, 194–197, 197–198, 205–207
   moderates 193–194, 199–201
   Native Americans 185, 187, 188, 191–193, 194, 197, 198, 202
   patriot unraveling 185, 194–198
   preemptive tyranny 187–194
   slave population 185, 187, 189–191, 195–196
   threat perception 192, 193–194, 195
   trade boycotts 187
Spain 122–123, 124–125, 128
Sparks, Jared 160–161
spoils of war 53
Stamp Act 65
Stark, John 142–143, 147–148
Stony Point, storming of 49
Sullivan, John 121–122, 154–156, 158, 213
Sumter, Thomas 199
Sycamore Shoals 109–110

Tarleton, Banastre 181–182, 197
Tecumseh 133
Tennessee 106, 109, 114, 127, 128, 131
terror and terrorism 24, 34, 214–215
Thirty Years War 42–43, 43–44, 63, 91, 107, 133, 209, 213, 216
trade boycott 67
Trans-Appalachian West 37–38, 103–133, **104**, 214
   atrocities 129–130
   Battle of Blue Licks 130
   Battle of the Clouds 130

British agents   113, 116, 128
British in   117, 117–118, 119–120, 120–121, 123–130
Clark's expedition   117–120
Continental Army in   116–117, 121–122, 127
counterattack   117–123
end game   131–133
existential warfare   133
expansion into   105–108, 111, 131–132
extirpative warfare   107–108, 133
Fort Laurens   117, 125
Fort Pitt   116–117, 122, 123, 124, 129, 131
Fort Sackville   120
geographical scale   103
Hamilton's surrender   119–121
hostilities   111–115
ideological concerns   115–116
Indian campaign   111–115
Indian wars   105–110
Indian-Anglo offensive   123–130
Native Americans   103–133
Native American neutrality   110–111
peace agreement   132
rebel responses   115–117
"squaw campaign"   116
state of terror   129
strategic situation   103, 105–111
Sullivan Expedition   121–122, 154–156, 158
Trenton   59
Trenton–Princeton campaign   74, 78
Tryon, William   91, 165
Turner House Massacre   207
Tye, Colonel (Cornelius, Titus)   90, 91

Upham, Joshua   177–178

Varnum, James Mitchell   176–177
Vattel, Emer de   45–46, 46–47, 51, 53–54, 55–56, 57, 58, 62, 74–75, 78, 83, 94, 133, 179, 179–180, 183–184, 216
violence
  blame   22–23
  familiarity with   31–33
  motivations   27–36
  pervasive   23
Virginia   170
  government   185
  Great Bridge   188
  invasion of   50–51, 52
  loyalists   188, 201
  Native Americans   191
  slave threat   189–190
  and Trans-Appalachian West   110, 111, 117, 127

war
  conduct   41–46
  motivations   27–36
Warren, Joseph   59
Washington, George   46, 47–48, 52, 73, 78, 79, 80, 85, 97, 105, 117, 121, 122, 130, 151, 154, 155–156, 168, 212
Waxhaws Massacre   181–182
Wayne, Anthony   49, 201–202, 213, 215
Welcher, Thomas   92
Westphalia, Treaty of   44
Williamson, David   130
Willing, James   123
Winthrop, John   32
Wright, James   188, 189, 205

Yorktown, siege of   51, 98, 181